THE INTERNMENT OF ALIENS IN TWENTIETH CENTURY BRITAIN

Edited by
DAVID CESARANI and TONY KUSHNER

FRANK CASS

First published in 1993 in Great Britain by
FRANK CASS AND COMPANY LIMITED
Gainsborough House, 11 Gainsborough Road,
London E11 1RS, England

and in the United States of America by
FRANK CASS
c/o International Specialized Book Services Inc.
5804 N.E. Hassalo Street
Portland, OR 97213-3644

British Library Cataloguing in Publication Data

Internment of Aliens in Twentieth Century
Britain. – (Special Issue of "Immigrants
& Minorities" Series, ISSN 0261-9288;
Vol.11, No.3)
  I. Cesarani, David II. Kushner, Tony
III. Series
305.800941

ISBN 0-7146-3466-2 (hb)
ISBN 0-7146-4095-6 (pbk)

Printed in Great Britain by
Antony Rowe Ltd, Chippenham, Wiltshire

Library of Congress Cataloging-in-Publication Data

The Internment of aliens in twentieth century Britain / edited by
  David Cesarani and Tony Kushner.
      p.   cm.
    "First appeared in a Special issue . . . [of] Immigrants &
  minorities, vol. 11, no. 3"—T.p. verso.
    Includes bibliographical references and index.
    ISBN 0-7146-3466-2 (hard) : £25.00. — ISBN 0-7146-4095-6 (pbk.) :
  £13.50
    1. Aliens—Great Britain—History—20th century. 2. World War,
  1914–1918—Prisoners and prisons, British. 3. World War, 1939–1945
  —Concentration camps—Great Britain. 4. Immigrants—Great Britain—
  History—20th century. 5. Great Britain—History—George VI,
  1936–1952.   I. Cesarani, David. II. Kushner, Tony (Antony Robin
  Jeremy) III. Immigrants & minorities. Vol. 11, no. 3 (Special
  issue)
  D636.G7I57   1993
  940.3'1741—dc20   92-21176
                                                                CIP

This group of studies first appeared in a Special Issue on 'The Internment of
Aliens in Twentieth Century Britain' of *Immigrants and Minorities*, Vol.11,
No.3, published by Frank Cass & Co. Ltd.

To Dawn and Mag

Contents

Editors' Note

This volume emerged from a conference organized by the Wiener Library (London) and Parkes Library (University of Southampton), 'Internment Remembered'. It was held in London in May 1990 to commemorate the fiftieth anniversary of the mass detentions of 'enemy aliens' in Britain during the Second World War. We should like at this stage to thank all those at both libraries and also the Association of Jewish Refugees who hosted the event. The conference was successful not only due to the efforts of all the speakers, but also because of the contributions made by the audience which included many former internees, both refugee and Italian.[1] Thanks are also due to Nicholas Jacobs of Libris Books who reprinted in 1990 the classic work by François Lafitte, *The Internment of Aliens*. We were delighted that Professor Lafitte, who did so much to alert the British public in 1940 of the abuses caused by internment, was able to speak at the conference. It was Nicholas Jacobs who initially suggested the idea of the conference.

The gathering proved to be a stimulus for further work. Some of the articles published in this volume were commissioned after the conference and the others have been greatly amended and expanded. It should be emphasized, however, that there are still many areas of the internment process and experience that are yet to be researched. We hope that not only will new work be carried out, but that the British government, following its promise of greater liberality with public records, will help the process of writing the history (and thereby increasing popular awareness) of the internment process by releasing withheld documentation.[2]

The introductory essay in this volume was split between the two editors. Section I was written by Tony Kushner and Section II by David Cesarani. We are pleased to publish in the Appendix testimonies of internees from both world wars and also the recent Gulf War. The use of these pieces stresses the essential need to include the voice of the minorities themselves in historical work – often a feature missing in studies of race and immigration. Thanks are due to George Duckworth for permission to include an extract from Paul Cohen-Portheim's autobiography in this section.

Finally we are grateful to Lydia Linford at Frank Cass for her usual helpfulness and efficiency and to Sybil Lunn for compiling the index to the book form of this collection.

TK and DC

NOTES

1. For a summary of the day's proceedings see David Cesarani, 'Internment Remembered', *The British Journal of Holocaust Education* Vol.1 (Summer 1992), pp.91–5.
2. R.M. Cooper in his interesting *Refugee Scholars: Conversations With Tess Simpson* (Leeds, 1992) includes an excellent section on the internment of roughly 500 refugee scholars in 1940. He points out that 'Unfortunately, even in 1991, the public has not been given access to all the relevant Home Office records' (see Chapter 7 and p.148 specifically).

Alien Internment in Britain During the Twentieth Century: An Introduction

TONY KUSHNER and DAVID CESARANI

Alien internment in Britain remains unexplored and its significance at most is seen as limited, as 'an unimpressive footnote' in modern British history. The introduction explores how internment has been remembered (and forgotten) in a general process of marginalization. It highlights the weaknesses of existing literature and indicates how the essays in this volume confront many of the untouched or unanswered questions of this tragic, comic and often very frightening subject.

I. The Memory of Internment

Britain has a tradition of alien internment in the twentieth century. It is a tradition that is easiest to follow within government administration where there has been bureaucratic continuity from at least the First World War until the conflict in the Gulf in the 1990s. Officials in a range of government departments have been aware of precedents which they have responded to in a variety of ways (even if it appears that the *mistakes* of internment have yet to be learnt).[1] On a popular level, however, alien internment remains a hidden feature of British history. The history of the various episodes is still in its infancy and some of the attempts to reveal its nature have been met with incredulity.

In 1985 a docu-drama was shown on British television which focused on the experiences of refugee internees on the notorious boat, *The SS Dunera*, en route to Australia in 1940. Affronted viewers complained that the manner in which the British soldiers in charge of the internees was shown was grossly unfair, it was 'a complete travesty'. The film by Ben Lewin actually played down the brutality and dishonesty of the British troops on the boat who were, in fact, drawn from a criminal population. The image of British unfairness was too much for some to accept: 'I don't believe that the British *could* have behaved as they were portrayed here'. It was 'wrong' and 'flabbergasting'. Younger viewers were less affronted and less surprised, seeing the treatment as part of a tradition of insensitive 'control' of immigrants and minorities in Britain today. Those sympathetic to the contemporary relevance of Lewin's film were, nevertheless, equally ignorant about the history of alien internment in the Second World War as the individuals who denied that such injustices could possibly have taken place.[2]

Lewin's film, several more serious documentaries and popular semi-scholarly works (as well as some fiftieth anniversary events in 1990) have at least started the process by which alien internment in the Second World War has been pushed into popular consciousness.[3] Biases have developed (some of which this volume will try to correct) but there is now the makings of a scholarly debate and some public awareness of the British treatment of 'enemy aliens' in the anti-Nazi war. The same cannot be said of the parallel story from 1914 to 1918. Indeed the authors of what are the only two major studies of internment in the First World War have complained that

> In the vast corpus of literature devoted to Great Britain's involvement in the First World War one of the more intriguing issues of domestic policy which has previously attracted little more than cursory attention from historians is the treatment of the small minority of the population . . . who found themselves classified as enemy aliens.[4]

Furthermore, 'Despite the enormous amount of attention aroused by the refugees who fled from the Nazis, the question of Germans in Britain before 1933 has never received sufficient attention.'[5]

It has been suggested that the neglect of alien internment in the First World War reflects the more general marginalization of immigrant and minority studies within the writing of British history. Such an explanation has much strength, particularly with reference to the absence of debate in First World War historiography, but more specific factors are also at work.[6] Immediately after the end of the war many thousands of 'enemy aliens' remained interned and there was a determination inside and outside of parliament to remove the alien presence altogether. There was certainly no self-reflection on the justice of the measures taken during the war. In fact there was a move in some military and security circles to continue the wartime measures and to expand them to include other aliens with radical sympathies.[7]

The net result was that 'The First World War destroyed the German communities which had thrived throughout Britain during the Victorian and Edwardian periods'.[8] With the continuation, as Cesarani suggests, of anti-alienism *after* 1918 and the removal of most of those interned, it is perhaps unsurprising that little was written about the internment process or experience in the First World War.[9] In a work produced at the start of the Second World War, the social commentator and travel writer H.V. Morton illustrated how much popular ignorance there was about the impact of internment and other measures taken against 'enemy aliens' in the earlier conflict:

> Nowadays one rarely sees the almost mediaeval wayfarers whom I dimly remember; the Italian with a hand organ and a monkey in a red flannel petticoat; the Punch-and-Judy man; the man with a dancing bear . . . Those characters, and with them the German band, seemed to fade away with the War and have never returned to England.[10]

Morton wrote with no malice, in fact the reverse, at this loss of ethnic diversity on the highways of Britain, but the innocence of his remarks concerning the German bands is remarkable. He appeared unaware of the intolerance of state and public that had removed almost anything of German origin in British society during the war. Morton's naivety is perhaps more surprising given that one of his contemporary travel writers, Paul Cohen-Portheim, had published a detailed account, *Time Stood Still: My Internment in England 1914–1918* in 1931. Cohen-Portheim was inspired to record his internment experiences because he believed that the catastrophe of the war was so immense 'that it can only be reconstructed by a vast number of single accounts of individual and limited experiences'. Moreover, Cohen-Portheim was convinced that it would be important that such 'accounts [not] be limited to those people who took an active part in the fighting' and should also include the civilian experience, including his own as an 'enemy alien'.[11]

It would take a long time for Cohen-Portheim's vision of a genuine social history of the war to be produced and his remained an isolated account of the specific issue of alien internment. Contemporary material such as the diary of another German, Richard Noschke, a resident in England since 1889, was accumulated by the new Imperial War Museum, but only fragments of information were published in the inter-war period.[12]

As the international crisis worsened in the late 1930s, the Home Office and War Office were forced to consider what measures would be taken against enemy aliens in a fresh conflict. Earlier discussions, such as that by the Committee of Imperial Defence in 1923, had suggested that on cost-effective rather than any humanitarian grounds, the mass internment of the First World War should be avoided and where possible the enemy aliens should be expelled. Limited internment should be prepared for, but not on the same scale of the 1914–18 conflict when up to 30,000 aliens lost their liberty.

With the arrival of tens of thousands of refugees from Nazism in the 1930s it became obvious that a new strategy was necessary since, on humanitarian grounds, expulsion back to Greater Germany was unthinkable.[13] As Kushner suggests, there were those in the military and security worlds who constantly distrusted the refugees and thus pressed for mass internment from the start of the war, but theirs was a minority position in the phoney war period. At this time policy was dominated by the Home Office which wished to avoid on administrative grounds (as well as for reasons of natural justice) the mass internment of the First World War. Thus whilst many of the errors of the previous conflict would be repeated in the summer of 1940, there was, at least in the Department most involved in the control of aliens, an awareness of the earlier episode and the public clamour that went with it.[14]

Louise Burletson in this volume highlights the informal government pressure, as well as blatant censorship, which led to the failure to discuss and debate all aspects of the 1940 internment process during the Second World War. Even now, with the destruction (mainly by accident) of much relevant material and continuing government reluctance to release relevant documentation, it is hard to reconstruct the exact nature of the decision-making process in the crisis period of May–July 1940.[15]

Nevertheless, unlike the First World War there was much contemporaneous public criticism of the internment process. In the late summer of 1940 particularly, the issue was widely discussed in liberal circles. Brilliant polemics such as François Lafitte's *The Internment of Aliens* and the anonymous *Anderson's Prisoners*, as well as debates and questions in parliament and criticism in the press, allowed many aspects of internment, including the deportation policy to Australia and Canada, to be discussed openly.[16] There is, therefore, a marked contrast between the situation in the months immediately following the implementation of a policy of mass internment and the almost complete absence of debate by the end of the war. Indeed, it could be suggested that the latter silence has only recently been broken. How did this silence come about and why has the episode again become, if only in a limited way, one of public interest?

During the Second World War itself several refugee memoirs of the internment episode were published. Although not uncritical in tone, their general attitude was benign towards British government and society.[17] Several factors were at work which also partly explain why the refugees from Nazism, the majority of those interned, did not want to dwell on the episode. First and perhaps foremost was the desire not to appear ungrateful – Britain had provided these individuals with asylum and if treatment by the British was not always considerate there was still a sense of debt to the country that had offered them refuge. From this came a desire to emphasize the more positive aspects of internment – the experience gained or the comic interludes rather than the more searching question of *why* their internment had been necessary in the first place.

Second, their position was still vulnerable. In the latter part of the war refugees became anxious over what was to be their future after the conflict. Few but the most politically motivated had any desire to return to the continent yet their status in Britain was uncertain. Many, for example, had come on temporary transfer visas and had been unable to continue their journeys because of the war. After the war the struggle for naturalization and the right to take up a range of occupations was slow and frustrating; the refugees were thus in no position to embarrass their somewhat reluctant hosts.[18]

It is interesting to contrast their unwillingness to criticize Britain with those in extreme-wing of the Zionist movement whose hatred of the British government in the immediate post-war years freed them of any restraint (and also made them anxious to use any ammunition against what they saw as their new enemy). Thus in the summer of 1947, when the British government was turning back the ships carrying survivors of the Holocaust which had reached the shores of Palestine, the Revisionist Zionist *Jewish Standard* produced a virulent article 'On the Subject of Hell-Ships' describing in graphic detail the abuses that had occurred on board *The SS Dunera*. Rather than treating them as an aberration, the article suggested that the deportations of 1940 and the current policy in Palestine were typical of an imperial people – as was the hypocrisy of presenting such policies 'framed in saintly halos'. Nevertheless, supporters of the line taken by the *Jewish Standard* were few in number and none of its contemporaries inside or outside the refugee world were prepared to make such forthright attacks on alien internment.[19]

The third point is that alien internment in the Second World War was, for the majority, a short-lived experience. Once it ended most wanted to get on with the difficult task of keeping together what family and friends they had and to struggle through the war and the difficult post-war austerity years. The fourth point related to the image of the war more generally in British culture. Angus Calder has written of the important role of mythology in Britain during the Second World War. The war was constructed from below and above, especially during the blitz, as one 'of British or English moral pre-eminence, buttressed by British unity'. Following Patrick Wright, Calder believes that these myths were essentially particularistic. The 'sense of national identity and belonging' was crucial in the war years and those immediately following. The war made clear who was and was not a real member of British society. For the refugees to complain about internment was not only to risk appearing disloyal, it would also emphasize their outsider status in British society.[20]

It is therefore significant that the monthly journal of the Association of

Jewish Refugees (AJR) published nothing on alien internment until 1951. The first overt reference to it was a short review of an early post-war memoir of internment, Eugen Spier's *The Protecting Power*:

> Most of us have already forgotten the days when we were guests of boarding houses at the Isle of Man or inhabitants of race course stables. Therefore at first sight it may seem a little odd that now, after 10 years, a book on the internment of aliens is being published. Whilst, however, for the majority of the then enemy aliens the funny aspects of the internment episode stand in the foreground of their recollection, Mr Spier belongs to that unhappy minority whose experience was a more serious one.[21]

Four more years passed before the AJR published a full article on internment (and this was in the form of a nostalgic report of a visit by a former inhabitant of the Hutchinson Camp to the Isle of Man).[22] Criticism of government policy was still unacceptable in refugee circles. In a review article of 1955 published in the refugee-dominated *Wiener Library Bulletin*, internment was put down to a 'misunderstanding'. Instead of concentrating on why it occurred, attention focused on the release process; 'an outstanding example of British fairness which was bound to reconcile even those who felt bitterness before'.[23]

In the summer of 1960 the AJR's journal decided to mark the twentieth anniversary of internment. The editors called for material on the event (with the significant proviso that it should not be 'from the political angle' and must relate only to 'personal interest'). As a result of this request, several pieces were published in the autumn of 1960 (reflecting, perhaps, the point two decades earlier when the releases rather than the internments were being implemented). The collection of articles showed internment 'in somewhat lighthearted reminiscences' as one commentator later put it.[24] The refugees left in Britain were almost all now naturalized and a good number had done well in British society. Internment had thus almost become part of an initiation test before full membership could be achieved: 'Was it not rather ridiculous, we tell each other, to take it as seriously as we did?' Stress was placed on 'the informal cameraderie of camp life, in mixing with all sorts of people whom they would not meet in their usual walk of life'.[25]

There was, however, in the lead article by Leo Kahn, a recognition that in 1940 'At a crucial and anxious time, internment brought additional stress into too many individual lives to be easily forgotten'. He also remarked that 'The "Arandora Star", the "Dunera" – that was serious'. Yet Kahn's conclusion on internment, despite these references, was adamant: 'it produced no lasting effects, and in the history of our community it remains an odd episode of small significance. There is no need to mark the occasion with much solemnity.'[26]

Internment in the Second World War, then, by 1960 had been sanitized into a jolly jape. Quite rightly the *achievements* of the internees had been stressed, but this was at the cost of any serious analysis of why the process had been instituted in the first place by the British state. Within the refugee community those with a more critical perspective were not encouraged to air their views. It was acknowledged that some, already perhaps in a distraught mental state or in physical ill-health, were badly affected by the experience, but the anger, bitterness and disappointment of 1940 (and, for some, much beyond) was put aside. As Leo Kahn remarked, 'we were rather unduly sorry for ourselves in that summer of 1940'.[27]

Kahn, however, was open enough to refer to the deportee ships and to acknowledge that 'in the internment story there were some incidents which even now we do not like to remember'.[28] If this was true of the refugee community (which, although shaken by the internment episode, was able to gather itself together quite soon after the crisis period in 1940), it was certainly the case for Italians in Britain. In no way could the Italians describe alien internment as an 'odd episode of small significance'. A shared silence was common to both groups but in the case of the Italians the reticence was not only due to fear of voicing ingratitude (like the refugees there was concern over status and freedom in post-war Britain and a struggle to obtain British citizenship). It was also because internment and especially the horrendous loss of life on *The Arandora Star*

> affected the pysche of the 'old' British Italian Community in such a deep and fundamental way that it is only now, 50 years on, that the Community is beginning to come to terms with these events. There is a long-standing but muted grief and humiliation within the 'old' Community because of these events.[29]

This was perhaps the case with only a minority of the refugee internees. Nevertheless, it is revealing that, in 1989/90, a significant number of former refugees also expressed bitterness in an open manner for the first time. A clear split occurred between those who felt indignant towards the British authorities and those whose feelings are still dominated by an overriding sense of gratitude towards Britain.[30]

In the case of the Italians, Terri Colpi suggests that for many who suffered 'An awkward taboo surrounding all aspects of the war-time experience seemed to develop'.[31] Here the experience of the British Italians is in contrast to the refugees who, from the 1970s, with the aid of national and local oral history projects, were anxious to record their recollections of life in Nazi Europe and, subsequently, in Britain. Colpi adds that those Italians who were young in the war and were subject to humiliation did 'not want to be reminded or to remember'. Moreover, given the shortage or oral and written testimony, the task of rediscovering the Italian wartime experience has been intensified by the reluctance of the British government to release relevant material. Discussion about the torpedoed *Arandora Star*, which led to the loss of over 400 Italian lives, was surpressed in the war and today documentation in the public domain on this disaster is still limited. The net result of both internal restraint and official reticence has been that 'very few British people admit to knowing much about the internment of Italians during the war and even fewer have heard of *The Arandora Star*'.[32]

As late as the mid-1970s, little or no progress had been made in discovering the roots of alien internment in the Second World War (or for that matter in the First World War – a topic which had fallen into obscurity). Lafitte's Penguin Special written and published in record time in the summer and autumn of 1940 along with its contemporary, *Anderson's Prisoners*, remained the only critical accounts and public memory of the events had almost totally faded. Angus Calder has stressed how the mythology of the war continued beyond 1945. The interning of the aliens, if not their release, did not fit the image of 'Britain Alone, fighting for democracy and freedom against totalitarianism'. He adds that 'the myth-making process . . . would eventually ensure that [the internment process] was rewritten with the aliens as an unimpressive footnote'.[33] This state of affairs was to be at least questioned in the early 1980s when the subject became a minor academic growth industry. Even then, however, the new work had little impact on 'mainstream' historiography. Moreover, the work produced was certainly not without distortions and omissions.[34]

Nevertheless, some individuals were willing to 'rediscover' alien internment. Two factors were particularly at work. The first, already briefly referred to, was the desire of refugees from Nazism to record their experiences. There was a parallel recognition from some in British society that the life stories of the refugees had great significance.[35] At around the same time, the first research on Allied responses to the crisis of European Jewry in the Nazi era was published. Alien internment was only one aspect of this new work, but the subject was for the first time studied seriously by academics and other investigators. The second factor further enabled the first to take place – the availability of records previously retained by a range of government departments.

As a result, a section of Bernard Wasserstein's 1979 work, *Britain and the Jews of Europe, 1939–1945*, focused on alien internment. The following year two books were totally devoted to the topic. The first was by Ronald Stent, himself a former refugee. The second was by Peter and Leni Gillman, investigative journalists working for the *Sunday Times*. The former was the first to provide a coherent account of camp life, including on the Isle of Man, Canada and Australia; the latter was the first attempt since Laffitte's to investigate the internal government debate about internment.[36] Other works published in the 1980s concentrated on the experience of internment, the deportations abroad and life on the Isle of Man. A major television documentary and several television plays were also devoted to the subject. Alien internment in the Second World War had been rediscovered, if only in a relatively specialist and fragmentary way.[37]

There were problems with this new material. First, the very fact of rediscovery led to a potential for sensationalism. There was still only limited documentation on the government decision-making process. In the mid-1980s a large amount of Home Office material was released. Whilst it gave an enormous amount of information on the administration of internment, the new files were almost silent on the implementation of policy in the crisis months of 1940. In the summer of 1940, conspiracy theories developed in left-liberal circles with regard to the internment of enemy aliens. It was suggested that right-wing elements inside and outside of government had turned attention to the refugees and others to hide their own subversive 'fifth column' activities. There was little evidence to support such an analysis, apart from the tenuous link that the strongest pro-appeasement papers in the 1930s were the same ones demanding mass internment in 1940. Yet with the continued shortage of hard information as late as the 1980s, conspiracy theories continued to circulate. A sober investigation of state policy was made difficult.[38] Matters were not helped by the continued reluctance of historians of Britain in the war, especially those concerned with political developments, to even mention alien internment. Angus Calder's *The People's War*, published in 1969, was a rare and partial exception.[39]

It was also only with the later releases of government files in the 1980s that a significant body of records became available on the Italian experience.[40] This, coupled with the bias towards the refugee aspect of internment, had previously led to a marginalization of the Italians – a distortion that is only now being corrected. Even the relatively voluminous work on refugee internment suffered from a continuing reluctance to offer an overly critical response. The literature on camp life itself was too celebratory in tone and at times lacked academic vigour. Thus it is not surprising that in a major collection of academic articles on German-speaking Jews in the United Kingdom published in 1991, which concentrated on the arrivals from Nazi Germany, not one piece was devoted to internment among the 36 offerings.[41] By the end of the 1980s there was a substantial body of literature and artistic output on alien internment (including a detailed investigation of state policy in the First World War), but there was still resistance to treating the subject with any great seriousness.[42] The commemoration of the fiftieth anniversary of mass internment in 1990 marked both the progress that had been made as well as the persistent limitations.

1989 and 1990 were years of major anniversary celebrations in Britain. The war remains the focal point in national memory and identity. It is, in Patrick Wright's words, 'that over-riding moment of national dignity and worth'. After 1945 an increasingly exclusive national identity (especially with regard to coloured immigration) became dependent on reference to the war years: 'We did make a terrible mistake letting them in. To think our men died to let that lot in.' As Wright adds, 'actual memories of the Second World War can be recuperated to a national mythologization and redeclaration of that war'.[43] Britain, of all countries, is most at ease with its self-image in the Second World War. There is no question of collaboration (with the minor exception of the Channel Islands) and a confidence and pride in knowing that Britain had remained steadfast against the Nazis for all of the conflict.[44] Myths, such as that of the blitz and communal spirit and 'taking it', are now so powerfully ingrained that questioning their reality is frequently labelled 'unpatriotic'.[45] Against this background it is hardly surprising that alien internment, and especially incidents such as *The Arandora Star*, are not given any serious attention. It was thus perhaps a sign of greater maturity that in 1990 events to mark the fiftieth anniversary of internment in spring/summer 1940 received some limited media interest. A reunion of Italian survivors of *The Arandora Star* was held at the Imperial War Museum and a serious academic conference (from which this volume indirectly originates) was organized jointly by the Parkes and Wiener Libraries.[46] These, however, were sideshows compared to the major war commemorations taking place almost simultaneously through the spring and summer of 1990. In particular, those most mythologized of British war episodes, Dunkirk, the Battle of Britain and the blitz received renewed and generally uncritical attention.

These events are still far too important in terms of contemporary definitions of 'Englishness' for any objective account of their real significance to be undertaken by British society.[47] It is therefore difficult in the 1990s for issues which would involve even greater self-criticism, such as alien internment, to receive the attention they deserve. It is true that compared to 1980 the discussion of alien internment a decade later was less prone to sensationalism and was no longer a hidden part of British history. There was still, however, little attempt to understand the implications of the earlier episodes as the tragic repetition (if on only a very limited scale) of internment in Britain, this time during the Gulf War, graphically illustrated.

The details of the Gulf War episode will be dealt with in the epilogue and conclusion. Here it is simply worth commenting that for many popular British commentators in the early months of 1991, the mistakes and hardships caused by the internment of enemy aliens in Britain during the previous world wars might just as well never have happened. To a minority, however, the lessons of the past were all too obvious. The campaigners for the release of the internees and prisoners thus gained strength from the hard-won knowledge and memory that had been so tortuously gathered in the post-war period.[48]

II. Introduction to the Contributions

The contributions to this volume are designed to establish the importance of alien internment in modern British history. They aim at least to begin the process of correcting the imbalance and omissions in existing work. That the literature is still so undeveloped reflects the manner in which the wider significance of alien internment has been too readily dismissed. For this reason the first studies by Cesarani and Panayi necessarily set out to establish the continuities in anti-alienism and the internment policy which inexorably grew out of it under wartime conditions. The intention is to show that the mass internment of aliens cannot be disregarded as aberrant or something confined to conditions in Britain in 1939–40, but should be seen as close to the core of political culture in Britain.[49]

Drawing on recent work undertaken by the historians of ideas, Cesarani demonstrates that the notion of the alien as a threatening presence was already evident in mid-Victorian social thought. It was greatly strengthened by socio-biological theories, such as eugenics, prevalent from the 1860s onwards.[50] Anti-alienism as a movement was the pre-eminent popular response to the first wave of mass immigration (apart from the exceptional case of the Irish) experienced by Britain in the modern era. Unlike the USA where powerful economic forces buttressed a liberal open-door policy, the perceived threat of cheap labour turned a substantial portion of English public opinion against unrestricted immigration. In the 1890s and 1900s, asylum and pro-alien feeling, which had been a distinctive if paradoxical feature of mid-Victorian society, gave way decisively to the demand for immigration controls. Politicians now discovered the potency of anti-alien rhetoric.[51]

The 1905 Aliens Act was a benchmark in the decline of liberalism and set in train the remorseless erosion of asylum as an ideal and a practice. The public learned that clamour, even localized and limited, could succeed in closing the doors to refugees and economic migrants. Politicians saw that there was much to gain and little to lose from appeasing anti-alienism. Officials in the Home Office acquired experience in the administration of entry controls and also the regulation of aliens inside the country. A dynamic relationship evolved in which each element radicalized the other. Hence, the regulation of enemy aliens in World War One fed off spy scares in the 1900s and 1910s while civil servants had already rehearsed the measures that were put into place. The first mass internment in 1915 represented the surrender of a Liberal government to xenophobic public opinion that articulated stereotypes of the foreigner as conspirator, criminal and degenerate that had been present in popular culture for decades.[52]

Anti-alienism was heightened by the war years and persisted into peacetime, accentuated by new fears such as the threat of revolution, drug scares and fear of miscegenation. Cesarani is at pains to demonstrate that anti-alien discourse was a seamless web: the same stereotypes of the alien Other encompassed groups such as Jews, Germans, Blacks, Chinese and Gypsies. Anxieties concerning class, public health, moral codes and, above all, national identity were projected onto immigrants and minorities.[53] The response to Jewish refugee immigration and the wave of internment in 1940 was, therefore, hardly atypical. It was consistent with a pattern of popular attitudes, political behaviour and official practice stemming from the turn of the century.

Nor was the experience of being an alien or undergoing internment a unique one in modern British history. Panayi forcefully objects to the way that British historians have marginalized or completely ignored the harsh treatment and considerable suffering of tens of thousands of Germans in Britain between 1914 and 1918.[54] Internment in the First World War was a complex operation involving several departments of state and the range of armed services. Germans were concentrated in an array of camps, several of which were vast agglomerations holding over 20,000 people. His detailed examination throws light for the first time on the intricacies of this massive operation: the size and lay-out of the camps, the conditions in them, the supply and quality of food, employment patterns amongst the inmates, leisure occupations and the human cost. This highly textured description is vital as the template for the events of 1940. Although at the start of the Second World War the Home Office was determined to avoid the expense and inconvenience of mass-internment, when its resistance crumbled the model and apparent lessons of 1914–18 were of crucial importance.

Panayi shows that the enactment of internment in 1915 cannot be divorced from patterns of anti-alienism before the war, notably the anti-German feeling coursing through the popular spy and war-scare novels of the Edwardian period. War led to the progressive suspension of liberal doctrines and removed the paramount obstacle to wide-ranging state intervention at the behest of public opinion and vociferous politicians.[55] The consequent impact on individuals was immense: deprivation of liberty, separation from family, loss of business and employment, poor health, mental distress and, ultimately, for many, expulsion from Britain. By 1919 the German population of the Britsh Isles had been forcibly reduced by over 20,000 souls. There are no means to calculate the misery involved in this ruthless policy of deportation.

The decision-making process (which culminated in mass internment and the transportation of aliens abroad) during the Second World War was marked by such confusion that it would have made a classic scenario for the Keystone Cops, except that it was in earnest and ended in tragedy. For the internees it was anything but funny, even if time and discretion mellowed their subsequent pronouncements on what they went through. The six contributions by Kushner, Burletson, Sponza, Kochan, Colpi and Hinrichsen move from Whitehall to the internment camps and convey both the muddled thinking of central policy-makers and the bewildered, pained responses of the internees.

As in 1914–18, internment was the product of official thinking and careful planning, even if this later went awry. Kushner delineates the mentality of politicians, civil servants and their advisers in the military and secret services. He shows how several powerful individuals fed clubland prejudices against foreigners, particularly Jewish refugees from Central Europe, into Whitehall policy-making.

At the start of the war, policy towards aliens had been informed by a traditional, if attenuated, liberalism and the lessons of the earlier conflict. Yet this liberal approach contained the seeds of disaster. The aliens were subjected to loyalty tests by the very tribunals which had been intended to forestall the necessity of mass detentions. They were further compromised by the refugee agencies which sought to reassure British public opinion by demanding rapid anglicization of those whom they were representing. This implicitly suggested that there was something at fault in being a Continental. It was only another short step to accepting the internment of refugee aliens as a prudent measure to allay 'understandable' public unease.

When the Fall of France generated a sense of national crisis, public opinion inevitably focused on questions of identity and loyalty: the unthinkable failure in battle was attributed to enemies within. The right-wing journal *Truth* inflamed animosity against Jews generally and refugees in particular, notably with the suggestion that they were potential subversives. *Truth* was directed by Sir Joseph Ball, a senior figure in the Conservative Party and an adviser to the Prime Minister, Neville Chamberlain. This obsession about spies was shared, not unsurprisingly, with the security services and MI5 in particular. Ball was a senior member of the Swinton Committee set up in May 1940 to prosecute internment while William Cavendish-Bentinck, the chairman of the Joint Intelligence Committee, was a key figure in the enactment of internment. It was thus in the hands of a small circle of men who operated with firm preconceptions about aliens. These ideas emanated from a cultural and political discourse which has already been described.

The familiar dynamic now reasserted itself. Initially the Home Office had intended to avoid mass internment, but it found itself beleaguered by the press, the military and security services, and worried politicians. Instead of defying the agitation and calling for a steady nerve, the government sent out signals that only incited public opinion and aggravated disquiet. Each stage of 'limited' internment fostered the impression that, indeed, there was something wrong about the aliens. The refugee organizations and the refugees themselves fell into the trap of attempting to prove their loyalty, thus only underlining the construction of the alien as a possible 'Fifth Columnist'.

Anxiety and rage, inflected by gender and class, were projected onto the hapless aliens. As Kushner illustrates, female refugee domestics were construed so as to embody simultaneously the peril of sexual subversion, class war and national humiliation. The liberal tradition represented by the Home Secretary, Sir John Anderson, was swept aside. However, it made a curious come-back late in 1940 when the short duration of mass internment was acclaimed as a 'victory' for liberalism at a time of national crisis. This triumphalism, along with the other factors mentioned above, may have long inhibited the former internees from protesting against their rough handling.

Yet internment was ultimately arrested and wound down, even if in an equally haphazard and gender-biased way. By August 1942 only about 5,000 persons were still in custody, of whom only a few hundred were refugees. To this extent liberal principles were not obliterated and were successfully mobilized in the campaign to rescind government policy. Burletson examines Home Office papers to reveal the sensitivity of officials to criticism. They were concerned not to alienate opinion in neutral countries, especially the USA, or allied states. It was also considered important to deny the Germans any pretext for maltreating any British citizens in their hands or handing them a propaganda victory.

Nor could the Red Cross be ignored. The most persistent and effective critique came from MPs including Eleanor Rathbone, George Strauss, Josiah Wedgwood, Frank Bellenger and Sidney Silverman. They were assisted by the liberal press and the Jewish newspapers.

However, as Burletson shows, the government consistently applied censorship or used misinformation to stifle public debate as well as to blunt and deflect criticism. Internees were lured into accepting 'voluntary' transportation overseas by the false promise that they would be reunited with their families. Ironically, the government also misled the Dominions in an attempt to get them to share the burden posed by the internees. Letters of complaint about their treatment or diaries of the 'hellish' journeys to Canada and Australia were ruthlessly censored. Editors and journalists were ceaselessly manipulated by the Ministry of Information and virtually blackmailed into whitewashing the affair with the plea that negative comment would damage the war effort. When the insensitive and unpopular commandant of the womens' camp on the Isle of Man was removed from her post, the government acted swiftly to curb adverse publicity.[56]

Together Kushner and Burletson expose the undemocratic, secretive and illiberal nature of mass internment. Their contributions, and those by Sponza and Kochan, also indicate the tragi-comic consequences. It was possible for the confusion, errors and blatant injustices which characterized the process to occur precisely because the secret service was allowed such influence in an operation that was made unaccountable to the public and concealed from either parliament or the press.

In their contributions Sponza and Colpi expose the arbitrariness and cruelty of the internment process. Colpi notes that there was no screening of Italians even during the tense months of 1939–40. When the order came to 'Collar the lot', the police relied on lists provided by central government which, in turn, obtained its information from the secret services. The result was disastrous: many Italians who were interned were British-born, while others were well over 60 years old. Most ludicrously, certain Italians ended up on MI5 lists as a result of their prior anti-Fascist activities. Men were torn from their families in the middle of the night or in dawn-raids, a practice more usually associated with the conduct of totalitarian regimes.

In another disturbing parallel, Sponza explains that the security services were assigned numbers of aliens to arrest on a quota basis. When these could not be filled, largely because they were set at random, names were plucked from any available source. These lists were compiled with scant knowledge of the Italian community or its social organization. There was little sensitivity to the function of Italian associations. Many of these had been colonized and exploited by the Italian embassy, but their superficial ideological allegiance bore no relation to the actual proclivities of their members. The majority of Italians had lived in the United Kingdom for decades and although they retained ties to their homeland, or more particularly to the towns, villages and regions from which they had emigrated, they considered themselves loyal to Britain.[57]

Class again played a part in the seizure of Italians: few were wealthy or had friends 'in high places'. It was not until the Home Office and the Foreign Office joined forces that there was any attempt at a proper screening of detainees. Even then, the head of the Home Office Advisory Committee, Sir Percy Loraine, was soon at odds with his Civil Service overlords and grew impatient with MI5's reluctance to release allegedly Fascist Italians. As with the workings of the Swinton Committee, there seems to have been a perceptible right-wing bias, combined with derogatory attitudes towards foreigners. Loraine's chief lieutenant was actually accused of pro-fascist sympathies! All in all it was a lamentable muddle, but it was not accidental just for being chaotic. Official attitudes were underpinned by certain predispositions about foreigners and an almost willful ignorance about the realities of a minority identity in Britain.

The devastating impact of internment is graphically described by Terri Colpi as she charts the traumatization and virtual destruction of Italian communities that had been present in Britain since the nineteenth century. By alighting on the discreet and neglected experience of women and children she throws a spotlight on to some of the most wounding aspects of the events in June–July 1940. Women, whose men had been arrested in the dead of night, were left defenceless as xenophobic mobs roamed the streets where Italian families lived. Shops were wrecked in several days of anti-Italian rioting that left families without a means of earning a livelihood at the same time as the chief breadwinner was wrenched away. The sons and daughters of interned Italian men were taunted with racist soubriquets when they attended school. For some the shock was so great that in later life they tried to disguise or eliminate their Italian identity.

While gender inflected the impact of anti-alienism and internment on the women left behind, varieties of sexism were as effectively at work as the forces of Anglo-Saxon supremacism in determining who would go behind the wire. The fact that only 4,000 of the internees were women indicates to Kochan that the authorities acted with patriarchal disdain for females. Most alien women were simply not regarded as being much of a threat to national security. As Kochan points out, the history of spying in the First World War should have given the secret service pause for thought in this respect, but on the whole gender stereotypes prevailed. The patronizing stereotype, treating women as harmless, could work to their benefit by protecting them from incarceration. But in the case of single women, particularly refugee domestics, they could operate in a malign fashion by constructing females as subversive, predatory and dangerous.

Even though the proportion of women amongst these interned was relatively low, for the thousands of women internees the experience was disorientating and in many cases humiliating. Many passed through the depressing, Victorian womens' prisons in London. When they arrived on the Isle of Man, Jewish women and anti-fascists found themselves sharing quarters with ardent German nationalists and Nazi sympathizers. Political hatreds added to the febrile atmosphere in which quarrels and fights became commonplace.

Yet, in many respects, the women were able to cope with their involuntary detention better than the men. Large numbers found employment as domestics inside the camps (enabling their employers to live in enviable comfort). They proved adept at organizing food supplies and preparing meals, provided excellent medical care for one another (including the pregnant women caught up in the internment net) and devoted considerable expertise to education programmes. Cultural activities flourished as much in the womens' camps as in the mens' and Kochan records that women previously involved in the theatre put on first-class productions.

These were compensations only in degree: the separation from loved ones, husbands and children caused misery. Unlike most of the male internees, women have also testified to the sexual frustration of incarceration and its effect on inter-personal relations. Kochan records that they fought over available males and, in one case, tried to rape an elderly gentleman found on the wrong side of the wire. There is a suspicious silence over the parallel aspect of life in the mens' camps.

Some light is thrown on this neglected subject by Hinrichsen in his examination of art and artists interned on the Isle of Man. 'Erotic nubile nymphs' were amongst the first subjects scratched into the black-out paint of the windows of the buildings in which the artists found themselves confined. Hinrichsen catalogues the capacity for improvization, resilience and humour of these dislocated painters and sculptors.

Many of them had seen their work proscribed by the Nazis as degenerate or politically incorrect. So they needed a good dose of flexibility and wry humour to withstand the disillusionment of being put behind wire by the authorities (whom they regarded as their protectors when they initially found refuge in Britain). However, they put the time to good use and, arguably, enjoyed a privileged life for the customarily insecure and impecunious creative personality. Once by ingenious means they had acquired the tools for their art they enjoyed free food and lodgings and were left to sculpt, sketch or paint at will.

Internment surely produced one of the most bizarre inventories of artistic materials. Linoleum was cannibalized for lino cuts, graphite from pencils and margarine were mixed together for ink, while a mangle was utilized to manufacture prints. After the camp commander provided the wherewithal for roneoed newsletters, the volume and quality of stencil productions rose dramatically and resulted in numerous enduring works. The famous Artists Café in the basement of a lodging house provided a focus for political and artistic debate as well as an informal seminar room for younger, aspiring members of the creative fraternity. It was here that the other, distinctive elements of internment were explored from an artistic perspective. In August 1940, a group of artists gathered in the café compiled a dramatic and heartfelt letter which was later published in the *New Statesman*. It was constructed around the desperate plea that art could not flourish in captivity. The note of despair was explored in many of the works which survive today. One sketchbook still in existence coolly depicts a man who hanged himself in the camp.

Hinrichsen notes that the artists were divided by political and religious allegiance as much as by fealty to particular schools. But they shared a feeling of estrangement from their homeland and a powerful sense of loss. If internment art produced a single, memorable image it was the barbed wire motif that appears in several works. Equally distinctive are the portraits of resignation and unhappiness. Beneath the jollity of the café and the high jinx of the artists in their search for materials, behind the façade of busy-ness in the preparation of exhibitions and running courses there was an appreciation that they had been unjustly deprived of their liberty and immured in the most painful and uncertain circumstances.

Nor did the experience of internment 'end' when individuals were released or even with the conclusion of the war. Colpi analyses the dramatic impact it had on the social structure and identity of the Italian communities in Great Britain. Those who had endured the prejudice and discrimination of the war years remained afraid of government agencies and kept a low profile. Many of the children who had grown up during the war, carrying the stigma of interned or deported fathers, sought to meld into British society by anglicizing their names and modifying their behaviour. For decades a distinction existed between the quiet and timid survivors of the damaged 'old' communities and the more confident and optimistic arrivals in post-war Britain.

The personal accounts of internment in the Second World War

contained in the Appendix, mostly written four decades after the events they describe, eloquently testify to the lasting effects of that experience. For the thousands of men and women in Britain today who underwent internment it remains lodged in their memory. The recollection may have been repressed, modified or still be raw, but it cannot be denied. Until British historiography and British society embraces this episode, what they endured will be continually rendered marginal or private. This will only serve to reinforce and perpetuate the negative connotations of having once been an interned alien and the sense of injustice at what occurred. Yet it will not be possible to make sense of mass internment without grasping anti-alienism as the root from which it sprang and this, in turn, poses a challenge to construct a genuinely heterogenous and pluralistic narrative of modern British history. This volume is intended as a modest contribution to that task. Finally it is hopefully intended, in small measure, as a balm for wounds inflicted in the past and a means to avert a repetition of the blows which caused them.

NOTES

1. There is no legal text surveying internment legislation but see Vaughan Bevan, *The Development of British Immigration Laws* (London, 1986); Ian Macdonald, *Immigration Law and Practice in the United Kingdom* (London, 1991); A. Dummett and Andrew Nicol, *Subjects, Citizens, Aliens and Others: Nationality and Immigration Law* (London, 1990) and, more polemically, Steve Cohen, *From The Jews to the Tamils: Britain's Mistreatment of Refugees* (Manchester, 1988). For bureaucratic continuity see Loiuse London, 'British Immigration Control Procedures and Jewish Refugees, 1933–1942' (unpublished Ph.D., University of London, 1992) and Cesarani's contribution to this volume. PRO HO 45/25754/863027/1, 10 Jan. 1940 for Home Office concern about the problems associated with internment in the First World War.
2. 'The Dunera Boys' was shown on 15/17 Oct. 1985 on Channel 4 television. The heated responses came in Channel 4's 'Right to Reply', 18 and 25 Oct. 1985. See also *Jewish Chronicle*, 18 Oct. 1985.
3. An interesting documentary, 'Jailed By the British', by Lavinia Warner and Terry Hughes was shown on Channel 4, 16 Feb. 1983. Plays which touch upon internment include David Pirie's 'Rainy Day Women' (1984). In January 1991 Tyne Tees and Border Television showed an excellent documentary on internment life, 'His Majesty's Most Loyal Enemy Aliens' which achieved a fine critical balance between the achievements of the refugees on the Isle of Man on the one hand and stressing the unnecessary nature of internment as a whole on the other. For a summary of the early literature see Paul Hoch, 'Gaoling the Victim', *Immigrants & Minorities* Vol.4, No.1 (March 1985), pp.79–83.
4. J.C. Bird, *Control of Enemy Alien Civilians in Great Britain 1914–1918* (New York, 1986), p.6.
5. Panikos Panayi, *The Enemy in Our Midst: Germans in Britain during the First World War* (Oxford, 1991), p.1.
6. Panayi, op. cit., p.1. A. Marwick, *The Deluge: British Society and the First World War* (London, 1965), pp.37-8 devotes one sentence to alien internment and the contributions in John Turner (ed.), *Britain and the First World War* (London, 1988) and Bernard

Waites, *A Class Society at War: England 1914–1918* (Leamington Spa, 1987) do not mention it all.

7. See the parliamentary debate on the Aliens Restriction Bill, *Hansard* (HC) Vol.114, Cols.2745–2818, 15 April 1919 and London, 'British Immigration Control Procedures', pp.56–7 and Sharman Kadish, *Bolsheviks and British Jews: The Anglo-Jewish Community, Britain and the Russian Revolution* (London, 1992), Ch.5 on the attempt to use internment and other measures against radical aliens.

8. Panayi, op. cit., p.283.

9. Cesarani contribution to this volume and idem, 'Anti-Alienism in England After the First World War', *Immigrants & Minorities* Vol.6, No.1 (March 1987), pp.5–29. For an early account of internment see Anna Thomas, *St. Stephen's House: Friends Emergency Work in England* (London, 1920), Ch.IV.

10. H.V. Morton, *I Saw Two Englands: The Record of a Journey Before the War, And After the Outbreak of War in the Year 1939* (London, 1943), p.32.

11. Paul Cohen-Portheim, *Time Stood Still: My Internment in England 1914–1918* (London, 1931), pp.1–3.

12. See Panikos Panayi, 'The Imperial War Museum as a Source of Information for Historians of Immigrant Minorities: The Example of Germans During the First World War', *Immigrants & Minorities* Vol.6, No.3 (Nov. 1987), pp.348-52. See A. Thomas, op. cit., for other, limited, published material.

13. For the shift in policy see R. Stent, *A Bespattered Page? The Internment of 'His Majesty's Most Loyal Enemy Aliens'* (London, 1980), pp.18–26.

14. See Kushner's contribution to this volume. For further evidence of the security world's suspicion of the refugees and Jews in particular see A. Masters, *The Man Who Was M: The Life of Maxwell Knight* (Oxford, 1984), pp.70–71, 110.

15. Peter and Leni Gillman, *'Collar the Lot!' How Britain Interned and Expelled Its Wartime Refugees* (London, 1980), pp.xi–xiv on the Home Office and internment records – released, withheld and destroyed. In 1986 more material was released. See Colin Holmes, 'Internment, Fascism and the Public records', *Bulletin of the Society for the Study of Labour History* Vol.52, No.1 (1987), pp.17–18 for a brief description. Some of the contributions to this volume make use of this new material.

16. François Lafitte, *The Internment of Aliens* (Harmondsworth, 1940); 'Judex', *Anderson's Prisoners* (London, 1940).

17. Alfred Lomnitz, *Never Mind, Mr Lom* (London, 1941); Alfred Perlès, *Alien Corn* (London, 1941) and Livia Laurent, *A Tale of Internment* (London, 1942) were the most prominent internment memoirs published in the war itself.

18. For post-war frustrations with the naturalization process and work restrictions see the monthly journal of the Association of Jewish Refugees, *AJR Information* from its first issue in January 1946. Marion Berghahn, *Continental Britons: German-Jewish Refugees from Nazi Germany* (Oxford, 1988), Chs. 6 and 7 for an analysis of refugee identity after the war.

19. A. Abrahams in *Jewish Standard*, 1 August 1947.

20. Berghahn, op. cit., pp.138–50 for the pressures operating on the refugees 'On being a guest'; Angus Calder, *The Myth of the Blitz* (London, 1991), p.10; Patrick Wright, *On Living in an Old Country: The National Past in Contemporary Britain* (London, 1985).

21. Werner Rosenstock, 'Record of an Episode', *AJR Information*, May 1951.

22. F.I. Wiener, 'Hutchinson Square Revisited', *AJR Information*, Sept. 1957.

23. H. Jaeger, 'Refugees' Internment in Britain 1939–40', *Wiener Library Bulletin* Vol.9, Nos.3–4 (May–Aug. 1955), p.31.

24. The request was in the July 1960 issue of *AJR Information*, the articles published in Sept. 1960 and the critique offered by Lucie Laquer in the same journal in Nov. 1960.

25. Leo Kahn, 'On Internment', *AJR Information*, Sept. 1960.

26. Ibid.

27. Berghahn, op. cit., pp.142–9 on the pressure *within* the refugee community to conform and show gratitude (as with the 'Thank-you Britain Fund' established in 1964/5); Kahn, 'On Internment'. Some of the most tragic cases of alien internment including

death through ill-health and suicide are highlighted in the HO 214 files released in 1986.
28. Kahn, 'On Internment'.
29. Terri Colpi, *The Italian Factor: The Italian Community in Great Britain* (Edinburgh, 1991), p.99.
30. This was partly reflected in two separate *Kindertransporte* (those who came to Britain as child refugees) anniversary reunions in 1989, one more celebratory in tone and the other more critical. See *Jewish Chronicle*, 30 June and 21 July 1989. In 1990 such debates continued with the internment anniversary. A strong division of opinion by former internees was expressed by members of the audience at the conference held in May 1990 from which this publication emerged. See *Hampstead and Highgate Express*, 11 May 1990.
31. Colpi, op. cit., p.100.
32. For Jewish refugee projects see Imperial War Museum, Department of Sound Records, 'Britain and the Refugee Crisis 1933–1947' carried out in the late 1970s and early 1980s. On a local level extensive interviewing of refugees took place at a similar time in Manchester through the Manchester Polytechnic Local Studies Unit and later the Manchester Jewish Museum and also in Birmingham through the Birmingham Jewish History Group; Colpi, op. cit; pp.100–01. For a comparatively rare British Italian autobiography which does cover internment see P. Leoni, *I Shall Die on the Carpet* (London, 1966). Some material on *The Arandora Star* was released in 1986 in the HO 214 and 215 series.
33. Calder, op. cit., p.117.
34. See Hoch, op. cit. for a review of the new literature of the early 1980s.
35. See the projects referred to in note 32. One product of this new interest was Zoe Josephs, *Survivors: Jewish Refugees in Birmingham 1933–1945* (Birmingham, 1988).
36. B. Wasserstein, *Britain and the Jews of Europe, 1939–1945* (Oxford, 1979), Ch.3; Stent, op. cit; Peter and Leni Gillman, op. cit.
37. M. Kochan, *Britain's Internees in the Second World War* (London, 1983); Erich Koch, *Deemed Suspect: A Wartime Blunder* (Toronto, 1980); Connery Chappell, *Island of Barbed Wire* (London, 1984). See also the important essay by Michael Seyfert, 'His Majesty's Most Loyal Internees', in G. Hirschfeld (ed.), *Exile in Great Britain* (Highlands, NJ, 1984), pp.163–93. For the plays and documentaries see notes 2 and 3.
38. Holmes, op. cit. for the government releases. For conspiracy theories see 'Judex', op. cit., p.121 quoting H.G. Wells' concerns and Lafitte, op. cit., p.27. These theories were raised in Stent, op. cit., Ch.17 and Peter and Leni Gillman, op. cit., *passim*.
39. Angus Calder, *The People's War: Britain 1939–45* (London, 1969), pp.130–33. There is the briefest of mentions in Paul Addison, *The Road to 1945* (London, 1977), p.104 and A.J.P. Taylor, *English History 1914–1945* (Harmondsworth, 1987), pp.598–9.
40. Holmes, op. cit.
41. W. Mosse (ed.), *Second Chance: Two Centuries of German-speaking Jews in the United Kingdom* (Tubingen, 1991).
42. Bird, op. cit. for the First World War. It is significant that Rudolf Rocker's, *The London Years* (London, 1956), which included an account of the author's internment in the First World War, received little attention or interest. See Bill Fishman, 'Jewish Immigrant Anarchists in East London', in Aubrey Newman (ed.), *The Jewish East End 1840–1939* (London, 1981), p.252. Progress (in terms of internment being incorporated into general surveys of the Home Front experience) is reflected in Jonathan Croall, *Don't You Know There's A War On? The People's Voice 1939–45* (London, 1989), pp.94, 129–35, 175, 178. There is no mention of internment, however, in the otherwise excellent collection of essays edited by Harold Smith, *War and Social Change: British Society in the Second World War* (Manchester, 1986).
43. Wright, op. cit., pp.167, 245.
44. For the rather sensational 'rediscovery' of atrocities committed on Alderney see the front page story in *The Guardian*, 4 May 1992.
45. Calder, *Myth of the Blitz*, preface and Ch.1 comments on the difficulty of writing about what is such an emotionally charged and sensitive subject.

46. For the Imperial War Museum event see *The Times*, 15 May 1990; *Hampstead and Highgate Express*, 11 May 1990; *Jewish Chronicle*, 27 July 1990 and the *Wiener Library Newsletter*, No.15 (summer 1990) for the conference. For other media interest see Chaim Bermant in *Jewish Chronicle*, 1 June 1990 and David Cesarani, 'The Fear Mongers Within', *The Guardian*, 2 July 1990 and correspondence in *The Guardian*, 5 July 1990.

47. Thus books such as Clive Ponting's *1940: Myth and Reality* (London, 1990) and Ronald Atkin, *'Pillar of Fire': Dunkirk* (London, 1990) are spoilt by an oversensational, muck-racking style, a reflection on the fact that discussion is still at an immature level between those that defend the war myths at all costs and those who want to demolish what might in reality be half-truths. The big war events of 1940 from a British perspective received major attention but 'side issues' such as alien internment, despite being intricately connected to the military crisis and the invasion panic, were rarely mentioned. See, for example, Martin Gilbert, 'Invader who decided not to', *The Guardian*, 7 Sept. 1990. On a local level, an exhibition and publication which did achieve a sensible balance was Claire Frankland, Donald Hyslop and Sheila Jemima (Southampton Oral History Team/Local Studies Section), *Southampton Blitz: The Unofficial Story* (Southampton, 1990).

48. Maya Vision Television Company produced 'Under Suspicion', screened on Channel 4, 18 March 1991 which made the explicit comparison between the detention of Iraqis, Palestinians and others in Britain during the Gulf War and alien internment in the Second World War. Similarly see the comments of Geoffrey Robertson, 'Tribunals That Cannot do Justice', *Observer*, 27 Jan. 1991. In contrast to the Maya Vision film, Joan Bakewell's 'Heart of the Matter', BBC 1, 17 March 1991 on the same topic only mentioned the Second World War in passing, commenting on how 'Britain rounded up some six thousand Germans here and interned them in camps'. That this brief statement could be so inaccurate in terms of the numbers involved and the omission of the fact that others such as the Italians were interned reflects how, as late as 1991, alien internment remains an obscure or non-existent part of British popular memory.

49. Raphael Samuel, 'History's Battle for a New Past', *The Guardian*, 21 Jan. 1989.

50. Daniel Pick, *Faces of Degeneration. A European disorder, c.1848–1918* (Cambridge, 1989).

51. John Garrard, *The English and Immigration: A Comparative Study of the Jewish Influx 1880–1910* (London, 1971) and Bernard Gainer, *The Alien Invasion: The Origins of the Alien Act of 1905* (London, 1972).

52. Stella Yarrow, 'The Impact of Hostility on Germans in Britain, 1914–1918', in Tony Kushner and Kenneth Lunn (eds.), *The Politics of Marginality* (London, 1990), pp.97–112; Panikos Panayi, 'Anti-German Riots in London during the First World War', *German History* Vol.7, No.2 (1989), pp.184–203 and his contribution to this volume.

53. For a brilliant account of the construction of the Other in culture, see Sander Gilman, *Difference and Pathology: Stereotypes of Sexuality, Race and Madness* (Ithaca, NY, 1985).

54. A notable exception is Stella Yarrow, 'The Impact of Hostility'.

55. On the strength and viciousness of wartime xenophobia, see Panikos Panayi, 'The British Empire Union in the First World War', in Kushner and Lunn, *The Politics of Marginality*, pp.113–28.

56. For a general account of the erosion of liberal values in the management of news in wartime, see Ian McLaine, *Ministry of Morale. Home Front Morale and the Ministry of Information in World War II* (London, 1979).

57. See Terri Colpi, *The Italian Factor*, pp.105–8 and her article in this volume.

I. PRECEDENTS

An Alien Concept? The Continuity of Anti-Alienism in British Society before 1940

DAVID CESARANI

Anti-alienism has usually been seen as a peripheral phenomenon in British society and politics. However, if anti-alienism is understood broadly as a form of discourse as well as a political movement it emerges as a continuous and central theme. Anti-alienism was the popular response to the first mass immigration into Britain, overwhelming earlier pro-alien traditions of asylum. Anti-alien legislation and the state apparatus for enforcing it established mechanisms for the transmission of anti-alienism as a concept, movement and set of practices from the 1880s to the 1940s. Seen in this context, internment in both world wars was made possible by accumulated administrative experience and a popular opinion habituated to anti-alien practices.

Although there are now several excellent histories of immigration into Britain, which include discussion of the responses encountered by settlers, there is no monograph or even an article on the history of anti-alienism itself. One reason for this curious absence may be the reluctance to give pride of place to a despicable movement. Another may be the genuine belief that anti-alienism is a marginal phenomenon in British political culture and deserves only to be treated as such.[1]

A further explanation lies with the difficulty of defining anti-alienism as a discrete subject, a problem inherent to the term itself. In its most familiar usage it connotes popular movements, party policy and actions by the state directed at foreign residents.[2] At another level, anti-alienism forms part of socio-biological discourse in Britain from the 1860s onwards. As Daniel Pick has recently demonstrated, the notion of degeneration was central to nineteenth century social and political discourse. The concept emerged out of the condition of England debate in the 1850s and 1860s, when social commentators drew on social darwinism and socio-biology to explain the problems of industrial society. Thus from an early stage, aliens became inextricably linked with diagnoses that pointed to degeneration. The occurrence of crime, unrest, revo-

---

The author would like to thank Tony Kushner for his helpful comments on an earlier draft of this essay, although responsibility for the argument and conclusions is his alone.

lutionary politics, and anarchism, were all attributed in part, if not wholly, to the alien presence.[3]

Anti-alienism is also inseparable from the construction of national identity in the late-nineteenth century. Faced with internal social strain and external challenges, British politicians sought ways to knit together divided classes and instill in the people a sense of common purpose. Some opted for a variant of German 'social imperialism' which included an appeal to workers on the basis of xenophobia and the exclusion of foreign labour. At the same time, the status of the monarchy was built up as a unifying institution.[4] Greater emphasis was laid on the distinct expression of Englishness in literature, the arts and music. Historiography became important for the construction and dissemination of the myth of an Anglo-Saxon race. So, by the turn of the century, racial thought, social darwinism and eugenics had given an exclusivist edge to English national identity. The corollory of this was the accentuation of alien characteristics attributed to foreigners and immigrants.[5]

Yet the protean nature of anti-alienism led to its erratic appearance in a variety of historical and cultural studies. It has been mentioned in the consideration of eugenic thought, imperialism, British historiography and the machinations of politicians. But in each case it has been incidental to the main story. This necessarily reflects the nature of monographs, but it is also an indication of the difficulty in assigning a place to anti-alienism. Without a discrete field of study of the phenomenon there has been a tendency to leave it hanging from the margins of history.[6]

However desirable it may be to see anti-alienism as a dark force on the periphery of British society, arguably this perspective inverts reality. Moreover, the predisposition to characterise anti-alien movements as aberrant or exceptional creates discontinuities at the expense of understanding the mechanisms for transmission and continuity. Our appreciation of British history, not just the history of minorities or minority movements, is thus partial and skewed. The purpose of this essay is to propose a narrative in which the rhetoric and practices of anti-alienism are located centrally in British society and political culture.

It is not intended to suggest here that anti-alienism in Britain has always been pervasive and institutionalized. As Bernard Porter has shown in *The Refugee Question in Mid-Victorian Politics*, dislike of foreigners does not preclude the practice of giving them refuge. To the contrary, in the mid-nineteenth century contempt for foreign powers actually fostered sympathy for those fleeing them.[7] Yet concern for the plight of refugees does not necessarily entail offering them homes and jobs, either. In July 1938, a Gallup Poll asked 1,000 British people if they thought refugees, mainly German and Austrian Jews, should be allowed to enter the country. Seventy per cent answered in the affirmative while only 26 per cent said 'no'. When those who replied 'yes' were asked if refugees should be admitted freely or subject to 'restrictions designed to safeguard British workers and taxpayers', only 15 per cent said 'freely' in contrast to 84 per cent who said 'with restrictions'.[8] By way of a caveat one can do no better than point to Peter Pulzer's remark, in an essay on immigrants in Britain, that 'Real life is muddled and complicated.[9]

An integrated approach to anti-alienism as a form of rhetoric, political action and state policy may help to sort out the confusion. Anti-alien discourse is a fusion of all those elements of political, cultural and social thought where the Other is constructed as part of the process of self-definition. It is also a movement and a set of practices. In this sense it is neither provocative nor perverse to situate anti-alienism at the heart of British political culture. Rather, by stressing the continuities of anti-alienism as a concept in the idea of the nation, public health and social stability as well as an evolving political tradition and set of administrative practices we may enhance our understanding of British history.

I. Aliens and the Principle of Asylum

During the mid-nineteenth century, Britain was a haven for political refugees and economic migrants from the Continent. The number of aliens was small. Although it rose from 50,289 in 1851 to 118,031 in 1881 aliens remained a tiny percentage of the whole population. The Irish, who were a distinctly foreign presence, vastly outnumbered them. In 1851, for example, there were 520,000 Irish in England.[10] The insignificance of these aliens amidst a sea of Scots, Irish and English rural migrants helped to prevent their presence becoming a matter of public interest or concern.

All the same, they were not well-liked. British administrations maintained an open door policy because it suited the country's liberal self-image. By a curious act of perversity, asylum was safeguarded from 1851 to 1881 precisely because the British despised foreigners. According to Bernard Porter,

> To this policy of asylum a great deal of obeisance was paid, and a moderately wide and deep attachment probably felt; but the attachment was deeper and wider to certain principles of the British constitution which affected Englishmen more intimately and which it was thought would be endangered by any effective action taken against the refugees. All these principles were supposed to demonstrate Britain's moral and political superiority over her continental neighbours . . .[11]

British society was not innocent of xenophobia. There is abundant evidence of prejudice against foreigners. Foreigners appeared in an array of stereotypes during the mid-nineteenth century.[12] However, in the expansive economic climate of the 1850s and 1860s, anti-alienism was a null force. In 1858, when Palmerston, the Prime Minister, tried to introduce a Conspiracy Bill to deal with European revolutionaries based in England, the proposed legislation was dubbed an 'aliens bill' and quickly attracted obloquy. Although temporary Aliens Acts had been in force from 1792 to 1826 and in 1848, such measures had subsequently become associated with the infringement of English liberties and, perhaps more important, bullying by foreign powers. The outcry contributed to Palmerston's fall from office and it appeared that the principle of giving refuge to aliens was inviolable.[13]

Bernard Porter argues suggestively that up to the late 1870s, xenophobia was chiefly directed outwards at nations which were deemed to possess fundamentally different characteristics to those prized by the British. When the gap between British society and that of continental countries narrowed, this hostility lessened. At the same time, sympathy for refugees and economic migrants was eroded. The prolonged economic depression from the 1870s finally knocked away the props for an unquestioning endorsement of free access to the United Kingdom. From then on, attitudes towards aliens changed fundamentally.[14]

II. Anti-Alienism as the Response to Mass Immigration

The mass immigration of Jews from Eastern Europe after the pogroms of 1881–82 was a watershed in popular feeling and government policy towards aliens. Previously there might have been friction with individual foreigners, but public opinion was broadly positive towards aliens as refugees. Now the pattern was reversed. While relations with individual immigrants may have been good, bad or indifferent, the dominant attitude towards immigration was negative. This was not only due to actual or perceived conflicts such as competition for jobs and housing. The reasons must be sought in the wider currents of contemporary social thinking and the transformations within culture. A set of 'Anglo-Saxon attitudes' crystallized in opposition to alien immigrants that was as much about the self-definition of individuals and classes in British society. Preeminent was the definition of the nation itself. The concept of the alien became a touchstone for the elaboration of the values of British society and political culture. They were an object on which to project anxieties as well as aspirations.

Jewish immigration coincided with a 'conjunctural crisis' in Britain. The economy was stalled. Recurrent bouts of unemployment focussed attention on both the plight of the working class (casual labour, poor housing, overcrowding) and their efforts at organization. Social commentators and politicians understood the crisis in ideological terms. They approached it through the medium of current social thinking in which social darwinism and eugenics played a crucial part.[15]

Jews settled in inner city districts, particularly East London, which symbolized the interlocking problems of modern industrial society: urban squalor, the degeneration of population and fear of the mob. At a moment when imperialist politicians felt it was critical to secure social cohesion, this instrusion was doubly unwelcome. It allegedly accentuated poverty and hence class conflict, while simultaneously diluting the Anglo-Saxon people who formed the kernal of the nation and the empire. Anti-alienism was thus one strand in the weaving of a British national identity that would integrate all classes into the nation and assuage class divisions.[16]

Theories of degeneration, associated with eugenic and racial thinking, carried the alien to the centre of social and political debate by the 1900s. Daniel Pick maintains that

> Edwardian legislation was characterized both literally and metaphorically by the dream of national insurance: a desire to tighten the supervision and welfare of the national stock, to exclude and eliminate degenerate 'foreign bodies'. Indeed the Royal Commission on Alien Immigration in 1903 and the ensuing Act of 1905, should not be seen as a mere anomaly, nor, exclusively, as part of some timeless centuries-old phenomenon of anti-semitism, but in relation to that wider contemporary attempt to construct a racial-imperial identity, excluding all 'bad blood' and 'pathological elements', literally expelling anarchists, criminals, prostitutes, the diseased, and the hopelessly poor – all those now declared 'undesirable aliens'.[17]

Anti-alienism as a movement surfaced in the London press in 1886 and was first voiced in Parliament a year later. In 1888, it helped to precipitate two Parliamentary inquiries touching on immigration. By 1892 the first anti-immigrant association flickered into life and there were regular calls for legislation to restrict the entry of aliens. Bills were introduced into the House of Lords by Lord Salisbury, the leader of the opposition, in 1892, and by the Earl of Hardwick in 1898. Salisbury's bill targeted 'destitute aliens' and anarchists, a significant coupling. Although these bills won only limited support, anti-alien rhetoric found its way to the heart of political debate in East London. It featured heavily in the General Election contests of 1892 and 1894. In the 'Khaki Election' of 1900 anti-alienism was part and parcel of the chauvinistic appeal of the Conservative Party following Britain's apparently victorious conclusion of the Boer War. Local feeling was articulated through the British Brothers' League, an aggressive, mass based movement with direct links to Tory MPs in Parliament. Pressure from East London MPs led to the establishment of a Royal Commission on Alien Immigration in 1902. Its report the following year laid the basis for an Aliens Bill introduced into Parliament in 1904. This bill was savaged by the Liberals and had to be re-introduced in a changed form in 1905, whereupon it passed into law.[18]

What did anti-alienism entail in practice? The Royal Commission proposed limited restrictions on the entry of aliens. It recommended the establishment of prohibited areas where, in view of overcrowding and ill-feeling, immigrants should not be allowed to settle. Its report also endorsed current notions that aliens were responsible for crime and vice. The Conservative Government introduced a bill in 1904 to implement the Commission's conclusions. It proposed to empower immigration officers to exclude criminals, prostitutes, destitute aliens and those of 'bad character'. A special court would be granted the power to expel aliens, with no right of appeal. Finally, prohibited areas would be established. This bill was wrecked by the Liberal opposition and withdrawn; but its controversial provisions would not be forgotten.[19]

The bill which was re-introduced in 1904, and passed as the Aliens Act the following year, was less stringent. It forbade an alien from landing at any but a designated port and then only with the permission of an immigration official. These officers were empowered to refuse an alien leave to land. However, the scope of their attention was limited to ships carrying 20 or more passengers in steerage. Well-to-do immigrants could avoid inspection. Immigration officers were given the power to exclude aliens who, due to illness, were liable to become a charge on the public purse or whose presence would be detrimental to the public good. The latter included those convicted of crimes in a country with which Britain had an extradition treaty. Aliens who lacked means of support could also be refused leave to land. But in an important concession to the principle of asylum, impoverished aliens would be permitted entry if they could prove they were fleeing religious or political persecution. The Home Secretary acquired the power to deport 'undesirable aliens' who became a charge on the rates or were found guilty of criminal offences.[20]

The results of the 1906 General Election indicated that anti-alienism had considerable appeal in several East London constituencies. The anti-Tory tidal wave broke around those constituences where the Conservative candidate had endorsed restrictionism. To this extent, it was proven to be a popular movement. However, the strength of anti-alienism should be kept in perspective. Although the Trades Union Congress passed resolutions in favour of restrictionism in 1892, 1894 and 1895, the support for such declarations was largely confined to traditional craft-based unions which faced (or feared) Jewish competition. Anti-alienism was always a complex coalition of interests, often highly local in nature.[21]

Public concern, demonstrations and the anti-alien vote may have been localised, but anti-alienism had an exaggerated effect. The opportunism of politicans, the vociferousness of the anti-aliens and the fear which gripped the immigrants combined to raise the movement's profile. This was to be a continuous feature of anti-alien agitation: it was consistently more feared in the imagination than it was confronted in the flesh. Unscrupulous politicans hoped it could deliver electoral success while pro-aliens feared the strength of its appeal. Above all, anti-alienism was never met head-on by a policy of public enlightenment led by government agencies. It is significant that after the 1906 General Election the benefit of the doubt would always go to the anti-alien movement.

III. Continuities in Anti-Alienism, 1906–14

The passing of the Aliens act was a 'landmark in the decline of Liberal England'.[22] It also needs to be seen as an upward ratchet in the rise of anti-alienism as discourse and practice. Henceforth, the stakes would inevitably be higher. Bernard Gainer has observed perceptively that

> From the day the Aliens Act of 1905 passed into law, the Liberal consensus of opposition to it began to erode and the anti-alien faction to increase . . . The principle having been admitted by Act of Parliament that the nation had a right to control the immigration of undesirables, there could only be a practical argument, and none in principle, for admitting any immigrants at all. By slow degrees the Liberals were forced to concede this premise.[23]

Furthermore, anti-alienism developed a momentum, dynamic and logic of its own. The existence of a statute and the administrative machinery to enforce it provided the basis for continuity. Politicians and civil servants began to amass experience in operating anti-alien measures and laid down precedents for future development. Anti-alienism was carried forward by the inexorable workings of the Home Office bureaucracy. Nor was the issue allowed to lapse by public opinion. During the years before the First World War the appetite of the anti-alienists increased. Having demonstrated the possibility of barring the entry of some foreigners and even expelling certain of them, sections of public opinion, the press and politicans now clamoured for measures against other groups.

In practice, the Act quickly led to a fall in the number of Jews attempting to enter Britain either as prospective settlers or transmigrants. For example, the volume of transmigrants declined from 110,700 in 1907 to 61,680 in 1908. This was the first, and perhaps the most important, discovery for officials and politicians in the new era of state interference in the free movement of population into the United Kingdom. The utility of aliens legislation as a deterrent would become a cornerstone for future policy-making.[24] In addition, the administrative machinery was invented, put in place and tested. Between 1906 and 1910, over 5,000 aliens were refused leave to land on grounds of means or illness. Over roughly the same period, nearly 400 'objectionable' aliens were expelled while hundreds of aliens convicted of crimes were deported annually. Whatever the criticisms of the working of the Act, from its proponents or opponents, these figures showed that it was operable and effective.[25]

A final, critical element in the continuity of aliens policy lay with the Home Office which was responsible for its administration. John Pedder, the official responsible for aliens in 1904 when the Aliens Bill was being drafted, was still in charge of matters concerning aliens three decades later. He served as the private secretary to three Home Secretaries over a period of six years and finally retired as a principal assistant secretary in 1932. By this time he and his staff had acquired a mass of data and experience which was passed on regardless of the transitory political figures flitting through the portals of the Home Office.[26]

The Aliens Act confirmed in the public as well as the official mind the notion that the alien presence was problematic. In the press and popular literature, aliens were identified with crime, vice, degenerate behaviour, economic competition leading to social unrest, miscegenation and spying. As Bryan Cheyette has shown, the stereotype of the alien Jew ran through Edwardian literature.[27] It was not just Jewish aliens who were constructed in this way: Germans, Africans, Afro-Caribbeans and Chinese were equally embraced by the discourse of anti-alienism. Although there were significant inflections in particular cases, the same themes cropped up time and again with respect to each group. It says much about the insecurity of British society at this time that the fear of subversion – of the nation, the race, the constitution, etc. – unifies this bleak catalogue.[28]

Anti-alienism was not monolithic, nor did pro-alien or pro-asylum feeling evaporate. Both tendencies were supported by shifting alliances in the press, in public opinion and in politics. Yet the very existence of debate ensured the perpetuation of the alien as a notion. Continuous discussion of anti-alien legislation in the late 1900s and 1910s hardened preconceptions about aliens for a new generation.

Between 1906 and 1914, both pro- and anti-alien lobbies continued to contest the definition of the alien. The *Jewish Chronicle* and members of the Jewish communities in London and Manchester campaigned for the repeal of the Act. They naturally stressed the utility, industry and law-abiding character of Jewish aliens along with the principle of asylum. However, even though the Act came into force at the same time as the Liberals took office, it was evident that the party which had fought the bill while in opposition had no intention of repealing the Act once it was in government. Lobbying only accomplished some amelioration of its application.[29]

The pro-alien lobby was greatly weakened by the occurrence of terrorist acts associated with East European immigrants in London. The 'Tottenham Outrage' of 1909 and the 'Siege of Sidney Street' in 1911 enabled the press to conjoin murderous crimes with anarchism and aliens. Haia Shpayer-Makov notes that 'The anti-alien and anti-anarchist sentiments fed upon one another'.[30] Anti-aliens were fired up by the incidents and found less resistance amongst disillusioned Liberals. In February 1911, E.A. Goulding, a Unionist MP, introduced a bill that would have obliged all aliens covered by the Aliens Act to register with the police. The Home Secretary was to be given the right to expel any alien convicted of a crime, even if no court had recommended that this be done. The criteria for determining what was an immigrant ship, and therefore subject to inspection, were to be lowered to just one steerge passenger. No alien would be allowed to carry a firearm. Finally, to show that the economic issues had not been forgotten, Goulding proposed a minimum wage for aliens – presumably to prevent undercutting by immigrants.[31]

Winston Churchill, the Home Secretary, sought to outflank Goulding's bill with a measure of his own. The Criminal Bill of 1911 was an attempt to prevent crimes by foreigners by creating penalties for carrying unlicensed pistols. It also sought ways to preclude illegal immigration and proposed sureties for aliens admitted to the country who possessed criminal records. Churchill included in the bill the means by which the Home Secretary could ask judges why they chose not to expel convicted aliens, doubtless to encourage greater rigour.[32] Both the government's and the private member's bill fell in committee, but again the proposals would not be forgotten.

Running alongside the alien-anarchist hysteria was the German alien/spy scare. Numerous books and articles peddled the fantasy that Britain was riddled with German spies in the guise of bankers, industrialists, barbers, waiters and humble clerks. David Stafford has commented that 'Germanophobia was a central feature of the British spy novel, feeding upon and fuelling popular hatred of Germany in particular and foreigners resident in Britain ("aliens") in general; the most conspicuous of these happened also to be Germans both Gentiles and Jews'. Constant harping on this theme affected foreign and domestic policy. The Home Office began to monitor and secretly register aliens. This was psychologically and practically the essential first step towards the arrest and mass detention of so-called enemy aliens.[33] At the same time, the tiny Chinese population ominously attracted antagonism far out of proportion to its size or activities. Opium-smoking was a well-established element in the theory of degeneration and was characterised as a threat to the strength of the empire no less. To local conflicts between British and Chinese seamen, was added the national issue of opium dens.[34] In each case, the ubiquitous alien was the target of demands for stricter controls, surveillance or expulsion. While in practice little may have been achieved (overtly), the medium term effect on the implementation of anti-alien policies was substantial.

By the outbreak of the First World War, the notion of tighter controls over aliens was not foreign to public opinion or government. On the contrary, British society had become habituated to immigration restrictions and the identification of foreigners as bearers of disease, criminal proclivities or dangerous ideas. It cannot be maintained any longer that the wartime regulations against aliens came like a bolt of lightning from a clear sky. Nor was the harsh treatment of Germans, Russian Jews, Chinese and Blacks in Britain during or immediately after the war simply a result of temporary jingoism or the understandable frustrations which four years of suffering had fostered. Rather, the roots of wartime and post-war anti-alienism are to be found in the construction of the alien in British political culture and society in the late Victorian and Edwardian eras. Policies and practices post-1914 were merely an extension of those which were tried and trusted or which had previously been mooted and experimented with.

IV. Anti-Alienism during the First World War

The First World War accelerated the decline of liberalism as a political philosophy and a set of principles for governance. *Laissez-faire* economics and individual liberties were sacrificed as relentlessly as the waves of infantrymen stumbling across no-man's land.[35] As a consequence, the intellectual and political resistance to anti-alienism was weakened still further. However, it never entirely disappeared; the principle of the free movement of peoples and the ideal of asylum had many doughty, if isolated, champions. Their persistent, admirable and at times quite effective advocacy of asylum should not be forgotten even if, on the whole, it only served to throw into relief the Gaderene charge towards ever tighter controls on aliens and more drastic anti-immigration measures.

On 5 August 1914, the Home Secretary, Reginald McKenna, rushed through Parliament an Aliens Restriction Act. The speed with which it was enacted resulted from years of prior planning inspired by war scares and spy mania. Its provisions also reflected earlier draft bills and recommendations dating back to 1904. Under the Act, the executive was empowered to control and prevent the landing of aliens. Prohibited areas were set up where aliens were not allowed to reside, although for security rather than economic reasons.[36]

From August 1914 to May 1915, the government implemented a policy of selective arrest and internment of Germans and Austrians of military age. The number in captivity reached 10,000 by late 1914. In addition, women and children and men above or below military age were encouraged to return to their countries of origin. After news of the sinking of the *Lusitania* on 7 May 1915, a wave of popular anti-alienism prompted the government to order the internment of all enemy alien males and the systematic repatriation of women and children unless a tribunal exempted them. The number of those interned rose to 32,000 and over the next two years, 10,000 were forcibly deported. Enemy aliens still at liberty were subject to elaborate practices of registration and regulation.[37]

If the core of the legislative practices and the pattern of anti-alien agitation were well-estabished, the experience of internment and forced repatriation was new. In her sensitive evaluation of the impact of anti-German hostility Stella Yarrow has shown that it had a differential effect depending on class and wealth. Interned German workers lost their jobs, their families, the breadwinner. Wives and children were repatriated while husbands and fathers languished behind barbed wire. Wealthy and naturalized Germans were able to insulate themselves to some extent and extended help to needy compatriots; but as the intensity of anti-alienism increased, relief networks were overburdened and broke down. The division between the rich and the poor was replicated inside the internment camps. They were a microcosm of the tensions in the wider society and also the political rivalry between sections of the German population.[38]

The anticipated use of the powers which the 1914 Act gave to government agencies rested on the premise that friendly and enemy aliens could be distinguished. This proved difficult in practice. Russian Poles and Belgian refugees all found themselves caught up in the web of regulations.[39] Nor was public opinion sensitive to the differences between aliens. After news of the sinking of the *Lusitania*, there were attacks on Germans and other foreigners, including Russian Jews and Chinese, in several British cities.[40] Gradually, all distinctions collapsed. In 1916, regulations were promulgated under the Defence of the Realm Act enabling the police to monitor and search premises suspected of use for the consumption of distribution of narcotics. This was a new step in the tightening of control over the Chinese communities.[41] British-born Jews and naturalized Germans were equally the targets of anti-alien feelings. In 1918, the 1914 British Nationality and Status of Aliens Act was amended to make it possible for the government to strip former enemy-aliens of their citizenship and deport them.[42]

Russian Jews were amongst the aliens affected by the riots in 1915, but this was accidental as compared to the sustained animosity aroused by their reluctance to serve in the allied forces. Jews who had fled Tsarist Russia had no desire to fight on the same side as their former country of oppression. They took advantage of their Russian nationality to evade both voluntary military service and conscription. As British losses on the Western Front mounted, the anomalous position of Russian Jews became increasingly galling to British public opinion. The resentment towards them was a variant of anti-alienism, even though they were 'friendly aliens'.[43]

Herbert Samuel, the Jewish Home Secretary, responded to the escalating hostility by proposing a drastic measure by which Russian Jews of military age could be forcibly deported to Russia to serve in the Russian army. The prospect of mass deportations was too much for Liberal Party backbenchers who helped to wreck the proposal. However, in 1917 the government concluded a convention with the Russian authorities by which Russian Jews could be compelled to serve in either the Russian or the British armed forces. 'The Convention' was eventually put into operation and several thousand Russian Jews and non-Jews returned to Russia and an uncertain future. Although they were 'friendly aliens', it transpired after the war that the British administration had no intention of allowing them back afterwards.[44]

Thus wartime chauvinism and xenophobia could not be limited to 'enemy aliens' or to the war itself. This was because anti-alien discourse by definition had no boundary: it comprehended everything that was 'Other' to Britain and Englishness. Military conflict heightened the intensity of its expression and gave it legitimacy; but, like the genie, it could not be popped back into the bottle on the cessation of hostilities. Meanwhile, the government found itself equipped with a wider range of powers which it had no reason to surrender, even if public opinion had allowed it to do so. Anti-alienism reached a new plateau as concept, movement and practice: but there was nothing innovative or exceptional about its content.

V. Continuities, 1919–39

Anti-alienism persisted with undiminished ferocity after the First World War ended. It was fuelled by wartime animosities, the repercussions of the Russian Revolution, economic dislocation and a prolonged socio-political crisis. Anti-alien rhetoric figured prominently in the General Elections in December 1918 and October 1924. Between 1919 and 1929, aliens were subject to a set of draconian practices extending from registration to expulsion. They and even their children were the victims of systematic discrimination by the state.[45]

During the war, the non-white alien population had expanded rapidly. Hundreds of seamen from Sylhet and East Africa arrived in British port cities. The labour force in the munitions industry was augmented with imported labour from the West Indies. Thousands of servicemen from India and the Caribbean served in the British Army and were quartered in Britain.[46] This contribution to the war effort was welcomed, but with the armistice the climate changed. Unemployment caused by the closure of munitions factories and retooling was aggravated by demobilization. Trade unions strove to eliminate female labour and non-white workers in order to ensure jobs for ex-servicemen. Industrial relations deteriorated while political tension heightened: riots by demobbed and unemployed soldiers occurred in Liverpool; workers around the country expressed sympathy for the Bolshevik Revolution and set up workers' councils.[47] It was against this background that clashes occurred between white and non-white troops in the summer of 1918. 'Racial' incidents continued throughout the winter months.

Serious rioting against non-white aliens broke out in several cities in the spring and summer of 1919. In East London disturbances took place in April, May and June 1919. The last incident climaxed in an exchange of gunfire between Black sailors and white rioters. The house owned by a Chinese family was sacked and set on fire. The disturbances spread to Liverpool and Cardiff in June. In Liverpool, mobs roamed the dockside districts setting upon African seamen. One Black man was killed during the ensuing street fighting and 700 were taken into protective custody by the police. Widespread rioting in Cardiff and Newport resulted in the death of one man and the injury of several more. Four non-white seamen were shot by Canadian servicemen in an exchange of gunfire. Street battles also occurred in Glasgow, Salford and Hull.[48]

While each incident had its own aetiology, it would be wrong to localize these occurrences and so foreclose an appreciation of how anti-alienism was a universal phenomenon. Chinese were the targets of hostility because of the alleged effects of opium smoking, brought to national attention by the death of the music hall star Billie Carlton. Black seamen were attacked due to rivalry for jobs and the fear of miscegenation. Jews were decried as the importers of subversive Bolshevik ideas. But anti-alien discourse was a seamless web in which all were entrapped. This may be illustrated by an editorial in the *East London Observer* in April 1919 which complained that the Aliens Bill, then in Parliament, was not stringent enough. The leader writer protested that 'nothing at all is intended to be done to meet the demand of the country to be protected from floods of alien spies, enemies and traitors, the mentally, morally and physically diseased and the parasitical scum of the earth.[49]

Moreover, Parliament and central government responded directly to local feeling: the riots assumed national significance and fed into Whitehall's policy making. The 1918 Nationality Act gave official sanction to the mood of xenophobia and intolerance. Government personnel who visited Liverpool in the wake of the anti-Black riots in June 1919 concurred with municipal officials that it was desirable to deport Blacks in order to defuse local conflict.[50] The very existence of such powers in the hands of central government was an incitement for their use to be demanded in certain localities. Thus between the riots in the summer of 1919 and the passing of the Aliens Bill in December, over 600 mainly African seamen were deported from Liverpool and Cardiff, while dozens of Jews were expelled for allegedly engaging in subversive activities. The implementation of repatriation/deportation measures proved their feasibility for future usage on a national plane.[51]

Above all, anti-German feeling, anti-Semitism and racism blended in the debates on the Aliens Restriction (Amendment) Bill in Parliament during the summer and autumn of 1919. The Act, passed at the end of the year, extended into peacetime and widened the 1914 aliens legislation. Initially, it was promoted as retribution against the subjects and citizens of countries against which Britain had been at war. To this extent it was a sop to the violent, hysterical and unremitting anti-German feeling that had been fostered during the war and whipped into a frenzy during the 1918 General Election. All former enemy aliens could now be deported unless a newly established aliens advisory committee deemed them exempt. For a five-year period no former enemy alien was allowed to enter the country. Until 1921, former enemy aliens were barred from acquiring land or a stake in key industries. Nor were they permitted to serve on British ships.[52]

The Act went still further. It made it a criminal offence for any alien to foster disaffection amongst British soldiers or civilians, or to promote industrial unrest. An alien found guilty of such acts could be deported. To ensure that aliens could not evade the regulations easily, those resident in the country since 1914 were prohibited from changing their name. Finally, all aliens were excluded from employment in the civil service, on juries, as pilots and senior officers on British merchant vessels.[53]

The political clauses of the 1919 Aliens Act can be seen as a fulfilment of the clamour against anarchists dating back to Lord Salisbury's bill in 1894. They were precipitated by the Bolshevik Revolution, but there was nevertheless a strong element of continuity with previous alien/spy scares. Russian Jewish anarchists, German spies and 'Jewish Bolsheviks' simply merged in popular opinion and public policy. A similar continuity may be detected in the 1920 Aliens Order, promulgated under the 1919 Act, which stipulated that in future any alien seeking work in the United Kingdom would be required to obtain a permit from the Ministry of Labour. This was of tremendous significance. It finally established a linkage between economic conditions in the UK and the control of immigration. The principle enshrined in the 1920 Order became a cornerstone in the regulation of immigration for decades to come. In effect it was the logical conclusion of the process begun with the 1888 Parliamentary investigation into 'sweating'.[54]

The 1919 Act elevated anti-alienism to a new level of viciousness which was then sustained throughout the 1920s by constant public debate and a series of aggressive measures against aliens in general and specific groups: Jews, Chinese and Blacks. The 1920 Aliens Order also empowered the police to detain aliens at their discretion, with no need of an arrest warrant. They were permitted to enter and close restaurants and places of entertainment where aliens gathered. All aliens were obliged to register with the police and to carry their certificate of registration along with their passport and an identity photograph at all times. Failure to comply with this ordinance could result in prosecution and deportation.[55]

Under the 1925 Aliens Order, alien seamen were made subject to the 1920 Order. Black seamen now had to register with the police and carry identification papers; if challenged by the police they had to prove their nationality. Even British-born Blacks were liable to be stopped and questioned. This left them open to petty harassment by the police and, ultimately, the threat of deportation.[56] Public alarm about the use of opium remained at a high level. The 1920 and 1923 Dangerous Drugs Acts gave the police wide powers to search and arrest suspected drug dealers. Chinese convicted of drug-dealing were routinely expelled. Since drug raids often revealed illegal immigrants, the anti-opium legislation conveniently buttressed the controls over aliens.[57]

Non-naturalized east European Jews who had arrived before 1914 formed the largest body of aliens in Britain. They found themselves labouring under a humiliating body of regulations, vulnerable to deportation for committing trivial offences. Non-British born Jews, even if they were naturalized, and their children were denied employment in the civil service and local government. In London they were also barred from council housing and council scholarships. Alien Jews were held in second-class status by the long delays in and high cost of naturalization. If the cost was accidental, the delays were deliberate. As Sir John Pedder explained to the Labour Home Secretary, Arthur Henderson, in May 1924, Home Office officials covertly operated a racial hierarchy by which 'Slavs, Jews and other races from Central and Eastern Europe' were obliged to await far longer than the statutory period before naturalization was bestowed upon them.[58]

The vivacity of anti-alienism was ensured by the fixed nature of the 1919 Act and a series of contingent events. Since the Act had to be renewed annually it was the subject of intermittent debate in the House of Commons. Opponents of aliens legislation regularly made use of these opportunities to challenge its extension, never with any success. Most pro-alien arguments deployed in these debates centred on asylum and the unfair treatment of Jews, especially. Such was the strength of anti-alienism inside and outside the House of Commons that no MPs argued for unrestricted immigration and it was taken for granted that controls had to stay.[59]

Anti-alienism intruded significantly into the 1924 General Election. The campaign featured a 'Red Scare' and allegations of foreign subversion that echoed the spy-mania of the 1910s. Unalloyed anti-alienism featured strongly in Conservative Party election strategy. In his election broadcast on 16 October 1924, Stanley Baldwin, the Tory party leader, warned that Britain could not afford to tolerate 'revolutionary agitation' and promised to 'examine the laws and regulations as to entry of aliens into this country'. This was a low-key but unequivocal use of the anti-alien card and a deliberate invocation of the furore in 1918 and before.[60]

The Conservative victory brought into office Sir William Joynson-Hicks, a key-figure in the continuity of anti-alienism from before the First World War through to the end of the 1920s. Joynson-Hicks had espoused anti-alienism when running for election in Manchester in 1908 and played his part in anti-Germanism during the war. During debates on the Middle East and Zionism in the House of Commons in 1921–22 he regularly invoked the language of anti-alienism against Jews in Britain and Palestine. Soon after his appointment as Home Secretary, Joynson-Hicks received an anti-alien delegation from the National Citizens' Union and pledged firm measures against aliens. A series of prominent anti-alien articles appeared simultaneously in *The Times* adding to the pressure for action. With much attendant publicity Joynson-Hicks called meetings of police and met with immigration officers to discuss the 'alien problem'. Under his auspices, the lives of aliens, mainly Jews, were fraught with insecurity. All efforts by the Jewish community and friendly MPs to meliorate the regulations were rebuffed. In 1927, Joynson-Hicks tried to make the Aliens Act permanent, but the proposal was dropped due to pressure of business and finally died with the election of a Labour government in 1929.[61]

The new administration proved more sympathetic to the plight of aliens and agreed to set up an appeals procedure for aliens subject to a deportation order. However, the essentials of the 1919 Act remained in place. One reason for this was the presence of Pedder at the Home Office and the prevalence of what was, by now, the standard Home Office view. Calls by Jewish organisations for the restoration of asylum were dismissed by civil servants as special pleading and humbug.[62] To justify their stance, obdurate civil servants and timerous politicians needed to do no more than refer to the unpopularity of aliens and the public demand for controls on immigration. In 1928, Col A.H. Lane, the chairman of the National Citizens' Union, published *The Alien Menace*, a book which went into five editions over the subsequent six years. The Jew remained a bogey amongst the myriad of groups on the radical right, but the influence of the anti-alienists spread far wider.[63] As unemployment rose after 1929, the pressure to maintain barriers to immigrants was well-nigh insuperable. Unlike the periods of high-unemployment before 1919, the government now had control mechanisms which could be geared to levels of economic activity or necessity. Knowledge that such devices existed aggravated the clamour; government had little option but to keep immigration down to a mere trickle.

Anti-alienism during the 1930s had few new ingredients. However, the scale of its expression was transformed by the existence of a mass-based fascist movement. Its impact was more severe due to the growth of Jewish emigration from central Europe after 1933. Yet anti-alienism should not be treated as a phenomena confined to the radical right or regarded simply as a response to Jewish refugee immigration. Popular attitudes towards aliens and immigration were heavily influenced by the concurrent debate on population. Notions of the English race and eugenic ideas which contributed to the demarcation and exclusion of aliens fed into popular opinion and, in turn, helped to shape government policy.

Mosley's policy on Jews, immigration and aliens has been exhaustively discussed. Stephen Cullen has concluded that by 1932–33 the policy of the British Union of Fascists was that 'all "aliens" in Britain should be treated as foreigners, and those who had been actively enegaged in anti-British activities were to be expelled'.[64] But who were the aliens? Articles in *Blackshirt* in September and November 1933 entitled 'The Alien Menace' consciously echoed A.H. Lane, whose book defined an alien as 'One who is not British born and did not serve in the British Empire or its Allies in the Great War'. Gizela Lebzelter notes that in 1933–34 the BUF attacked Jews, Poles and Lascars without discriminating between them. However, after 1933 Mosley's references to 'alien financiers' and 'internationally minded' bankers were unambiguously about Jews.[65] Taken at face value, Mosley was proposing nothing more drastic than the policy and practice of the Tory Home Secretary between 1924 and 1929: his anti-alien rhetoric and policy was a striking example of continuity. The tradition of anti-alienism was self-consciously evoked during the BUFs East End campaign, too.[66]

As well as transmitting anti-alienism through the 1930s, the presence of a well-organized Fascist Party with extensive propaganda resources at its disposal ensured that the treatment of aliens remained an issue in political debate that other parties, including the government, could not ignore. Although the real strength of the fascists may have been slight, their spectre loomed large and provided a crucial justification for maintaining barriers against foreigners seeking to enter the country.

Popular and official responses to the influx of Jewish refugees after 1933 have been as thoroughly dissected as the history of British Fascism over the same period. The main features of anti-alienism in the 1930s were no different from previous waves. Indeed, the continuity is at times astounding. Aliens allegedly threatened the jobs and homes of Englishmen, undermined the country's security, brought with them diseases (or ill-considered methods of treatment) and crime. German, Austrian and Czech Jewish immigrants were the objects of an anti-alien rhetoric that harked back to the turn of the century. In June 1938, for example, the *Sunday Express* pronounced that 'just now there is a big influx of foreign Jews into Britain. They are overrunning the country'. A less well-known weekly declared that 'Most alien doctors and dentists are Jews who are fleeing from the terror in Germany and Austria . . . And the methods those aliens are bringing into England are not always in accordance with the professional etiquette of this country.' A characteristic headline in the *Daily Mail* in August 1938 ran 'Aliens Pouring into Britain'.[67]

The period of Jewish refugee immigration coincided with a prolonged debate on British population policy. This important, but neglected, aspect of the response to immigration shows another strong element of continuity with earlier phases of anti-alienism marked by concern about the size, structure and health of the British people. Between the wars the rate of increase of the British population slowed dramatically. Family size shrank and the age of the population rose.[68] This gave rise to an anxious discussion of population and, by implication, immigration policy. If the population was shrinking, how could its quality be preserved or raised? How could people be induced to have more children and, if that were possible, what could be done to ensure that they were of optimum intelligence and physique? This debate was informed by the eugenic theories of Francis Galton, Karl Pearson and Benjamin Kidd. Their ideas on race, heredity and selective breeding inevitably fostered a sharp sense of 'racial' or national identity. All three had, at various times, looked at or commented specifically on Jews. Their research and its popularised expression reinforced notions of the homogeneity of the British at the expense of the alien. Although some economists called for increased immigration, the state never seriously considered this option as a salve to the apparent crisis of depopulation. The desire for national cohesion again predominated over the economic argument.[69]

The continuities of anti-alienism were evident in practice, too. Although the government evinced sympathy for the refugees, it insisted on adhering to the highly restrictive conditions established by the 1919 Act. In some cases, the very same personnel who had been administering the 1905 and 1919 Acts now determined the fate of Jews queuing to escape from Germany. The hostility of sections of the British press and public opinion to Jewish immigration were used by the government to justify retention of the ungenerous provisions established in 1919–20. In particular, the same case for restriction based on domestic unemployment recurred again and again. The principle of asylum was obliterated by economic arguments and the claim that immigration would lead to an anti-alien (anti-Semitic) backlash. Without any concerted government effort to educate or lead public opinion this became a self-fulfilling prophecy. Yet the possibilities for a more open asylum policy, backed by a substantial slice of public opinion, were to be demonstrated in 1938–39.[70]

The initially unpropitious climate had an effect on Anglo-Jewish

responses to the refugee crisis. Jewish organisations, aware of the
unpopularity of Jewish aliens and the vulnerability of even limited
immigration to the pressure of anti-alienism, accepted and worked within
the provisions of the 1919 Act. Unlike the 1910s or the early 1920s, they
did not contest the legislation, possibly because they were cowed by the
existence of a powerful anti-alien fascist movement. Instead, they assured
the government that Jewish immigration would not become a burden on
the public purse or displace native labour. This promise obliged the
Jewish communities to find large sums of money for relief work and to
secure jobs for Jewish arrivals. It was a gigantic task which slowed down
the rate at which Jews could enter Britain. When emigration turned to
flight following the German annexation of Austria in March 1938, the
pledge turned into a fatal bottleneck.[71]

Public opinion was aroused by the scenes of Jewish degredation in
Vienna in March 1938 and the anti-Jewish violence in Germany in
November. Confronted by evidence of brutal persecution and egged on
by powerful advocates of asylum in Parliament and the press, the
government relented. Strict controls were relaxed in order to cope with
the tidal wave of penniless refugees streaming out of central Europe. This
is indicative of the volatility of pro- and anti-alienism and the tenacity of
asylum as an idea and a practice. Yet, at the very same time that it
virtually abandoned controls on immigration, the government was
exploring an international solution to the Jewish refugee crisis and
investigating ways of diverting the flow of Jews to other countries or parts
of the British Empire. The fear of anti-alienism remained as pervasive
and persuasive as ever.[72]

VI. War and Internment 1939–45

By the outbreak of war, about 55,000 Jews from Central Europe had
found homes and refuge in Britain. Several thousand exiled Germans,
Austrians and Czechs had also arrived in the country. The government's
wartime policy on aliens was initially designed with the trials and errors of
earlier experience, particularly during 1914–18, in mind. All enemy aliens
were compelled to register with the police and some were obliged to move
from areas of military sensitivity. Tribunals categorized them according
to whether they were to be interned (category A), subject to restrictions
(category B) or exempt from both (category C). The bulk of refugees fell
into the last category.[73]

It may be considered a remarkable act of tolerance that during the
'Phoney War' period no other action was taken against the bulk of aliens.
However, after the fall of France in May 1940 scare stories began to

appear in the press about the alleged German 'Fifth Column'. Public opinion was transformed. In a Gallup Poll taken in May 1940, 64 per cent of those interviewed thought that government policy towards foreigners in Britain was 'too lenient'. Yet incarceration did not appear to be considered unequivocally as the favoured solution. A month later, when mass internment was in full swing, 43 per cent agreed that all aliens should be in interned while 48 per cent believed that 'only those who may be unfriendly and dangerous' needed to be confined.[74]

Indeed, the government decision to begin mass internment was powered as much by internal considerations as fickle public opinion. Driven on by the security services and Churchill, the Prime Minister, the Home Office reluctantly extended internment from Category A to B and then to a large slice of all those in class C. By the end of the process, around 27,000 aliens, including Jewish refugees, non-Jewish Germans and Austrians, and Italians were interned and over 7,000 deported abroad to Canada and Australia.[75]

As in 1914–18, anti-alienism during the Second World War was nurtured in pre-war spy stories and the alarums about a 'Fifth Column' which had been in vogue since the Spanish Civil War. Likewise, the internment policy was a continuity of peace and wartime measures considered and implemented since 1904. Despite the good intentions not to repeat the mistakes of the First World War, mass internment in 1940 was equally unsatisfactory. The experience of the internees was less awful in terms of their physical conditions, but it was more psychologically gruelling.

Anti-Nazi exiles and Jewish refugees were scooped up along with German nationalists. They were dispatched to hastily erected and ill-equipped collection centres before being moved on to better established camps where they helplessly pondered what their fate would be if the Germans invaded the British Isles. Those who were shipped abroad suffered humiliations from their guards en route and found themselves dumped in isolated camps in some of the most climatically inhospitable parts of the world. In despair, several camp inmates in Britain and elsewhere killed themselves. Nearly seven hundred deported Germans and Italians died when their ship, the SS Arandora Star, was torpedoed in the Irish Sea. As in 1914–18, Anglo-Jewry did not initially distinguish itself in the relief of those who were interned or in the campaign to free them. Opposition to internment was led by a brave group of Liberal and Labour politicians, churchmen and publicists. Assisted by the outrage following the sinking of the Arandora Star, they eventually prevailed and by the autumn the government began the selective release of internees.[76]

As in the First World War, the internees eventually established a sort of life for themselves. Political, cultural and educational activities flourished in the internment camps. However, there was no repatriation either as a one-way process or by way of exchange. The majority of the internees were Jewish and there was no question of their return to Germany; nor was there any possibility of a reciprocal arrangement. In another significant departure from 1918, most were allowed to remain in the United Kingdom whereupon they formed an important addition to the population.[77]

VII. Conclusion

If Bernard Porter is correct, between the mid and the late nineteenth century a profound shift in attitudes towards aliens took place in British society. It is difficult to assess whether this movement occurred due to the way aliens were understood, because their numbers increased dramatically or because this escalation coincided with a period of economic recession. Probably no one reason suffices in itself; it was the conjuncture of forces which was critical. Had the mass immigration of Jews in the 1880s and 1890s taken place during a period of sustained economic growth, it may not have aroused such opposition. In the USA, anti-alien or nativist feeling was contained until the 1920s due to the strength of the industrial and business interests which placed a premium on maintaining a supply of cheap labour.[78]

In Britain, at this crucial moment, countervailing voices within the business community were muted. Politicians faced pressure from their constituents to restrict immigration while the appeal to free trade and asylum was effectively countered by arguments around protection, population and social policy. As a result, if the special case of the Irish is excepted, Britain never became a country that experienced a period of sustained, free and broadly accepted mass immigration. It must be stressed that this is distinct from being a country of refuge. Asylum always remained a potent case for allowing some foreigners in. This was shown most powerfully in the case of refugee immigration from central Europe between 1938 and 1939. But because the economic and social arguments for mass immigration were lost at the first challenge, asylum would always be compromised by the alleged threat which immigrants posed to the availability of housing, jobs and welfare.[79]

It may now be possible to venture a schematic analysis of the pattern of anti-alienism over the century up to 1940. From the 1850s to the 1870s, public opinion was broadly pro-alien or, perhaps more accurately, pro-asylum while the state sought ways to control the influx of foreigners. Between the 1880s and 1900s, the expression of popular feeling towards aliens became predominantly negative. It was possible for anti-alien activists to mobilize substantial numbers of people against the alien and to give the impression of still greater antipathy. The state was ambivalent, largely because of the doctrine of free trade and the reluctance to embark on collectivist measures. However, in the two decades after the 1905 Act, the state finally embraced anti-alienism and immigration controls. There was a high degree of harmony between public opinion and state action: hence the consensus on the 1914, 1919, 1920 and 1925 measures. During the 1930s public opinion towards aliens fluctuated. The state appears to have erred towards a liberal interpretation of alien controls, but its scope for relaxing the legislation was limited.

The turning point in this cycle occurs in the 1880s and 1890s. Anti-alienism was the popular response to mass immigration. A set of policies and practices previously confined to government for specific purposes now became the goal of a mass movement. Henceforth, the dynamic between public opinion and government was reversed. By 1940 the cycle had turned fully. Public opinion now helped to trigger an anti-alien measure that the government (barring certain powerful individuals) opposed. Of course, this is a highly schematic approach to a complex phenomena and does not assess the weight of liberal, pro-alien feeling. For example, in the twentieth century the Liberal and Labour Parties and the trades union movement repeatedly defended the principle of asylum. But, in practice, these forces were marginalized in the debates on aliens and immigration. During the 1920s and 1930s, in particular, the solid body of pro-alien opinion counted as little against the fear of an anti-alien backlash should controls be relaxed.

What may account for this dramatic inversion? It appears that pro-alienism was closely related to public confidence and optimism. Anti-alienism was most intense during periods of economic insecurity, political instability and external threat. Yet the fear of subversion and antagonism towards the alien Other cannot be reduced to a convulsive reaction to economic trends or foreign affairs. Anti-alienism is a mirroring of national identity and sense of self.[80] In so far as nationalism in politics and culture is central to the existence of any nation state, then anti-alienism must be seen as central, too. The construction of the alien is a nodal point where ideology and politics intersect. In the definition of the alien, the state and the people act in collusion: popular attitudes and official policy are fused to produce a coherent account of the nation. During the long period of Britain's decline as a world power and the concurrent stress within society, the forging of the nation was critical.[81] To omit anti-alienism from this process is like playing 'Macbeth' without the ghost.

NOTES

1. James Walvin, *Passage to Britain* (London, 1984); Colin Holmes, *John Bull's Island* (London, 1988). One interesting exception is the local study by C. Husbands, 'East End Racism 1900–1980: Geographic Continuities in Vigilantist and Extreme Right-Wing Political Behaviour', *London Journal* Vol.8 (1982), pp.3–26. The cool and judicious treatment of immigration in British history by Colin Holmes, *A Tolerant Country? Immigrants, Refugees and Minorities in Britain* (London, 1991) comes close to a study of anti-immigrant feeling, but Holmes is concerned to show that anti-alienism is one strand within a wide spectrum of responses.

2. John Garrard, *The English and Immigration: A Comparative Study of the Jewish Influx 1880–1910* (London, 1971), Ch.3 and Bernard Gainer, *The Alien Invasion. The Origins of the Aliens Act of 1905* (London, 1972), Chs.3, 5.

3. Daniel Pick, *Faces of Degeneration: A European disorder, c. 1848–1918* (Cambridge, 1989), Chs.6–7. See also Haia Shpayer-Makov, 'Anarchism in British Public Opinion', *Victorian Studies* Vol.31 No.4 (1988), pp.511–15 and Anthony S. Wohl, *Endangered Lives. Public health in Victorian Britain* (London, 1983), pp.329–36.

4. Bernard Semmel, *Imperialism and Social Reform. English Social-Imperial Thought 1895–1914* (London, 1960), Chps.4–5; David Cannadine, 'The British Monarchy, c. 1820–1977', in Eric Hobsbawm and Terence Ranger (eds.), *The Invention of Tradition* (Cambridge, 1983), pp.120–38.

5. Robert Colls and Philip Dodd (eds.), *Englishness Politics and Culture 1880–1920* (London, 1986); Keith Robbins, *Nineteenth-Century Britain, England, Scotland and Wales. The Making of a Nation* (Oxford, 1989), Chs.1–2; Hugh A. MacDougall, *Racial Myth in English History* (Hanover, 1982), Ch.5; P. Levine, *The Amateur and the Professional. Antiquarians, Historians and Archeologists in Victorian England 1838–1886* (Cambridge, 1986), pp.81–5; Billie Melman, 'Claiming the Nation's Past; The Invention of an Anglo-Saxon Tradition', *Journal of Contemporary History*, Vol.26, Nos.3–4 (1991), pp.575–95. On the character of national identity, see Michael Howard, 'Empire, Race and War in Pre-1914 Britain', in Hugh Lloyd-Jones *et al.* (eds.), *History and Imagination: Essays in honour of Hugh Trevor-Roper* (London, 1981), pp.340–55 and Paul B. Rich, *Race and Empire in British Politics* (Cambridge, 1986), pp.12–27. For a concise synthesis of this argument, see David Feldman, 'The Importance of Being English: Jewish Immigration and the Decay of liberal England', in David Feldman and Gareth Stedman Jones (eds.), *Metropolis London: Histories and Representations since 1800* (London, 1989), pp.56–84.

6. See, for example: Greta Jones, *Social Darwinism and English Thought* (London, 1980) and G.R. Searle, *Eugenics and Politics in Britain 1900–1914* (Leyden, 1976); J.W. Burrow, *A Liberal Descent: Victorian Historians and the English Past* (Cambridge, 1981), p.192; G.R. Searle, *The Quest for National Efficiency* (Oxford, 1971) and Semmel, *Imperialism and Social Reform*.

7. Bernard Porter, *The Refugee Question in Mid-Victorian Politics* (Cambridge, 1979), pp.67–71.

8. George H. Gallup, *The Gallup International Public Opinion Polls: Great Britain 1937–1975*, Vol.1, *1937–1964* (New York, 1976), p.22.

9. Peter Pulzer, 'Foreigners: The Immigrant in Britain', in Werner Mosse (ed.), *Second Chance: Two Centuries of German-speaking Jews in the United Kingdom* (Tübingen, 1991), p.4.

10. Bernard Porter, *The Refugee Question*, pp.4–5. On the Irish, see Lynn Hollen Lees, *Exiles of Erin: Irish Migrants in Victorian London* (Manchester, 1979).

11. Porter, *The Refugee Question*, pp.111–12.

12. For example, James Walvin, *Black and White: The Negro in English Society, 1555–1945* (London, 1973); Douglas Lorimer, *Colour, Class and the Victorians: English Attitudes to the Negro in the Mid-Nineteenth Century* (Leicester, 1978); Colin Holmes (ed.), *Immigrants and Minorities in British Society* (London, 1978); Peter Fryer, *Staying Power: The History of Black People in Britain* (London, 1984); Lucio Sponza, *Italian*

Immigrants in Nineteenth Century Britain: Realities and Images (Leicester, 1983); Pauline Pauker, 'The Image of the German Jew in English Fiction', in Werner Mosse *et al.*, (ed.), *Second Chance*, pp.315–33; Harry Stone, 'Dickens and the Jews', *Victorian Studies* Vol.2, No.2 (1959), pp.223–53.

13. Porter, *The Refugee Question*, Ch.6.
14. Porter, *The Refugee Question*, pp.218–27. In a later article, Porter argues that English dislike of foreigners may have been powered by real perceived differences between themselves and the subjects – or victims – of 'backward' and illiberal Continental states. Yet he acknowledges that whether or not this antipathy was the product of xenophobia or rational judgments, the effect was much the same. Bernard Porter, ' "Bureau and Barrack": Early Victorian Attitudes Towards the Continent', *Victorian Studies* Vol.26, No.1 (1982), pp.407–33.
15. Gareth Stedman Jones *Outcast London* (London, 1971), Ch.16; Bernard Semmel, *Imperialism and Social Reform*, Chs.2, 4, 5.
16. David Feldman, 'The Importance of Being English', in Feldman and Stedman Jones (eds.), *Metropolis London*, pp.56–84.
17. Pick, *Faces of Degeneration*, pp.215–16; Douglas Lorimer, 'Theoretical Racism in Late-Victorian Anthropology, 1870–1900', *Victorian Studies* (Spring 1988), pp.421–4, 429–30. Cf. Searle, *Eugenics and Politics in Britain 1900–1914*.
18. Garrard, *The English and Immigration*: Gainer, *The Alien Invasion*: I. Finestein, 'Jewish Immigration in British Party Politics in the 1890s', in A. Newman, (ed.), *Migration and Settlement* (London, 1971), pp.128–44.
19. J.M. Evans, *Immigration Law* (London, 1983), pp.5-8; Garrard, *The English and Immigration*, Ch.2.
20. Ibid.
21. Husbands, 'East End Racism 1900–1980', pp.9–12; Feldman, 'The Importance of Being English', pp.70–74.
22. Feldman, 'The Importance of Being English', p.79.
23. Gainer, *The Alien Invasion*, pp.209–10.
24. Eugene C. Black, *The Social Politics of Anglo-Jewry 1880–1920* (Oxford, 1988), p.315. V.D. Lipman, *A History of the Jews in Britain Since 1858* (Leicester, 1990), p.73, notes that the decrease may have had other causes and was reversed during 1910–14 when immigration reached levels comparable to two decades before the Act was passed.
25. Garrard, *The English Immigration* pp.106–7; Black, *The Social Politics of Anglo-Jewry* p.315.
26. Jill Pellew, *The Home Office 1848–1914: From Clerks to Bureaucrats* (London, 1982), pp.91, 190; Black, *The Social Politics of Anglo-Jewry*, p.311; Louise London, 'British Immigration Control Procedures and Jewish Refugees 1933–1939', in Mosse (ed.), *Second Chance*, pp.494 n.28.
27. Bryan Cheyette, 'Jewish Stereotyping and English literature, 1875–1920: Towards a Political Analysis', in Tony Kushner and Kenneth Lunn (eds.), *Traditions of Intolerance* (Manchester, 1989), pp.12–32; idem., 'Hilaire Belloc and the "Marconi Scandal" 1913–1914; A Reassessment of the Interactionist Model of Racial Hatred', in Tony Kushner and Kenneth Lunn (eds.), *The Politics of Marginality* (London, 1990), pp.131–42; idem, ' "Jewgreek is Greekjew": The Disturbing Ambivalence of Joyce's Semitic Discourse in Ulysses', *Joyce Studies Annual*, Vol.3 (1992), pp.32–56; idem, 'Superman and Jew: Semitic Representations in the work of Bernard Shaw', *Shaw. The Annual of Bernard Shaw Studies*, Vol.12 (1992), pp.249–68; idem, 'Beyond Rationality: H.G. Wells and the Jewish Question', *The Wellsian*, No.14 (Summer 1991), pp.41–64.
28. For example, M. Banton, *The Coloured Quarter* (London, 1955), Ch.2; Rozina Visram, *Ayahs, Lascars and Princes: Indians in Britain 1700–1947* (London, 1986), pp.55–71; Gregory Anderson, 'German Clerks in England 1870–1914: Another Aspect of the Great Depression Debate', in Kenneth Lunn (ed.), *Hosts, Immigrants and Minorities: Historical Responses to Newcomers in British Society* (Folkestone, 1980), pp.201–22; George K. Behlmer, 'The Gypsy Problem in Victorian England', *Victorian Studies* Vol.28, No.2 (1985), pp.213–54. For reflections on the 'foreboding and fear'

underlying Edwardian imperialism, see Bernard Porter, 'The Edwardians and the Empire', in Donald Read (ed.), *Edwardian England* (London, 1982), pp.128–44.

29. Geoffrey Alderman, *The Jewish Community in British Politics* (Oxford, 1983), pp.75–85.
30. Shpayer-Makov, 'Anarchism in British Public Opinion', pp.514–15. On the pro-alien lobby and administration of the act, see Black, *The Social Politics of Anglo-Jewry*, pp.309–16; Garrard, *The English and Immigration*, pp.103–13; Gainer, *The Alien Invasion*, pp.199–210.
31. Gainer, *The Alien Invasion*, pp.205–7.
32. Ibid.
33. Christopher Andrew, *Secret Service* (London, 1985), pp.68–108. See also, A.A. Morris, *The Scaremongers: The Advocacy of War and Rearmament 1896–1914* (London, 1984), Ch.12; D.H.T. Stafford, 'Spies and Gentlemen: The Birth of the British Spy Novel 1893–1914', *Victorian Studies*, Vol.24, No.4 (1981), pp.489–509. The French did not escape either: Gerald Newman, 'Anti-French Propaganda and British Liberal National-ism in the Early Twentieth Century', *Victorian Studies*, Vol.18, No.4 (1975), pp.385–418.
34. Virginia Berridge, 'East End Opium Dens and Narcotic Use in Britain', *London Journal*, Vol.4, No.1 (1978), pp.15–16 and idem, 'Victorian Opium Eating: Respon-ses to Opiate Use in Nineteenth Century England', *Victorian Studies*, Vol.21, No.14 (1978), p.460; J.P. May, 'The Chinese in England', in Holmes (ed.) *Immigrants and Minorities in British Society*, pp.114–20.
35. Arthur Marwick, *The Deluge. British Society and the First World War* (London, 1965), Chs.5, 7; John Stevenson, *British Society 1914–45* (London, 1984), pp.57–60, 67–74.
36. The 1914 Act effectively supplanted the 1905 Act which was formally repealed in 1920. Evans, *Immigration Law*, pp.9–10.
37. Stella Yarrow, 'The Impact of Hostility on Germans in Britain, 1914–1918', *Immigrants and Minorities*, Vol.8, Nos.1–2 (1989), pp.106–7 and the contribution to this volume by Panikos Panayi. It would be interesting to investigate whether any connnection exists between the policy of internment practised during the Boer War and that applied in Britain during the 1914–1918 War.
38. Stella Yarrow, 'Germans in England and the First World War', unpublished M.A. in Social and Industrial History, Middlesex Polytechnic, 1987, pp.63–100.
39. Marwick, *The Deluge* pp.36–8. David Saunders, 'Aliens in Britain and the Empire During the First World War', *Immigrants and Minorities* Vol.4, No.1 (1985), pp.5–27.
40. Panikos Panayi, 'Anti-German Riots in London during the First World War', *German History*, Vol.7, No.2 (1989), pp.184–203; Marwick, *The Deluge*, pp.131–2; Stevenson, *British Society 1914–45*, pp.55–7.
41. Berridge, 'East End Opium Dens and Narcotic Use in Britain', pp.15–16.
42. Holmes, *John Bull's Island*, p.112. For the erosion of distinctions between aliens and naturalised subjects, see David Cesarani, 'An Embattled Minority: The Jews in Britain During the First World War', in Kushner and Lunn (eds.), *The Politics of Marginality*, pp. 60–81 and Yarrow, 'The Impact of Hostility on Germans in Britain, 1914–1918', pp.104–5.
43. Sharman Kadish, *Bolsheviks and British Jews* (London, 1992), pp.45–52.
44. Kadish, *Bolsheviks and British Jews*, pp.172–212; David Cesarani 'Anti-Alienism in Britain After the First World War', *Immigrants and Minorities*, Vol.6, No.1 (1987), pp.9–14.
45. Kadish, *Bolsheviks and British Jews*, Ch.1; Cesarani, 'Anti-Alienism in Britain After the First World War', pp.4–29; K.O. Morgan, *Conflict and Disunity. The Lloyd George Coalition Government* (Oxford, 1979), esp. Ch.10.
46. Fryer, *Staying Power*, pp.294–7; Caroline Adams (ed.), *Across Seven Seas and Thirteen Rivers* (London, 1987), pp.31–8 and *passim*.
47. A.J.P. Taylor, *English History, 1914–1945* (Oxford, 1965), pp.138–46; Morgan, *Conflict and Disunity*, Ch.3.
48. Banton, *The Coloured Quarter*, Ch.3; Fryer, *Staying Power*, pp.298–326; Holmes, *John Bull's Island*, pp.107–12. See also Jacqueline Jenkinson, 'The Glasgow Race

Disturbance of 1919', *Immigrants and Minorities* Vol.4, No.2 (1985), pp. 46–37 and idem, 'The Black Community of Salford and Hull 1919–21', *Immigrants and Minorities* Vol.7, No.2 (1988), pp.166–83.

49. *East London Observer*, 26 April 1919, p.2.
50. *Liverpool Daily Post and Mercury*, 11 June 1919, pp.3, 4 and 13 June 1919, p.3.
51. *Liverpool Daily Post and Mercury*, 18 June 1919, p.4; *Liverpool Echo*, 16 June 1919, p.6 and 17 June 1919, p.6. Cesarani, 'Anti-Alienism in Britain After the First World War', pp.9–14,; Holmes, *John Bull's Island*, p.110.
52. Evans, *Immigration Law*, pp.11–12.
53. Ibid.
54. Rich, *Race and Empire in British Politics*, Ch.6; Ron Ramdin, *The Making of the Black Working Class in Britain* (London, 1987), pp.76–7.
55. Ramdin, *The Making of the Black Working Class in Britain*, pp.76–7; Cesarani, 'Anti-Alienism in Britain After the First World War', pp.15–16.
56. Fryer, *Staying Power*, pp.358–8; Neil Evans, 'Regulating the Reserve Army: Arabs, Blacks and the Local State in Cardiff, 1919–45', *Immigrants and Minorities*, Vol.4, No.2 (Special Issue) (1985), pp.86–106.
57. Berridge, 'East End Opium Dens and Narcotic Use in Britain', pp.21–2; Annie Lai, Bob Little, Pippa Little, 'Chinatown Annie: The East End Opium Trade 1920–35: The Story of a Woman Opium Dealer', *Oral History Journal*, Vol.14, No.1 (1986), pp.22–3. See *The Times*, 1 Feb. 1928 and 14 March 1928.
58. Cesarani, 'Anti-Alienism in Britain After the First World War', pp.14–18; Elaine Smith, 'Jewish Responses to Political Antisemitism and Fascism in the East End of London, 1920–1939', in Kushner and Lunn, *Traditions of Intolerance*, pp.55–7; Geoffrey Alderman, *London Jewry and London Politics 1889–1986* (London, 1989), pp.66–68.
59. Cesarani, 'Anti-Alienism in Britain After the First World War', pp.18–21.
60. Charles Loch Mowat, *Britain Between The Wars 1918–1940* (London, 1955), pp.187–94; David Cesarani, 'Joynson Hicks and the radical right in England after the First World War', in Kushner and Lunn, *Traditions of Intolerance*, pp. 127–8.
61. Cesarani, 'Joynson Hicks and the Radical Right in England after the First World War', pp.118–39.
62. Cesarani, 'Anti-Alienism in Britain After the First World War', pp.21–2.
63. See G.C. Webber, *The Ideology of the British Right 1918–1939* (London, 1986), Ch.4.
64. Stephen Cullen, The Development of the Ideas and Policy of the British Union of Fascists, 1932–40', *Journal of Contemporary History*, 22 (1987), p.127.
65. A.H. Lane, *The Alien Menace* (London, 1928), p.9. See also, Gizela Lebzelter, *Political Anti-Semitism in England, 1918–1939* (London, 1978), p.91; cf. Robert Skidelsky, *Oswald Mosley* (London, 1975), pp.379–84.
66. See C. Husbands, 'East End Racism in 1900–1980; Geographical Continuities in Vigilantist and Extreme Right-Wing Political Behaviour'.
67. Quoted in Andrew Sharf, *The British press and the Jews under Nazi rule* (London, 1964), pp.155–74. See also, A.J. Sherman, *Island Refuge, Britain and the Refugees from the Third Reich, 1933–1939* (London, 1973), pp.48, 94, 123–6, 217.
68. Stevenson, *British Society 1914–45*, pp.143-67.
69. Paul Hayes, 'The Contribution of British Intellectuals to Fascism', in Kenneth Lunn and Richard C. Thurlow (eds.) *British Fascism* (London, 1980), pp.173–82; Rich, *Race and Empire*, Ch.5 and idem, 'The Long Victorian Sunset: Anthropology, Eugenics and Race in Britain, c.1900–48', *Patterns of Prejudice*, Vol.18, No.3 (1984), pp.3–17; Michael Freeden, 'Eugenics and Progressive Thought: A Study in Ideological Affinity', *Historical Journal*, Vol.22, No.3 (1979), pp.661–71.
70. See Louise London, 'British Immigration Control Procedures and Jewish Refugees, 1933–1939', in Mosse (ed.), *Second Chance*, pp.485–518; idem, 'Jewish Refugees, Anglo-Jewry and British Government Policy, 1939–1940', in David Cesarani (ed.), *The Making of Modern Anglo-Jewry* (Oxford, 1990), pp.163–90; idem, 'British Government Policy and Jewish Refugees, 1933–1945', *Patterns of Prejudice*, Vol.23, No.4 (1989), pp.26–43. In general, see Sherman, *Island Refuge*.

71. For the impact of popular prejudice on immigration policy, see Tony Kushner, 'The Impact of Anti-semitism, 1918–1945' in Cesarani (ed.), *The Making of Modern Anglo-Jewry*, pp.195–9; idem, 'Beyond the Pale? British Reactions to Nazi Anti-Semitism, 1933–39', in Kushner and Lunn (eds.), *The Politics of Marginality*, pp.154–5 and 'Politics and Race, Gender and Class: Refugees, Fascists and Domestic Service in Britain, 1933–1940', in ibid, pp.49–58.
72. Sherman, *Island Refuge*, Chs.4, 5, 7 and 8.
73. Peter and Leni Gillman, *Collar the Lot!* (London, 1980), Ch.5. And see the contributions to this volume by Tony Kushner, Louise Burletson and Lucio Sponza and Terri Colpi.
74. Gallup, *The Gallup International Opinion Polls*, pp.33–4.
75. Tony Kushner, *The Persistence of Prejudice* (Manchester, 1989), pp.143–52; Peter and Leni Gillman, *Collar the Lot!*, Chs.8–11. See also the contributions by Bernard Wasserstein and Ronald Stent in Gerhard Hirschfeld (ed.), *Exile in Great Britain. Refugees From Hitler's Germany* (Leamington Spa, 1984). On the Italian experience, Terri Colpi, *The Italian Factor. The Italian Community in Great Britain* (London, 1991), pp.105–8.
76. Peter and Leni Gillman, *Collar the Lot!* Chps.17, 20, 23; Colpi, *The Italian Factor*, pp.101–5, 108–26.
77. Miriam Kochan, *British Internees in the Second World War* (London, 1983); Hirschfield, *Exile in Great Britain*. Many aspects of internment and the post-war experience are dealt with in Mosse (ed.), *Second Chance*.
78. John Higham, *Strangers in the Land. Patterns of American Nativism 1860–1925* (New York, 1955).
79. Cf. Holmes, *A Tolerant Country*, pp.97–8.
80. The literature on the construction of national identity is enormous; but see especially, Benedict Anderson, *Imagined Communities* (London, 1983) and Patrick Wright, *On Living in An Old Country: The National Past and Contemporary Britain* (London, 1985), notably pp.81–7, 119–29.
81. Robbins, *Nineteenth-Century Britain. England, Scotland and Wales* loc. cit.; Donald Read, 'Introduction: Crisis Age or Golden Age', in Read (ed.), *Edwardian England*, pp.40–55 and Bernard Porter, 'The Edwardians and their Empire', loc. cit.; Mary Langan and Bill Schwarz (eds.), *Crises in the British State 1880–1930* (London, 1985). The point is also made in J.H. Grainger, *Patriotisms, Britain: 1900–1939* (London, 1986), pp.19–21, although he inexplicably omits any discussion of anti-alienism.

An Intolerant Act by an Intolerant Society: The Internment of Germans in Britain During the First World War

PANIKOS PANAYI

The German community in Britain during the Great War, which numbered approximately 60,000, and which had developed during the course of hundreds of years, found itself under attack both officially and unofficially during the course of the 1914–18 conflict. The most potent of the official responses involved the introduction of a policy of wholesale internment and repatriation, which reduced the size of the German community in Britain to 22,254 by 1919. In order to fully understand this development we need to put it within the context of the intolerance which gripped Britain during the First World War.

I

Since the 1960s numerous books have appeared on the domestic affects of the Great War in Britain. However, none of them has systematically dealt with one of the most fundamental socio-political developments of the War: that is the growth of intolerance and the decline of liberalism. Some historians of the conflict acknowledge this change and outline the extension of government intervention. We can say this about John Turner's edited collection of essays and about Arthur Marwick, for instance, who recognizes that war leads to changes in 'social cohesion', 'customs and behaviour', 'intellectual ideas and practices', and 'social and political values, institutions and ideas'. But his study of Britain in the First World War is basically a social history rather than a work which takes detailed account of ideological and political changes. Trevor Wilson's massive narrative study, meanwhile, illustrates many aspects of British intolerance, but does not bring the threads together. A similar assertion can be made about John Bourne's work. The best attempt to tackle the decline of liberalism systematically can be found in John Stevenson's *British Society 1914–45*, in a chapter entitled 'War, Patriotism and the State'.[1]

Contemporaries, meanwhile, clearly recognized that fundamental changes had taken place in Britain. Norman Angell, for instance, the liberal journalist, writing in 1915, wrote that the country had entered the

conflict as the 'antithesis of all the Prussian doctrines . . . It was agreed
that the political doctrines of Prussia, which it was our mission to destroy,
were a menace to human freedom'. Nevertheless, within six months
Britain had begun to adopt the militaristic characteristics which it had
originally entered the War to fight. To support his position, Angell
quoted an article from the radical Unionist *Morning Post* which asserted
that, 'Militarism, said to be so bad a thing in itself, is become the sole
business of the nation . . . Democracy may still exist, but it is no longer in
evidence'. Angell himself accepted this to some extent by writing:

> We may be fighting for democracy, freedom, parliamentary govern-
> ment, against despotism, government by a military caste, and
> restraint of free speech; yet if we are to wage the war efficiently, our
> government must be autocratic, free speech must be suspended,
> and the military order must have arbitrary power.[2]

How do we demonstrate that Britain became intolerant during the
Great War? Three developments will help to illustrate the transfor-
mation: political changes; the extension of the role of the state; and
government and public persecution of three outgroups, 'socialists',
'pacifists' and immigrants. If we deal with political changes the most
important of these is the growth of power of the 'Radical Right' and its
ideas. This group, which has received extensive attention from scholars of
modern Britain, originated at the turn of the century but only 'really came
into its own' during the First World War. At this point the basic tenets of
its ideology, revolving around extreme nationalism and xenophobia
acquired greater purchase. The fringe groups which had existed during
the pre-war period began to increase their influence while new ones
developed. More importantly, the Radical Right entered the centre of the
political spectrum, since in an environment of 'Total War', anti-
Germanism and jingoism became a national obsession. Candidates who
put forward strong nationalistic views did well at successive by-elections,
while the 1918 General Election, conducted in extremely jingoistic
fashion, resulted in the biggest landslide victory in twentieth century
British history, and saw major gains for the Radical Right.[3]

At the same time, the state increased its role in the life of the citizen.
While this process may have begun before the war, the conflict entailed
government intervention on an unprecedented scale. For instance,
the state established controls over the pricing and distribution of food
and drink. The Defence of the Realm Act meant that through the introduction of subsequent Orders in Council the government could undertake
virtually any action it wished in the interests of public safety and national
defence. David Englander has rightly described it as 'the most Draconian

legislation ever enacted by a British Parliament'. Meanwhile, new Ministries came into existence, including those dealing with Munitions, Labour and National Service. The state also controlled information through the development of the Press Bureau and the Secret War Propaganda Bureau. The Security Services also expanded significantly.[4]

At the same time certain minorities came under attack from both the state and the public. One target was socialists, especially those in the Labour Party who had not fully supported the war. At the 1918 General Election, although 59 Labour MPs obtained seats, the anti-War section, including Arthur Henderson and Ramsay MacDonald, failed to do so. MacDonald felt that he had 'become a kind of mythological demon in the minds of the people'.[5] Pacifists also faced attack. John Stevenson has written that, 'With the introduction of conscription the state had undoubtedly crossed a new threshold in its relationship with ordinary citizens'.[6] The liberty of the individual seemed to have disappeared, as the state could *compel* him to enter its service. During the war some 16,000 men objected to armed service although 90 per cent of them accepted alternative service. A total of 1,298 refused and faced imprisonment and brutal treatment, which, in 70 cases led to their deaths. The government also suppressed anti-war leaflets and launched propaganda campaigns against Pacifists, while speakers at Pacifist meetings faced constant physical attack.[7] Furthermore, immigrants endured violence, for instance, Jews in Leeds and east London.[8]

But the minority which faced the most intense hostility in Britain during the First World War, from both the government and public opinion, consisted of the 60,000 people of German birth who had made their way to Britain during the late nineteenth century for primarily economic reasons. By the outbreak of the First World War they had developed communities in many British cities, particularly London, Manchester and Liverpool. Although animosity had begun to develop towards them during the Edwardian years, with the rise of Anglo-German political and economic rivalry, this hostility remained mild compared with what they would face after 1914.[9]

In the opening months of the conflict, 'spy-fever', a belief that all Germans acted as agents on behalf of their homeland, became widespread. As the war dragged on fear of spies developed into a more sophisticated conspiracy theory which argued that Germans controlled all sections of the British establishment and were frustrating the attainment of military victory. Individuals with German connections faced constant vilification in the press, including Prince Louis of Battenberg, the First Sea Lord, and Sir Edgar Speyer, Sir Ernest Cassel and Baron Bruno Schroeder, all prominent merchant bankers. German employees, meanwhile, faced anti-German strikes or lost their positions while social bodies and trading organizations expelled individuals of enemy alien origin. Worst of all, German property was attacked on a large scale throughout the country. In October 1914, for instance, violence broke out in south London and Crewe. But the most serious disturbances took place in May 1915 following the sinking of the *Lusitania*. German-owned shops in every part of Britain, from Glasgow to Exeter and from Liverpool to London, suffered damage. In the capital alone the Metropolitan Police received 1,950 claims for compensation. Press reaction to the sinking of the *Lusitania* played a part in sparking off the disturbance.

This was the background against which the government made efforts to control the activities of Germans in Britain. On 5 August 1914 it passed the Aliens Restriction Act which allowed the government to introduce subsequent Orders in Council to control many aspects of the lives of alien enemies. These covered movement, residence, and social activities; Germans could not travel more than five miles, could not live in 'prohibited areas', and had their social institutions closed down. Later, the British Nationality and Status of Aliens Act of 1918 allowed the Home Secretary to revoke the naturalization certificates of Germans in certain cases and also forbade Germans from becoming British citizens for a period of ten years after the conclusion of hostilities. At the same time, the Trading with the Enemy Acts closed down hundreds of German-owned businesses in Britain.[10]

II

It is within this context of rising intolerance and the extension of state intervention in Britain after 1914, that we need to look at the policy of internment of Germans in Britain. We can do this in two parts. First, by looking at the development of internment policy, and then by carrying out a survey of the camps established and conditions within them.

During the years immediately before the outbreak of the First World War, no plans existed for the internment of alien enemies. However, on 7 August 1914, three days after war broke out, the General Staff decided that all Germans and Austrians between the ages of 17 and 42 should be interned. Yet on the following day a conference of the War Office, Foreign Office, Home Office and Colonial Office agreed to rescind this decision. Chief Constables received instructions to arrest only those suspected of being in any way dangerous to the safety of the realm, although if they could obtain sureties from two British residents of standing they would be released. This remained government policy until the end of August. By 13 August, 1,980 people had been interned.

This figure reached 4,300 by the 28th.

On 27 August the War Office received a Home Office letter which stated that the Public believed that the German and Austrian reservists remaining in the country might become a source of danger. The letter stated that because enemy aliens had lost their employment, they could cause acts of sabotage 'in the central portion of London'. Reginald McKenna, the Home Secretary, proposed 'to instruct the Police . . . to arrest those most likely to be dangerous . . . and to hand them over to the Military Authorities for internment as prisoners of war'. Only those of military age would be affected. After the despatch of this letter the Home Office issued instructions to the Police and arrests were made freely until 20 September.[11]

The arrests of late August and September meant that the number of people in internment camps increased from 4,300 on 28 August, to 6,600 on 7 September, and 11,000 on 16 September. By 23 September there were 13,600 internees of whom 10,500 were civilians, while the rest had been captured on the battlefield. But by 20 September arrests were suspended because the War Office had made use of all available accommodation. Only those perceived as an immediate danger would be arrested.

However, during the course of October 1914, serious anti-German hostility reached a peak. This manifested itself in press comment as well as in anti-German riots in Deptford on 18 and 19 October. These events had an immediate effect on internment policy. In 'the interests of public safety and public order' the Home Office decided to resume wholesale internment. But the amount of available internment space quickly ran out and on 22 October, the War Office asked for the suspension of arrests because of a lack of space. The suspension was intended to last for a few days until further space became available and did not apply to the east coast, regarded as a sensitive area because of its proximity to the North Sea, or to any alien enemy whom the police regarded as dangerous. In fact, general internment did not begin again until May 1915.

Meanwhile a decision was reached whereby each Chief Constable would have to contact the War Office via the Home Office before making arrests. The War Office would indicate the amount of space available and arrests would proceed accordingly. Yet few arrests actually took place between November 1914 and April 1915. In fact, at the beginning of November, Lord Kitchener, who had become Secretary of State for War at the outbreak of hostilities, had decided that alien enemies could be released from internment camps. Therefore between November 1914 and early February 1915 approximately 3,000 alien enemies were released.[12]

Certain groups of people did not face internment. The most important of these were women and children and those men not of military age.

Other groups included ministers of religion and doctors of medicine, together with those men unfit for military service. During October and November 1914 the British and German Governments made reciprocal arrangements for the exchange of people in these categories. At this stage such people could not be compelled to leave and many decided to remain. Nevertheless, by January 1915 between 6,000 and 7,000 females had left together with 2,000 males over fourteen.[13]

Throughout the early months of the war both the government's internment policy and the Home Secretary attracted much criticism from the press and the Radical Right. Nevertheless, until May 1915 the government resisted the demands for a stricter internment policy. In that month the situation changed due to the sinking of the passenger liner *Lusitania* by a German submarine on the 7th, leading to the loss of over 1,000 lives. This act led to a crescendo of anti-German hysteria which seriously affected the Germans within Britain. The hostility resulted in widespread rioting against them as well as an overwhelming chorus for their internment.[14]

Consequently, on the afternoon of 13 May, the Prime Minister, Herbert Asquith announced a new internment policy. 'Persons of hostile origin residing in this country' were divided into two classes – 'those who have been naturalized and have therefore become British subjects, and those who have not'. He continued:

> Dealing first with the non-naturalized aliens, there are at this moment 19,000 interned and there are some 40,000 (24,000 men and 16,000 women) at large. We propose that in existing circumstances, *prima facie*, all adult males of this class should, for their own safety, and that of the community, be segregated and interned, or, if over military age, repatriated. This will not require fresh legislation. We recognize that there will be cases which call for exceptional treatment. The women and children in suitable cases will be repatriated, but there will, no doubt, be many instances in which justice and humanity will require that they should be allowed to remain.

An advisory body 'of a judicial character' was to be set up, 'by which applications for exemption from the general rule of internment can be considered'. As soon as 'the naval and military authorities' had provided the necessary accommodation, 'those who do not secure exemption from the advisory body' would face internment. 'In the case of the naturalised aliens, who are in law British subjects' (numbering about 8,000), they would not be interned unless it could be ascertained by the advisory body that it would be dangerous if they were allowed to remain free.[15]

The process of internment was necessarily slow because, as Asquith mentioned, space had to be found. Germans from London went to the camps at Frimley, Stratford, and the Isle of Man, and to the ships anchored off Southend, while those from Liverpool went to Hawick and the Isle of Man. Up to 5 June 3,339 additional males had been interned. By the end of July 'internment was proceeding at the rate of 1,000 cases a week, and there still remained 6,000 aliens to be interned'.[16] Repatriation had also started apace. The Home Office estimated that there were 14,400 registered 'German female adults'. Of these, 'about 5,000 are single or unattached women, 4,500 are German born wives, and 5,000 are Englishwomen married to Germans'. In addition to these were children and men above military age. The Home Office informed the police forces that the only group which should be allowed to remain was those women who had gained enemy nationality through marriage. The rest received notice that, unless they obtained an exemption certificate from the Advisory Committee, they should 'voluntarily leave the country'; otherwise a deportation order would be issued against them.[17]

Two Advisory Committees were set up: one for Scotland and one for England and Wales. The latter consisted of two High Court Judges, Sir John Sankey (Chairman) and Sir Robert Younger, in addition to four Members of Parliament, Colonel Lockwood, Sir Donald Maclean, Stanley Baldwin, and J.J. Mooney. It had two sections. One, which dealt with exemptions from internment, under Justice Sankey, and the other, dealing with exemptions from repatriation, under Justice Younger. Because repatriation affected mostly women, the second of these received two additional female members, Maude Lawrence and Meriel Talbot.[18]

It is not clear when the Committees finished their work. They were still meeting regularly in July of 1915 and less frequently by the following spring. A total of 16,000 applications for exemption from internment were considered, of which 7,150 were granted, and 16,456 for exemption from repatriation, of which 14,939 were granted. The Committee dealt firstly with unnaturalized alien enemies and then looked at '14B cases'. This referred to regulation 14B of the Defence of the Realm regulations which stated that the Home Secretary could intern any person of 'hostile origin or associations' on 'the recommendation of a competent naval or military authority or of one of the advisory committees'.[19]

During the summer of 1915 internment proceeded at the rate of about 1,000 per week so that by 22 November the number of internees had reached 32,440, an increase of 12,871 from the figure of 13 May. The number of people interned then remained steady until the summer of 1916. At this time approximately 22,000 enemy aliens were at liberty, including 10,000 women. Of the 12,000 men, exemption from internment had been granted on the following grounds. First, 4,000, who, although technically of German or Austrian nationality, were 'violently hostile to Germany and Austria'. These included Czechs, Poles, Alsatians, Italians from the Trentino, Southern Slavs, as well as 'a certain number of Armenians who have fled here from Turkish oppression'. Second, 1,500 men over 70 years of age. Third, a few individuals whose sympathies lay with the Allies, and who carried out 'valuable scientific or industrial service to the country in connection with the war'. And, fourth, 'About 6,000 others . . . mostly persons of long residence'. About two thirds of them had resided for 30 years and upwards – and many of them had sons fighting in the British Army.[20]

Approximately 10,000 people were repatriated (many voluntarily) between May 1915 and June 1916. This figure consisted of men who were not of military age, women, and children. The only class of people automatically deported was, as previously mentioned, single women of less than five years residence. Otherwise, exemptions could be granted in any of the following cases. First, applicants of either sex with English born dependant children between five and 15 years of age. Second, men and women with English born children irrespective of age, who had been resident in England for 35 years or over. Third, people, without English born children, who had lived in England for 40 years or over. Fourth, women in pregnancy, invalids, or persons nursing invalids. Fifth, persons involved in developing an industry in Britain. And, sixth, technical alien enemies such as Czechs and Poles.[21]

Further progress on repatriation occurred in January 1917, when, after much correspondence, the German and British governments agreed to the repatriation of all civilian internees over 45 except 20 who could be retained by either side for 'military reasons'. Retired officers and crews of merchant ships were included and the agreement was extended to overseas possessions. The agreement resulted in the exchange of only 350 Germans for 70 Englishmen because, in February of 1917, the German government proclaimed a war zone in waters surrounding the United Kingdom and declared that every ship in the area would be sunk by submarines.[22] Later, in June, the Cabinet agreed to send three representatives to a conference on the question of Prisoners of War at The Hague. An agreement was signed on 2 July. This provided for repatriation to be resumed, as before, under the auspices of the Netherlands government. The Dutch also agreed to intern, within their own borders, 1,600 invalid civilian prisoners of war from Great Britain and 400 from Germany. These would be chosen 'by the medical authorities of the captor State' in accordance with a 'new schedule of disabilities for the internment of sick and wounded combatants'. The Dutch authorities agreed to provide the necessary transport in the form of two paddle-wheel steamers which were painted as hospital ships and 'ran on an assigned course between Rotterdam and Boston'. Voyages were resumed in October 1917 and from that date until November 1918, 3,662 interned civilians returned to the Continent, 'making a total of 6,840 between the beginning of the war and signing of the Armistice'.[23]

Meanwhile, a strong campaign for more widespread internment reached a climax in the summer of 1918. From 5 June the *Daily Mail* launched a campaign against Home Office aliens policy. Other sections of Fleet Street quickly joined the bandwagon. At the same time organizations of all descriptions throughout the country passed resolutions against the alien enemy.[24] The Prime Minister, David Lloyd George, 'keenly sensitive to newspaper agitation', had apparently appointed a Committee of six MPs to look into the aliens question. In fact the Cabinet papers show that Lloyd George had, strictly speaking, not done this at all. What he did was to 'ask those particular Members of Parliament who had taken an active part in the agitation for increased stringency to state definitely what suggestions they would themselves make'. They 'had not taken any evidence from the Departments concerned, though they had no doubt a mass of information before them from other sources'.[25]

The 'Committee' presented a report to Lloyd George on 8 July which made 15 recommendations including a call for every male enemy alien over 18 to be interned immediately unless there existed national or medical reasons for exemption. The definite national reason should be made known to the public, while the medical reason should be certified by three doctors. The second recommendation concerned alien enemy women who were to be repatriated unless their husbands had been exempted from internment. Furthermore, in 'certain cases it may be necessary to consider the alternative of internment, while in other cases justice and humanity may dictate exemption from both these courses.'[26]

The Home Secretary reacted favourably. In a Cabinet Memorandum he wrote that the Advisory Committees should be reconstituted so that all the exemptions which had previously been made could be 'carefully and drastically revised'.[27] The reconstituted Committee for England and Wales held its first meeting on 21 July. By the end of the war it had recommended 257 fresh internments and 220 repatriations out of more than 3,200 cases which were considered. One German historian later commented that this was a poor return for the amount of shouting, ink, paper, and energy expended by the anti-aliens.[28]

During the course of the war much public attention had been devoted to the question of 'what action the Government intend to take to prevent enemy aliens now interned in this country remaining here after the signing of peace'.[29] When the armistice was signed there were still 24,255 enemy aliens in internment camps and the figure remained stable until the end of December owing to the 'military position' and the lack of available shipping facilities. During the 1918 General Election campaign Government Ministers made speeches promising action.[30]

TABLE 1

DECLINE OF GERMAN POPULATION OF BRITAIN, 1914–19[a]

Year	Males	Females	Total
1914	37,500	20,000	57,500
1917	32,012	16,326	48,338
1919	8,476	13,778	22,254

(a) The female totals include those women who were British born but had married Germans and therefore assumed their husband's nationality. In 1917, the figure was 10,078 and in 1917 8,457. No separate total is given for 1914.

Source: The 1914 figure is from PRO HO45 11522/287235/81; 1917 is from figures in PRO HO45 11522/287235/98. The 1918 total is based on figures in PRO HO45 11522/287235/148 and in Parliamentary Papers: Report of the Committee Appointed to Consider Applications from Compulsory Repatriation Submitted by Interned Enemy Aliens (Parl. Papers, 1916, X).

By February 1919 the number of internees remaining had been reduced to 19,831, of whom 16,442 were Germans, and by May the total figure was down to about 5,000. This last figure consisted mainly of individuals unwilling to leave Britain. An advisory Committee was set up during this month, under Sir Robert Younger, to which Germans could apply for exemption. In fact, 4,300 applications were submitted, of which 3,890 were granted on grounds such as friendly origins, family ties, or long residence. Therefore, of the alien enemies interned at the date of the armistice, 84 per cent had been repatriated by the middle of October.[31]

Is it possible to work out the numerical decline in the number of Germans in Britain during the War years? Table 1 gives approximate figures which graphically illustrate the consequences of the anti-German campaign during the Great War.

III

The confinement of adult men within camps and away from their families, for periods of perhaps four years and more, proved a distressing experience leading, in some instances, to insanity. We can now deal with life behind barbed wire. We can begin with a general survey of the various places of internment and then move on to deal with the conditions within them, emphasizing food, work, leisure, and health.

Little information survives about the earliest of the internment camps. The available material suggests that the War Office, through its Directorate of Prisoners of War, headed by Lieutenant-General Herbert Belfield, held responsibility for both the requisition of buildings and sites, and their administration.[32] The camp at Olympia became one of the first places to receive internees whose numbers included a wide range of people, from merchant sailors, who had been brought ashore from German, Austrian and British ships, to tourists and permanent residents of London. It acted as 'a clearing house for concentration camps', until its closure in December 1914, and many people were brought here before being subsequently transferred elsewhere. During its existence as a place of internment, at any one time Olympia held anything from 300 to 1,500 men.[33]

Among other early War Office camps were those at Frimley and Newbury. Like Olympia, these lasted for only a short time. The former housed prisoners in either 'quarters built of galvanized iron' or bell tents. It was heavily guarded, surrounded by three fences and many sentries. In mid-October, when the Home Office decided to step up arrests, more prisoners arrived here from London and Brighton. By the beginning of November the total number of internees in both Frimley and Newbury reached 5,600. The latter camp was actually established on the race course with the prisoners being housed in the horse boxes, which had neither heat nor light. Many inmates at both places resented the conditions, a fact of concern to the War Office which had intended to close the camps before the onset of cold weather at the end of October. In fact, they remained open until the beginning of 1915 when alternative quarters became available.[34]

Due to the lack of suitable accommodation the War Office decided to make use of nine trans-Atlantic liners which the Admiralty requisitioned on its behalf at a cost of between £7,000 and £12,000 per month according to tonnage. The ships were divided into three groups and lay near three coastal towns: Ryde, Gosport and Southend. Each locality held both civilian and military internees. John B. Jackson inspected all the vessels in early 1915 as part of a general survey of places of internment in Great Britain on behalf of the American Ambassador in Berlin who, in turn, acted for the German Government. Jackson pointed out that of the three vessels at Ryde, the *Canada*, *Tunisian* and *Andania*, the first two housed civilians and the third military prisoners of war.

The *Canada* contained a total of 1,026 internees, most of whom came from the camp at Newbury, who were divided into three classes. The

Tunisian, meanwhile, held a total of 795 in one class. The War Office had dispensed with this group of ships by March 1915. Those at Gosport and Southend, however, remained in use until later in the year. At the former, the *Scotian*, *Ascania* and *Lake Manitoba* had come into operation from 1 December 1914 and collectively housed about 3,600 prisoners when Jackson made his inspection. At Southend, the *Invernia* held military prisoners while the *Saxonia* and *Royal Edward* looked after civilians. In March 1915 the total numbers for the three vessels stood at 1,575, 2,300 and 1,200 respectively. Both the *Royal Edward* and *Saxonia* remained in operation until the end of May 1915 when many of the prisoners moved to the camp at Alexandra Palace.[35]

In August 1914, the War Office had also requisitioned an old wagon works in Lancaster, which had been empty for seventeen years, for use as an internment camp. This began to take prisoners from early September. When Jackson visited it, at the start of 1915, it held 2,000 internees, including 200 boys under seventeen, some of whom had been taken from fishing boats. Similar to the camp at Lancaster was the one at Handforth, near Manchester, which had also formerly acted as a factory. By November it held about a thousand men. This figure had increased to approximately 2,000, including 400 sailors who lived separately, in early 1913. The Commandant and his Adjutant administered the camp, which continued to hold civilian internees until 1916 when it became a centre for just military and naval prisoners.[36]

The War Office had also requisitioned a former jute factory in Stratford, east London, which opened on 20 December 1914 and closed during 1917. Every individual who had spent some time here unequivocally condemned it, particularly because of the quality of the accommodation and the intolerance of the administration.[37] The War Office opened a further camp at Stobs, near Hawick, in Scotland, at the start of November 1914. This housed both military and civilian prisoners until the latter were transferred to Knockaloe in July 1916. The authorities kept the two groups separate by providing individual compounds for each of them: in April 1916, for instance, compounds A and B held 1,102 and 1,098 civilians respectively while C and D contained 1,081 and 1,209 military and naval internees. The accommodation consisted of huts which were 120 feet by 20. Each held 33 men.[38]

One of the most unusual War Office camps was Lofthouse Park, near Wakefield which lay on the site of an unsuccessful 'pleasure park' which had originally been 'a country house surrounded by fine grounds'. The camp had three sub-divisions, each of which held about 500 prisoners who could not move out of their own section without a pass obtained one day ahead of the proposed visit from 'the second officer in command'. All the inmates came from wealthy backgrounds because they had to pay the authorities ten shillings a week 'for the privilege of being there'.[39]

The War Office opened its last civilian internment camp in May 1915 at Alexandra Palace, a 'cultural and entertainment centre in North London'. The first prisoners arrived on 7 May 1915 and the last did not leave until May 1919. During the intervening years the largest number held at the Palace at any one time reached nearly 3,000. In total, about 17,000 men 'passed through this camp at ages varying from 8 to 80, criminals released from prison, as well as missionaries, men from the remotest parts of the world and practically of all nationalities and social standings'. The War Office made an effort to use the camp for people from the London area in order to facilitate visits from their families.[40]

Having looked at the War Office camps it is now time to turn to those mainly administered by the Home Office, particularly those on the Isle of Man which housed the overwhelming majority of alien enemies for most of the war. The Home Office handed its responsibilities in this matter to a subsidiary body, the Destitute Aliens Committee, formed in August 1914. In early September 1914 the Destitute Aliens Committee had written to the Home Office proposing the transfer of Germans to the Isle of Man. A holiday camp in Douglas 'was at once thought of, and before long this camp was in the hands of the government. Barbed wire fences were speedily erected, gas and electric standard lamps were introduced for lighting the compounds at night, various guard-rooms were built, and other alterations made.' The first 'consignment' of 200 prisoners arrived on 22 September. By 24 October the total number of internees in the camp had reached 2,600 'but, in order to assist in relieving congestion in temporary places of internment in London and elsewhere, a temporary increase to 3,300 prisoners was authorised'. However, the Destitute Aliens Committee believed that the camp could only hold 2,400 and so by February 1915 figures had declined to this level where they remained for most of the war. The internees initially slept in tents but later moved into huts. The camp had three sub-divisions: first, the privilege camp; second, the Jewish camp; and third, the ordinary camp.[41]

In October 1914 the Destitute Aliens Committee recommended the establishment of a second camp on the Isle of Man on a farm called Knockaloe Moor, near Peel Harbour, which had formerly acted as a base for 16,000 Territorials. Both the Insular and Central Governments had originally planned a camp for 5,000 but, following the decision to intern all alien enemies after the sinking of the Lusitania, Knockaloe expanded to take 10,000, then 15,000 and, finally, 23,000 prisoners, who lived in unsatisfactory huts.[42] As one might expect, a camp with over 20,000 prisoners had sub-divisions. In fact, four camps exisited, each of which contained between five and seven sections called compounds. Administration of the camps was complex since the War Office, Home Office (through the Destitute Aliens Committee) and the Isle of Man government all played a role. In addition, the prisoners themselves had a part in running their own affairs.

Apart from the Isle of Man camps, the Home Office also detained men in a former workhouse in Islington, North London. This held between 600 and 700 prisoners, most of whom had wives of English birth. A committee chosen by the interness ran the entire camp. Although a senior soldier acted as Commandant of the camp, the guard consisted of four police constables and their sergeant. It remained open until November 1919 as it held individuals who had applied to Justice Younger's Committee for exemption from repatriation. Closely related to the Islington camp was one at Hackney Wick which shared the same Commandant.[43]

The Home Office established some unusual internment camps. For example, the premises of the German Industrial and Farm Colony were taken over for such a purpose. This happened at the start of 1915 because of 'an urgent need for an institution for elderly, infirm and rheumatic men whose health is likely to be very seriously injured by detention in Military Camps'. By May 1915, Libury Hall contained 188 internees and continued to operate as a farm colony producing most of its own requirements. The management remained in the hands of W. Müller, the pre-war director, who now acted under the supervision of a British Commandant, and a few police officers. This institution still had 83 inmates in February 1920.[44]

During the early part of the war about one hundred alien enemies found themselves in Brixton Prison. They consisted of persons 'detained indefinitely under Deportation Orders or pending the enforcement of Expulsion Orders'. However, owing to the fact that conditions here compared unfavourably with those prevailing in camps, the Home Office, in consultation with the Prison Commission, decided to transfer the detainees to Reading Prison which would act as a 'special prison' for aliens awaiting deportation or expulsion. The inmates from Brixton, as well as others from Birmingham, Leeds, Liverpool, Wakefield, Stafford, and Manchester prisons, arrived at Reading between December 1915 and January 1916. The ordinary prisoners had departed in November. In 1917 many of the aliens became discontented and demanded an improvement in their conditions. The Home Office reacted by transferring about 50 to

Knockaloe where they would remain separate from the rest of the internees.[45]

Although the Home Office never interned women *en masse*, it did place a small number in one of the blocks of the Inebriate Reformatory in Aylesbury. They consisted of members of various nationalities 'who are of hostile origin or associations, and against whom Internment Orders have been made under the Defence of the Realm Regulations because they are suspected of espionage or other hostile proceedings and because it is contrary to the interests of public safety and the defence of the realm that they should remain at liberty'. In February 1918 only five women of German nationality were interned there.[46]

This description of Aylesbury concludes the survey of the major civilian internment camps and their administration. We can now move on to discuss other aspects of life behind barbed wire. For instance, the question of food attracted much attention. In most camps, the prisoners themselves actually held responsibility for preparing the meals but only dealt with the official ration. In addition, many camps had canteens which sold snacks for those who wanted them. The Isle of Man government controlled those at Knockaloe and gave a percentage of the profits to the internees. The Army Council decided the daily ration which caused some controversy. Throughout the war, internees received three meals per day and during the first two years of the war, complaints about food were relatively rare. In addition to the official ration and the extra supplies in the canteens, prisoners could also receive parcels from their relatives outside. However, the situation changed with the German submarine blockade which resulted in food shortages and rationing. Eventually the prisoners could only receive food packages from relatives outside England, while the range of items on sale in canteens decreased. Furthermore, internees had to endure constant reductions in their rations during 1917 and 1918 which led to numerous, and often bitter, complaints from the prisoners.[47]

Behind barbed wire the internees had to find something new to occupy themselves during their period of internment, which, in some cases, lasted from 1914 until 1919. A certain number of men played a part in the internal administration of each camp. In addition, groups of prisoners volunteered to undertake the everyday duties in the buildings. Each institution had internees acting as cooks, cleaners, refusemen, hospital attendants, clerks and postmen. But no more than a small percentage of internees would ever have held these positions.[48]

Therefore, many prisoners tried to make money for themselves. For example, some acted as valets to prisoners who could afford to pay them while others tried to continue their former occupations.

Various groups, such as barbers, succeeded, although not in places where supply exceeded demand such as Camp II at Knockaloe where over 80 barbers were interned. Many tailors and cobblers continued with their work either through their own initiative or with the help of the camp authorities who, as in Camp IV at Knockaloe, set up workshops for the repair and production of clothing and footwear belonging to prisoners. Meanwhile, some internees began to produce various 'fancy goods' such as rings made from silver foil, handbags, wooden models and children's toys but these proved difficult to sell.[49] At Douglas internees manufactured pipes, watches and, above all, brushes. In fact contractors established a brush making factory here which sold its goods to government departments and to the public. In August 1918 it provided jobs for 734 of the internees. The prisoners held at Islington also produced brushes, as well as wigs, postal bags and surgical equipment, for outside firms. By 1917, the wage they received ranged from 18/– to 39/– per week. The camp at Hackney Wick, meanwhile, contained highly skilled German mechanics selected from all the places of internment. Vickers and Co. employed these men in the manufacture of sewing machines. The company provided the machinery and paid the men an average of 45/– for a 54-hour week which rose to as much as £2 15s. with overtime. Only 15 of the 115 men interned here in March 1917 did not play a part in the manufacture of machinery.[50]

For much of the war the various authorities responsible for interning aliens devised schemes for employing prisoners outside their camps. For instance, they became involved in agricultural production on the Isle of Man, as well as on the mainland, where a few hundred also found employment with Lloyd's Ironstone Company in Northamptonshire and road building in Warwickshire.[51]

But, despite the numbers of internees employed both inside and outside camps, the majority did not secure any kind of paid work and had to occupy themselves in other ways. Many attempted to improve their education, for which opportunities existed in most camps. During the early stages of the war, in particular, speakers presented, usually informal, lectures on a wide range of subjects. The lectures at Douglas formed a part of the syllabi at the camp school which developed rapidly. It provided instruction in both technical subjects and academic disciplines. By May 1916 about 1,400 internees, constituting approximately 50 per cent of the total in the camp, occupied themselves either as teachers or students at the school. Other camps also possessed schools including Alexandra Palace. At Knockaloe each of the sub-camps possessed its own schools.[52] At Lofthouse Park a 'very thorough Educational scheme' was organized 'on University lines and equivalent to a University Standard, classes and lectures to meet all capacities'. It opened its first session on 1 October 1917 but did not last for long because Lofthouse Park closed during 1918.[53]

Some internees preferred to spend their time pursuing outdoor activities such as gardening for which the authorities usually provided land. At the same time all the camps offered opportunity for exercise. This could simply mean route marches which at Lofthouse Park, for instance, took place three or four times a week. However, some places, such as Alexandra Palace, possessed a gymnasium and most had fields for outdoor sporting activities. Football proved particularly popular but other prisoners played cricket, fistball and tennis. Towards the end of the war food rationing meant that many internees did not have enough energy for sports. Some prisoners decided to try painting and sculpting while others tried to play musical instruments.[54]

Nevertheless, despite all the available recreational opportunities, lack of opportunities for real work became one of the factors which affected the mental condition of the prisoners. Before discussing this, we must look at their physical health, which largely depended upon the sanitary situation of the camps. Although hygiene arrangements differed in each camp, they came under the control of the medical officer in charge who frequently communicated with the local medical officer of health. Furthermore, two 'experts in sanitation' constantly visited the various places of internment 'with a view to making the conditions as nearly perfect as possible'. Although this did not happen initially, by the middle of 1916 complaints about hygiene had almost disappeared. The series of American Embassy reports carried out in the spring of that year comment on the cleanliness of the camps.[55]

The *Manchester Guardian History of the War* stated that with regard to 'the sanitary arrangements of the camps and the general health of the prisoners the best tribute is the fact' that very few people actually died behind barbed wire. By April 1917 only 105 alien enemies had died in camps under Home Office control which meant an annual death rate of about three per thousand. The situation had changed little a year later when James Cantlie of the British Red Cross Society, after visiting Knockaloe, pointed out that the death rate there averaged about 2.5 per thousand whereas that for the Isle of Man generally came to 15.7 per thousand.[56]

Every camp possessed a hospital which treated patients with minor illnesses. At Knockaloe, each sub-camp had its own hospital. There also existed an isolation hospital for contagious diseases, situated at a distance from the main buildings. The total staff in all the institutions consisted of eight doctors and 40 German attendants. The sicknesses dealt with included tuberculosis, bronchitis and lunacy. Any serious cases went to local hospitals outside the camps. For example, between November 1914 and April 1917, 81 prisoners were moved to the Isle of Man lunatic asylum.[57]

This figure suggests a low insanity rate among internees and receives support from another report carried out into conditions in Knockaloe in October 1916 by the Destitute Aliens Committee. This claimed that the occurrence rate of 1.6 per thousand, 'is markedly less than the pauper lunacy incidence in the general population in 1914 – for males of the same ages'. Nevertheless, the report also referred to 'milder forms of mental derangement' whose incidence the investigators could not establish.[58] But these forms attracted the attention of other individuals, particularly Dr A.L. Vischer, of the Swiss Embassy in London, who regularly visited the British internment camps as Switzerland held responsibility for German interests in Britain from 1917. Vischer seems to have coined the phrase 'barbed wire disease' which he constantly referred to in his reports. He even produced a book on the subject.[59] At one point in this work Vischer claimed that 'very few prisoners who have been over six months in the camp are quite free from the disease'. But he continued: 'Of course, there are many degrees, varying from the easily excited to the introspective apathetic conditions.'[60] Various writers attempted to explain the causes of barbed wire disease and those put forward included lack of opportunity to work; complete absence of any chance of solitude; ignorance of the duration of captivity; irregularity of communication with the outside world and, especially, contact with women and children; and the influence of public opinion.[61]

If we try to assess the position of the German prisoners in Britain it can best be described as *fair*. Neither the Home Office nor the War Office set out to deliberately mistreat internees, but this did not prevent their mental and physical health from deteriorating. We therefore have to question the necessity of subjecting over 30,000 men to prison life merely because of the fact that they were unfortunate enough to reside in a country at war with their own. Much of the blame for this state of affairs lay with public opinion which constantly demanded wholesale internment.

IV

The government did not resist the clamour and we can understand this state of affairs by considering the fact that during the First World War, liberalism and intolerance within Britain exchanged their positions. The latter became dominant and the former took up its role as the belief of a minority. We must remember that along with Germans all other minorities which were perceived as a threat endured official and unofficial hostility during the First World War.

How do we explain the change during the First World War? We can answer this question by considering the foundations which supported British liberalism during the nineteenth century, that is, security. Britain had not faced a real threat of invasion since the Napoleonic Wars. After 1914 this threat became real and engendered the fear which leads to intolerance. To repeat the assertions of Norman Angell, militarism and its ideology and demands took control of the country both in terms of legislation and attitudes. The sense of national unity intensified and, in such circumstances, the state and the public turned on real and perceived enemies.[62] During the nineteenth century, when the fear of invasion remained distant, Britain had no need to resort to militarism, as the need did not exist.

Liberalism did not actually *die* in the First World War and intolerance faded into the background again after 1918. Certainly, much of the legislation of the war years was repealed. Perhaps we might agree that:

> The basic underlying values of British – and particularly English – society underwent no transformation. The British people were not 'militarized'. Wartime excesses of chauvinism, anger and hate became regarded with incredulous embarrassment and were then forgotten. Patience, tolerance and generosity returned.

These words come from the most recent academic history of Britain during the Great War[63] and imply that the First World War experience in Britain was simply an aberration. To interpret modern British history in this way seems erroneous. The mere fact that the country did behave as it did during the Great War means that it had traditions of intolerance upon which it could draw (for instance the growth of Germanophobia during the immediate pre-war period). In addition, we could mention the experience of Irish immigrants throughout the course of the nineteenth century as well as the hostility towards Russian Jews between 1885 and 1905.[64] At the same time, anti-Semitism and Germanophobia certainly did not disappear after 1918. The mere fact that Fascism did rise in Britain, albeit on a small scale, indicates this, as does the hostility towards Jewish refugees entering the country during the 1930s.[65] However, we can say that after 1918 the pre-war equilibrium was re-established. Liberalism became the predominant ethos but intolerance still had a significant role to play, as it always has had in British history. During the Second World War intolerance returned, resulting in the reintroduction of internment, but it did not grip Britain in the way that it had done in the previous conflict.

NOTES

1. John Turner (ed.), *Britain and the First World War* (London, 1988); John Stevenson, *British Society 1914–45* (Harmondsworth, 1984), pp.46–77; Trevor Wilson, *The Myriad Faces of War: Britain and the Great War 1914–1918* (Cambridge, 1986); Arthur Marwick, *War and Social Change in the Twentieth Century* (London, 1974); idem, *The Deluge: British Society and the First World War* (London, 1986 reprint); John Bourne, *Britain and the Great War, 1914–18* (London, 1989).
2. Norman Angell, *The Prussian in Our Midst* (London, 1915).
3. G.R. Searle, 'Critics of Edwardian Society: The Case of the Radical Right', in Alan O'Day (ed.), *The Edwardian Age* (London, 1979); Panikos Panayi, *The Enemy in Our Midst: Germans in Britain during the First World War* (Oxford, 1991).
4. David Englander, 'Military Intelligence and the Defence of the Realm: The Surveillance of Soldiers and Civilians in Britain During the First World War', *Bulletin of the Society for the Study of Labour History*, 52 (1987), p.24; F.W. Hirst, *The Consequences of the War to Great Britain* (Oxford, 1934), p.106; Stevenson, *British Society*, pp.57–60.
5. David Marquand, *Ramsay MacDonald* (London, 1977); Marvin Swartz, *The Union of Democratic Control in British Politics During the First World War* (Oxford, 1971).
6. Stevenson, *British Society*, p.64.
7. John Rae, *Conscription and Politics: The British Government and the Conscientious Objector to Military Service 1916–19* (London, 1972); Panikos Panayi, 'The British Empire Union in the First World War', in Tony Kushner and Kenneth Lunn (eds.), *The Politics of Marginality: Race, the Radical Right and Minorities in Twentieth Century Britain* (London, 1990), pp.119–22.
8. Colin Holmes, *Anti-Semitism in British Society, 1876–1939* (London, 1979), pp.121–40.
9. Panayi, *Enemy*, pp.9–41.
10. Ibid., *passim*.
11. PRO WO32/5368, letter of A.H. Dennis to the deputy assistant adjutant general, 12 Nov. 1914.
12. E. David (ed.), *Inside Asquith's Cabinet: From the Diaries of Charles Hobhouse* (London, 1917), p.206; PRO HO45 10760/269116/8, 25, 42; *Hansard*, fifth series, LXIX, 259–60, 8 Feb. 1915.
13. *Hansard* (Lords), fifth series, XVIII, 282–3, 6 Jan. 1915.
14. Panayi, *Enemy*, pp.223–57. Cate Haste, *Keep the Home Fires Burning* (London, 1977), p.111; *John Bull*, 31 Oct. 1914.
15. *Hansard*, fifth series, LXXI, 1842, 13 May 1915. Military age, mentioned by Asquith, was 17–55.
16. *The Times*, 15, 17, 18 May 1915; *Daily Graphic*, 15 May 1915; *Manchester Guardian History of the War*, Vol.II (London, 1915), p.362; *Liverpool Daily Post*, 13 May 1915; *Liverpool Weekly Post*, 22 May 1915; *Hansard*, fifth series, LXXII, 360, 10 June 1915.
17. PRO HO45 10782/278567.
18. *Hansard* (Commons), fifth series, LXXII, 4, 3 June 1915; LXXIII, 368–9, 7 July 1915; *The Times*, 10 July 1915; British Library (hereafter BL), Cave Papers, Add Ms 62477, 'List of Commissions, Committees, and other Bodies appointed to consider Questions during the Present War'; PRO HO45 11522/287235/12.
19. *The Times*, 20 July 1915; PRO HO45 11004/259527/227; PRO HO45 11025/410118/2; Defence of the Realm Regulations Consolidated and Revised to January 31st, 1917.
20. PRO HO45 11522/287235/12, 23; *Hansard* (Commons), fifth series, LXXXIII, 1069–73, 29 June 1916; *Hansard* (Lords), fifth series, XXII, 473–4, 29 June 1916; PRO CAB 37/150/3.
21. PRO CAB 37/150/3; PRO HO45 11004/259527/276a.
22. Parliamentary Papers: Conditions of Diet and Nutrition in the Internment Camp at Ruhleben (Parl. Papers, 1916, XXXIV); PRO HO45 11004/259257/338; Parliamentary Papers: Further Correspondence Respecting the Proposed Release of Civilians Interned

in the British and German Empires (Parl. Papers, 1916, XXXIV); Parliamentary Papers: Further Correspondence Respecting the Proposed Release of Civilians Interned in the British and German Empires (Parl. Papers, 1917–18, XXXVIII); PRO HO45 11004/259257/732; PRO HO45 11025/410118/1, 'Report on the Directorate of Prisoners of War', p.67; PRO HO45 11025/410118/2.

23. Lord Newton, *Retrospection* (London, 1941), pp.237–9; Parliamentary Papers: An Agreement Between the British and German Governments Concerning Combatant and Civilian Prisoners of War (Parl. Papers, 1916, XXXVIII); PRO HO45 11025/410118/1, 'Report on the Directorate of Prisoners of War', p.68; PRO HO45 11025/410118/2.

24. Panayi, *Enemy*, pp.90–91, 217–20.

25. Sir Charles Mallet, *Lord Cave: A Memoir* (London, 1931), p.212; Haste, *Home Fires*, p.135; J.C. Bird, *The Control of Enemy Alien Civilians in Great Britain, 1914–1918* (New York, 1986), p.125; PRO CAB 23/7, WC 443 (11), 10 July 1918.

26. House of Lords Record Office (hereafter HLRO), Lloyd George Papers, F170/3/1.

27. PRO CAB 24/57, GT 5067, 9 July 1918; PRO CAB 23/7, WC 443 (11), 10 July 1918.

28. Bird, *Enemy Aliens*, p.128; C.R. Hennings, *Deutsche in England* (Stuttgart, 1923), p.160; PRO HO45 11025/410118/1.

28. *Hansard*, fifth series, CX, 432, 21 Oct. 1918.

29. PRO HO45 10833/327753/36.

30. See PRO HO45 11025/410118/2; HLRO, Bonar Law Papers, 96/10/11, Memorandum by Edward Shortt, 25 Feb. 1918.

31. HLRO, Bonar Law Papers, 96/10/11, Memorandum by Edward Shortt, 25 Feb. 1918; Parliamentary Papers: Report of Committee Appointed to Consider Applications From Compulsory Repatriation Submitted by Interned Enemy Aliens (Parl. Papers, 1919, X); PRO HO45 11025/410118/3.

32. PRO HO45 10760/269116/8.

33. *Manchester Guardian*, 15 Aug. 1914; C.S. Peel, *How We Lived Then 1914–18* (London, 1929), p.42; Basil Thomson, *Queer People* (London, 1922), pp.59–60; PRO HO45 10760/269116/192; Peter and Leni Gillman, *'Collar the Lot!'* (London, 1980), pp.11–12; Hennings, *Deutsche in England*, p.161.

34. *East End News*, 11 Aug. 1914; *Daily Mail*, 17 Sept. 1914; *The Times*, 24 Oct. 1914; PRO HO45 10760/269116/25; Hennings, *Deutsche in England*, p.161; Anna Braithwaite Thomas, *St. Stephen's House: Friends Emergency Work in England 1914–20* (London, 1920), pp.46–7.

35. PRO HO45 10760/269116/192; *Hansard*, fifth series, LXX, 1769, 15 March 1915; Rudolf Rocker, *The London Years* (London, 1956), pp.261–2, 266, 275, 284–5.

36. *Manchester Guardian*, 7 Sept. 1914; PRO HO45 10760/269116/192; Robert Graves, *Goodbye to All That* (Harmondsworth, 1985 reprint) p.64; Bundesarchiv, Coblenz (hereafter BA), R85 2973, extract from the *Morning Post*, 23 Nov. 1914; PRO HO45 10760/269116/192; Hennings, *Deutsche in England*, p.161; Parliamentary Papers: Reports of Visits of Inspection made by Officials of the United States Embassy to Various Internment Camps in the United Kingdom (Parl. Papers, 1916, XV).

37. Paul Cohen-Portheim, *Time Stood Still* (London, 1931), p.27; PRO FO 383/35; BA R85 3152, reports of visits made by US Embassy Officials, 14 Feb., 31 May, 13 Dec. 1916; Reports of Visits of Inspection (PP, 1916, XV); Hennings, *Deutsche in England*, p.162; Imperial War Museum, 'The First World Diaries of Richard Noschke', pp.15–17, 25, 28, 30.

38. BA R85 3150, reports of US Embassy visits, 23 Feb. 1916, 28 Feb. 1918; Hennings, *Deutsche in England*, p.161; Reports of Visits of Inspection (PP, 1916, XV); PRO FO 383/33.

39. PRO HO45 10760/269116/192; Cohen-Portheim, *Time Stood Still*, pp.64, 65, 100, 104–9.

40. PRO FO 383/33; BA R85 3023, reports of US and Swiss Embassy visits, 26 Feb. 1916– 12 Oct. 1917; BL, Rudolf Rocker, 'Alexandra Palace Internment Camp in the First World War', Preface, p.1.

41. PRO HO45 11005/260251; PRO HO45 10946/266042/7a and 7b, 38; PRO HO45 10947/266042/341; B.E. Sargeaunt, *The Isle of Man and the Great War* (Douglas, 1922), pp.59, 62, 63–4; Reports of Visits of Inspection (PP, 1916, XV); Board of Deputies of British Jews, *64th Annual Report* (London, 1915), pp.30–31.
42. PRO HO45 10946/266042/22, 38; Sargeaunt, *Isle of Man*, pp.65–7; Thomas, *St Stephen's House*, p.66.
43. PRO HO45 10947/266042/307, 361; Adolf Vielhauer, *Das englische Konzentrationslager bei Peel (Insel Man)* (Bad Nassau, 1917), pp.1–2; PRO HO45 10946/266042/120; Hennings, *Deutsche in England*, p.163; BA R85 3087, 3106; PRO HO45 11025/410118/3.
44. PRO HO45 11006/264762; BA R85 3100.
45. PRO HO45 10948/267603.
46. PRO HO45 10785/297142.
47. Reports of Visits of Inspection (PP, 1916, XV); Thomas, *St Stephen's House*, p.51.
48. Rocker, 'Alexandra Palace Internment Camp in the First World War', pp.10, 12; Cohen-Portheim, *Time Stood Still*, p.91; PRO HO45 11025/410118/2; PRO HO45 10947/266042/361, 'Final Report on the Internal Administration of the Prisoners of War Camp IV, Knockaloe'; Reports of Visits of Inspection (PP, 1916, XV); BA R85 3112, Government Circular No.175, Repairs to Huts; Vielhauer, *Konzentrationslager*, p.6.
49. Cohen-Portheim, *Time Stood Still*, pp.44, 45, 97; BA R85 3112, report of US Embassy visit, 22 Jan. 1916; Reports of Visits of Inspection (PP, 1916, XV); PRO HO45 10947/66042/361, 'Final Report on the Internal Administration of the Prisoners of War Camp IV, Knockaloe'; PRO HO45 10946/266042/38; PRO FO 383/33; Rocker, ibid., p.13.
50. PRO HO45 11025/410118/2; Sargeaunt, *Isle of Man*, p.82; Society of Friends Library (hereafter SFL), FEWVRC/CAMPS/2/4; BA R85 3087, reports of US and Swiss Embassy visits to Islington, 13 March 1916, 15 March 1917; BA R85 3106, report of Swiss Embassy visit to Hackney Wick, 16 March 1917; BA R85 3112, report of US Embassy visit to Douglas, 22 Jan. 1917; BA R85 3115, report of Swiss Embassy visit to Douglas, 30 Aug. 1918.
51. Panayi, *Enemy*, pp.119–21.
52. PRO HO45 11025/410118/1; BA R85 3114, report of Swiss Embassy visit to Corby, 7 June 1917, report of Swiss Embassy visit to Whitley, 3 July 1917; PRO HO45 109047/ 266042/341, 361; *Camp Echo*, Oct. 1915; Benedix, *In England*, p.42; Reports of Visits of Inspection (PP, 1916, XV); Rocker, 'Alexandra Palace Internment Camp in the First World War', pp.15–21.
53. SFL, FEWVRC/CAMPS/2/3; Cohen-Portheim, *Time Stood Still*, pp.92–3.
54. SFL, FEWVRC/CAMPS/1/7; CAMPS/2/1 and 2; Reports of Visits of Inspection (PP, 1916, XV); Ron Carrington, *Alexandra Park and Palace* (London, 1975), p.162; Rocker, 'Alexandra Palace Internment Camp in the First World War', p.22; PRO FO 383/33; H.E. Benedix, *In England Interniert* (Gotha, 1916), pp.39–41, 44; BA R85 3023, report of US Embassy visit to Alexandra Palace, 26 Feb. 1916; Cohen-Portheim, *Time Stood Still*, p.93; Panayi, *London Years*, p.311.
55. R.F. Roxburgh, *The Prisoners of War Information Bureau in London* (London, 1915), p.x; Reports of Visits of Inspection (PP, 1916, XV); PRO HO45 10946/266042/141.
56. *Manchester Guardian History of the War*, Vol.IV (London, 1916), p.215; *Hansard*, fifth series, XCII, 1135, 3 April 1917; PRO HO45 10947/266042/307.
57. Reports of Visits of Inspection (PP, 1916, XV); Roxburgh, *Prisoners Bureau*, p.x; BA R85 3114, report of Swiss Embassy visit to Knockaloe, 30 May 1917.
58. PRO HO45 10945/266042/199.
59. This originally came out in German as *Die Stacheldraht-Krankheit* (Zurich, 1918) but was also published in English under the title of *Barbed Wire Disease: A Psychological Study of the Prisoner of War* (London, 1919).
60. Vischer, *Barbed Wire Disease*, pp.53–5.
61. These reasons are taken from Vischer *Barbed Wire Disease*, p.3, and Rocker, 'Alexandra Palace Internment Camp in the First World War', p.4. Each writer gives additional reasons.

62. See Anthony D. Smith, 'War and Ethnicity', *Ethnic and Racial Studies*, 4 (1981), pp.375–97; Panikos Panayi, 'National and Racial Minorities in Total War', *Immigrants & Minorities*, Vol.9, No.2 (1990), p.192.
63. The quote comes from Bourne, *Britain and the Great War*, p.236.
64. Colin Holmes, *John Bull's Island: Immigration and British Society, 1871–1971* (London, 1988), pp.56–84.
65. Tony Kushner, 'An Alien Occupation: Jewish Refugees and Domestic Service in Britain', in Werner E. Mosse (ed.), *Second Chance: Two Centuries of German-speaking Jews in the United Kingdom* (Tuebingen, 1991), pp.553–78; Richard Thurlow, *Fascism in Britain, 1918–87* (Oxford, 1987).

II. THE BRITISH STATE AND INTERNMENT

Clubland, Cricket Tests and Alien Internment, 1939–40

TONY KUSHNER

Alien internment in the Second World War has received only passing attention from general historians and is usually viewed as no more than a panic measure due to the military crisis in spring/ summer 1940. This article argues that ideological factors have not received sufficient attention, specifically the debate about 'Englishness' which was a constant issue in twentieth century Britain. In the crisis period, when most of the internments were carried out, forces whose ideology was shaped by the world-view of clubland dictated government policy over 'enemy aliens'.

'How much antisemitism was there [in Britain during the 1930s and 1940]? The refugees seldom complained of it. Of course, they had seen the real thing and knew how to differentiate between that and golf-club snobbery.'[1]

'There are worse forms of discrimination than not being allowed to play ball with the pompous nobs of Edinburgh [Honourable Company of Golfers]'.[2]

'If one looks at the treatment by the United States of its citizens of Japanese descent, with no substantial threat of invasion, the British decision about internment becomes easier to understand. The immigrants were interned not because they were Jews (that is, not as a result of antisemitism) but because they were Germans. And the reaction of the refugees themselves proved considerably more understanding than that of the historians who were not even born at that time, or who were infants then.'[3]

'[C]ompared with the vile conduct of the Vichy Government, which delivered every refugee to the Germans, our own Government's actions constitute a monument of generosity'.[4]

'Many continentals think life is a game; the English
think cricket is a game . . . It is important that you
should learn to enjoy simple joys, because that is
extremely English. All serious Englishman play darts
and cricket and many other games'.[5]

'The Committee may terminate the membership of a
member without giving any reason'.[6]

In 1954 the English Golf Union defended the rights of clubs 'to exclude
Jewish members'. The Council of Christians and Jews countered that
such discrimination was 'inconsistent with the spirit and the best interests
of British sportsmanship'. The Union replied that this attack missed the
point. Selection of members was important, they argued, because 'the
game of golf in many cases is merely incidental to the Club life'. In 1990,
the senior Conservative party statesman and ex-Chairman Norman
Tebbit posed 'an interesting test' – how many Asians in Britain cheered
the 'wrong side' in cricket matches against England. Tebbit added that
'When people move to a new country, they should be prepared to
immerse themselves utterly and totally in that new country'.[7]

Golf clubs and cricket tests seem on the surface a long way removed
from the explicit military crisis facing Britain in the spring and summer of
1940 which as a result led to the internment and deportation of 27,000
'enemy aliens'. To explain the *direction* and *scope* of internment in this
period, however, it is necessary, I will argue, to examine the ideology
behind those responsible for policies which led to the removal of freedom
for thousands of refugees from Nazism and members of Britain's Italian
community. Although the military and political situation provided the
specific context of the scale of internment in May–July 1940, most
specifically in the balance of power within government circles, more
fundamental was an ongoing and ever-developing battle over
'Englishness'. The crisis of spring 1940 brought into sharp focus in a most
dramatic manner the question of who did, and did not, 'belong' in British
society. The key to understanding this issue can be found in the world of
British clubland.

I. The Phoney War

To the journal *Truth* and its readership based across the elite institutions of
the country (in 1941 it was reported that it was 'still to be found in every club
of standing and in most of the messes of well-known regiments'), it was
clear who was not a proper member of British or more importantly, English
society. In a poem published in October 1939 the 'Refu-Spy' is unveiled:

To Germany I bid farewell
The country has become a hell
For anyone who won't conform
To the dull, regimented norm
I'd rather be a refugee
Than live where I'm not even free
To perpetrate from time to time
What prejudice describes as crime.
how can a fellow work in peace,
When he is wanted by the police
In several towns for fraud alone?
My finger-prints are too well known.
The only sensible solution
For victims of such persecution
Is a forged passport to acquire,
Accomplices on board to hire,
And as a stowaway set sail
Concocting some heart-rending tale
Wherewith asylum to implore
On England's hospitable shore.
O Promised Land of milk and honey,
Where people love subscribing money
To help the foreigner who robs
Their fellow-citizens of jobs!
Some heartless magistrate in court
May make an order to deport;
But I don't care. I know of course,
It never will be put in force,
And that I safely can betray
My hosts by off'ring to purvey
Secret and vital information
To agents of the very nation
Which, if my tale were accurate,
I ought most bitterly to hate.
A little quiet espionage
Helps to eke out my modest wage,
And no one will suspect that I
Am acting as a German spy.
How can the Englishmen whom sees
This teeming crowd of refugees
Distinguished in it sheep from goats,
Or the chaff winnow from the oats?

So I intend no more to roam;
Here I can make myself at home.
Particularly when I find
So many others of my mind
That – ere they know what we're about –
The English will be crowded out,
Regarded as intruders, while
We occupy their native isle[8]

For *Truth* there was no legitimate place in Britain for the refugee. Shortly
afterwards the weekly journal published an attack on leading *British*
Jews which made it clear that in its mind a Jew could not be a good
patriotic Englishman.[9] There was much worse anti-Semitism in Britain
than *Truth* in the form of the semi-pornographic British Fascist or
pro-Nazi press at this stage of the phoney war. *Truth*, however, was run
by Sir Joseph Ball who was also in charge of the Conservative Research
Department on behalf of Neville Chamberlain. It was, according to
an intelligence report of August 1940, 'run since the beginning of the
war . . . as a secret corridor where the ghost of appeasement could walk
and try itself out, while it clanked its muffled chains'. Moreover, it
was described by the Conservative party chairman in the middle of
the war as 'being nearest to a dependable organ' in the British press.[10]
In autumn 1939, however, Ball, despite his close links with Chamberlain,
had limited influence on government policy towards aliens. *Truth*
managed to play a major role in the destruction of the political career
of Leslie Hore-Belisha, the Minister for War, in January 1940. Hore-
Belisha was reported to have explained his dismissal in two words:
'Jew boy'. A vicious attack on him by *Truth* in the weeks following
ensured that Hore-Belisha would remain an outsider for the rest of the
war. Yet its constant attack on the refugees in the first six months of
the war had less of an impact.[11]

It is true that some very peculiar individual decisions were taken with
regard to 'enemy aliens' at the start of the conflict. Eugen Spier, a friend
of Churchill and bitter opponent of appeasement found himself interned
with several hundred aliens at Olympia in October 1939. Looking around
and seeing that half the internees were fellow German Jews or known
anti-Nazis, Spier wondered if the internment lists had not been drawn up
by the Gestapo. In fact Spier was at Olympia courtesy of the British
security world, but why he and other anti-Nazis had been admitted to this
exclusive club remains a mystery.

In a snippet of information released accidentally as part of the Mosley
papers in the 1980s, a hint of the membership rules qualifying aliens for a

stay at Olympia is given. Ewald Stern, a Jewish refugee, was apparently interned on the advice of MI5 because they were worried that the Gestapo had expelled him from Germany. Spier, therefore, if only indirectly, may have been right – to MI5 its enemy's enemy was not necessarily a friend, and certainly not one to be allowed the privilege of freedom in Britain. Elsewhere in this volume Lucio Sponza indicates how Italian anti-Fascists in Britain during the summer of 1940 believed that they were pursued by MI5 according to whether they were on lists of subversives provided by the Italian secret service.[12]

Fortunately for the refugees, during the phoney war period club rules in Britain were not being drawn up by Ball or his friends in the security forces. Policy towards enemy aliens at the start of the war was dominated by the Home Office and the Home Secretary, John Anderson. Anderson, later rather unfairly maligned by contemporaries for his role in the internment episode, stated in September 1939 that as the enemy aliens were guests in Britain and as a large proportion were refugees, there would be, he was sure 'a general desire to avoid treating as enemies those who are friendly to the country which has offered them asylum.' Anderson was appalled by the later mass internment of aliens and fondly reflected on the 'liberal policy [which he had outlined at the outbreak of war] . . . which gave me personally the greatest satisfaction'.[13]

Tribunals were set up to categorize the aliens. They were generally informal affairs which gave the enemy aliens a chance to put their own case and even bring a British friend to emphasize their suitability for freedom and their loyalty to the British cause. Here was a classic manifestation of a liberal aliens policy. It was local, individual and gentlemanly. The refugee children of Harris House in Southport recorded their experiences in their collective diary as such:

> When the country went to war with Germany, we were considered automatically as enemy aliens. The fairness of the English [is shown as it] set up Tribunals in every town, to give the Refugees the opportunity to prove themselves as loyal friends of Great Britain. We were very glad to get this chance not only because it would exempt us from certain restrictions, but also we hated to be considered as enemy aliens. Everything before the tribunal went very well. The chairman showed great understanding and sympathy and Mr Middleton and Mr Harrison [from the hostel] did their best to help us . . . So we all got exemption all[]right.[14]

Such policy was self-consciously liberal and the government had a great eagerness to show the world that this was indeed the case. In particular, there was a desire to prove to the United States how humanitarian British treatment of the refugees was. The key was to show the differences between Nazi treatment of 'aliens' and those of a liberal democracy. The early detentions at Olympia were an embarrassment to the liberal image, but it was stressed that 'internment *en masse* has not been our policy and we can state principles which will fully correspond with American ideas.' Furthermore the tribunals proved the decency of British policies and it was suggested by the Permanent Under-Secretary at the Home Office, Sir Alexander Maxwell, to John Anderson that the BBC cover one at work classifying a refugee 'with a view to giving the public, and particularly the American public, some information as to the methods we are following in dealing with the enemy aliens in this country'.[15]

At a conference of Christian and Jewish refugee bodies in December 1939 a letter was sent to the Home Office to express great appreciation 'of the liberal policy of His Majesty's Government towards the refugees'. Internment figures at this point appear to justify the enthusiasm of these refugee organizations. Just 486 aliens had been interned and of 62,000 dealt with by the tribunals, 53,000 had been place in 'C' category (that is their loyalty to the British cause was not in doubt). We have seen that the liberal approach had not been totally dominant and the 486 reflected the limited power of the security forces in this issue rather than the decisions of the tribunals. Nevertheless it is within the liberal approach typified by the use of tribunals that the most blatant pressures operating on the refugees in Britain can be located.[16]

Violence against the refugees during the 1930s and the phoney war period in Britain was almost totally absent. The fascists complained about the 'refu-Jews' and several of the Conservative popular papers called for restrictions against refugee entry on economic grounds. Trade union surveys and opinion polls carried out in 1939 and towards the end of the phoney war period would suggest that there was indeed concern about the refugees as economic rivals. With a few notable exceptions such as nursing and domestic service, the refugees were excluded by the British government from taking up any form of work. Many of the refugees, and especially those in the majority who had come to Britain as transmigrants, were thus dependent on the Jewish refugee organizations which in turn had made a pledge to the government that their charges would not be a burden to the British tax-payer.[17]

Much power thus rested with the refugee organizations. Their great fear, and that of the British government, was that a refugee influx would lead to an intensification of British anti-Semitism. The most powerful refugee organizations based at Bloomsbury House attempted to ensure that the new arrivals were made as invisible as possible, that they speak English and adapt themselves wherever possible to British ways. The 'benefits' of such anglicization were made clear in the tribunal system. Success at the tribunals (in the form of exemption from restrictions) depended in many cases on the adjustment made by the refugees to the British way of life. Those schooled by the Bloomsbury House approach and often with personal recommendations that they were learning or had learnt the rules of the game were thus at a distinct advantage. There were a few tribunal chairmen who were not convinced by such superficial displays of Englishness; to them the Boshe, and worse still those of Jewish origin, could never really be 'one of us'. Yet in the autumn of 1939 and the spring of 1940 such Colonel Blimps were in a small minority. More common was the approach of the chairman of the Stamford Hill tribunal; a man who was a true predecessor of Norman Tebbit.[18]

The approach adopted by the refugee organizations at Bloomsbury House was not one favoured by the Chief Rabbi's Emergency Council. Its leading figure was the remarkable Solomon Schonfeld who managed to save, through personal initiatives, several thousand Jews from central and eastern Europe. Schonfeld was concerned to rescue those whose Jewish religious background was intense – they were to the reservoir of talent to ensure the survival of Judaism if its leading centres on the continent continued to be destroyed.[19] One such group of young Jewish refugees aged between sixteen and twenty five (formerly in a German Talmudic school) was transferred to Stamford Hill before the war. In October 1939 these young men faced the Presiding Officer of Aliens Tribunal No. 8. With little or no English (the man in charge of the hostel was also a refugee) and 'no idea of exercise' they were in grave danger of failing their entrance test. It soon emerged that they were lacking even the rudimentary knowledge of the geography of Britain or, as an English Jew present at the tribunal put it: 'the slightest idea of anything English at all. They are living in a ghetto'. The Chairman of the tribunal thought it was a scandal and also a grave reflection on Anglo-Jewry itself that refugee youths were brought here 'without any attempt being made to Anglicize them'. He was prepared to intern the lot and would have done so had the English Jew present (who was the liaison officer at the tribunal) not intervened and 'given him my assurance that they would be in future looked after and guided by the Jewish community'.[20]

An attempt was made by the leading figures in the assimilationist wing of Anglo-Jewish politics, including the President of the Board of Deputies of British Jews, Neville Laski, to pressurize the Chief Rabbi, Joseph Hertz, into taking action regarding this particular refugee hostel.

Hertz refused and his response and the reply of the Jewish liaison officer to the Chief Rabbi are worth quoting at length; they expose the debates about Englishness that surrounds the whole aliens question in the war.

Hertz wrote that a mountain was being made out of a molehill and he did not

> regret, and certainly need not apologize for, my having rescued these Yeshivah students from Nazi concentration camps. Nor was it my first duty to teach them either British geography or English games, but to enable them to *live*. And I have yet to learn that ignorance of British geography or of English games on the part of a poor hounded human being is sufficient reason for him being interned.

The liaison officer responded that any aliens tribunal would be concerned

> that the people whom it exempts from internment are not only beyond suspicion, but are likely to prove loyal citizens. Rabbinic studies alone in a German-ghetto atmosphere can achieve absolutely nothing to this end.

> How can this loyalty be demanded of any body of young men who are taught nothing about English ways, English history, or the English outlook? If they are not to be trained in this loyalty from the very first week of their arrival, what chance have they of merely comprehending, let alone feeling, that love of England which is the veritable fountain-head of these traditions of Anglo-Jewry of which we English Jews are so proud and which is itself the strongest bulwark against the antisemitism in our midst?

It is clear that the Jewish community, and specifically the liberal-orientated refugee bodies around Bloomsbury House, played an essential role not only in the 1930s in the selection and treatment of those escaping from Nazi Europe, but also in the phoney war period. In the months before the fall of the low Countries and the invasion of France they acted as a crucial buffer between the state and the refugees; the informal mechanisms of the tribunals allowed the refugee organizations to have an important role in the decision-making process. As a Home Office Memorandum for the guidance of the tribunals stated with regard to Bloomsbury House: 'While care must be taken to check the information supplied by these representatives, full use should be made of such information as they can give and they should be given facilities to assist the tribunal.' The military crisis of spring 1940 was to drastically change that situation.[21]

II. The Panic Begins

A popular campaign against the refugees on security grounds was launched by certain right wing Sunday papers at the start of 1940. The *Sunday Express*, *Dispatch* and *Pictorial* all commented on the lack of internments being made by the tribunals yet the public was still to be convinced that a real problem existed. As late as the end of April 1940 only one in a hundred interviewed on the aliens question 'spontaneously suggested that refugees should be interned en masse'.[22] It is true that the threat of invasion changed public perceptions about aliens. More crucial, however, were two factors relating to the state. The first was the change in the balance of power at Whitehall in favour of the military and the security forces and against the liberal stance taken by the Home Office. The second was a shift within the Home Office relating to *perceptions* of the public mood.

The press campaign against the aliens gathered pace in April and May 1940: 'Act! Act! Act!' screamed the *Daily Mail*. Its leading journalist George Ward Price added 'The rounding-up of enemy agents must be taken out of the fumbling hands of the local tribunals.' Ward Price, a leading pro-appeasement journalist and an admirer of some aspects of the European Fascist dictatorships in the 1930s, had a particular animus towards the refugee Jews who he distrusted. In the 1930s, Ward Price had sympathized with Hitler and Germany's 'Jewish problem'. He wrote in October 1939 that 'many of these alien immigrants are Jews. They should be careful not to arouse the same resentment here as they have stirred up in so many countries.'[23]

Such comments outside the world of British fascism and extreme anti-Semitism were rare in the first few months of the war. In the spring of 1940, however, restraint in much of the right-wing popular press diminished and references were made explicitly outlining who were the insiders and outsiders in British society. To these papers all Germans were suspect, regardless of background. Categories such as 'refugee', 'alien' and 'enemy were blurred: 'In Britain you have to realize that every German is an agent'. Individualism was dead: 'I'd Intern My German Friends' wrote Beverley Baxter in the *Sunday Chronicle*. In an editorial in the *Sunday Dispatch*, 'Our Guests – and Others', it became clear that the tolerance of the 'host' had disappeared; all the 'guests' were to be removed.[24]

The days of liberty for the refugee aliens were over, as was the control of the situation by 'namby-pamby humanists'. Conspiracy theories were rife; the alien refugees, part of Hitler's Fifth Column, were according to the *Sunday Dispatch*, 'in league with Berlin and Moscow'. Here indeed we move into the world of 'Clubland Heroes', the inter-war thrillers and detective novels of John Buchan, Sapper, Dornford Yates and Agatha Christie. Foreigners could not be trusted. In peacetime they were a nuisance but they had their uses in fiction. If it was true, as George Mikes suggested, that the English, unlike the Continentals, had no sex life, only hot water bottles, then the foreign 'other' could be made to add spice to the anaemic, boring lives of the English upper and middle classes.[25] In wartime, however, what was previously comic now became threatening. Thus the pro-Labour Party *Daily Mirror* could publish a vicious attack on the Italian community in Britain as early as April 1940.

On the surface (with the exception of areas such as Edinburgh where Catholic–Protestant clashes were rampant throughout the 1930s) it does appear, as Terri Colpi has suggested, that the Italians of inter-war Britain 'had become an accepted minority'.[26] This may well have been true of ordinary everyday relationships, but there was still a vast difference between the real British Italian of the local community and that of the popular imagination. In the inter-war period the image of the Italian was complex: fascism was of course unBritish and episodes such as the Ethiopian campaign showed what cads foreigners could be, but Mussolini and Italians were a bit of a joke – babies at heart.

Thus in a popular work published in 1935 satirizing those who had the misfortune not to be English (despite some English faults 'it does just happen they are much the best nation'), Mussolini is pictured with full fascist regalia (including black leather and boots), but sucking a dummy in his mother's lap.[27] British children of the 1930s could be entertained with 'Sexton Blake: Greatest of all Card Games' where the Anglo-Saxon sleuth (worth 120 points) faced the might of the Yellow Peril in the form of 'Snowy King, Drug Trafficker' (110 points), the semitic 'Gus Lavery, White Slaver's Agent'(60 points) or his co-religionist 'Denis Goldring, crooked Financier' (100 points). The threat offered by the Italian 'Caesar Bombski, Assassin', was hardly serious. His unkempt whiskers (surely a false beard), ridiculous hat and smoking explosive was a giveaway. Caesar was only worth 20 points, even less than 'Diamond Tim, Assistant Jewel Thief'.

All this was to change with the war or at least the end of the phoney war. The joke was over and the menace had to be dealt with. Here is the *Daily Mirror* after the fall of the Low Countries:

> The London Italian is an indigestible unit of population. He settles here more or less temporarily . . . He often avoids employing British labour . . . Now every Italian colony in Great Britain and America is a seething cauldron of smoking Italian politics. Black

fascism. Hot as hell. Even the peaceful, law-abiding proprietor of the back-street coffee shop bounces into a fine patriotic frenzy at the sound of Mussolini's name.[28]

The attitudes reflected in this diatribe did not emerge from a vacuum. What was different in the spring and summer of 1940 was that these views extended beyond the world of English popular fiction and into the heart of state policy. The *Daily Mirror* article concluded that 'We are nicely honeycombed with little cells of potential betrayal. A storm is brewing in the Mediterranean. And we, in our droning, silly tolerance are helping it to gather force.'[29]

There are two key interlocking questions relating to the internment episode in May 1940. First, how did the 'namby-pamby humanists' and those with a tendency to 'silly tolerance' lose their influence over alien affairs? Second, how did those who were opposed to a liberal policy take control and instill their form of exclusive Englishness so easily? The first issue relates to the internal weaknesses of the liberal approach; the second to the fragility of British democratic structures during the war.

By the end of May 1940, and in a stark reversal of the situation just one month earlier, only one in a hundred of the British population objected to the government's internment measures and the majority wished that *all* aliens should be interned.[30] Osbert Peake, Parliamentary Under-Secretary for the Home Office, in the Commons on 10 July 1940 defended the government's alien internment measures on the grounds that they were designed to protect the aliens from a hostile British public. The latest research on the role of the intelligence world during the war has indeed stressed police concern in late May about potential attacks on aliens in the event of 'serious occurrences'. There is no doubt that this was a major consideration of the Home Office and it partly explains the creeping expansion of the internment net in the last days of May and early June 1940.[31] Yet the failure of Anderson and the Home Office to take any risks regarding public opinion and the aliens is hardly surprising.

As early as January 1940 (when the Home Office's Advisory Committee on aliens recognized that the public had little interest in alien matters), there was a fear that 'public opinion may flare up suddenly as in 1915. It will then be too late to expect reason to prevail.' It was thus necessary in a time of 'comparative quiet to make sure that the methods of dealing with enemy aliens are such that public opinion may be reassurred on the vital matter of national security and thus avoid the outbreak of unreasoning prejudice.' Anderson was worried at this point about the newspaper campaign against aliens and commented that he would 'have to do something about it'.[32] Thus even when there was little or no public concern about the aliens on grounds of security, the Home Office had decided to take actions to appease those hostile to the presence of the refugees.

In late May 1940, although there is no evidence of public violence against the refugees, the government intervened to assure the British populace that their prejudices or potential prejudices were being well taken care of. Measures were thus taken against the refugees and then the Italians as internment increased from a selective process to one with a mass, if still random, basis. The public clamour, encouraged by government action, increased. Such is the story of immigration restriction and control of aliens in twentieth century Britain; the state attempting to limit the forces of intolerance by taking intolerant measures. As in the summer of 1940, it helped legitimize hostility and helped intensify the demands for further action – ones which it had no resources to carry out properly.[33]

Was an alternative strategy possible? In the first months of 1940 Home Office policy was shaped by concern about the public mood yet there was no attempt to confront ignorance or latent fears. The idea of educating the public about the possible dangers of an unreasoning panic against the aliens did not occur to Anderson or his civil servants. A few months later at the height of the hysteria, the Ministry of Information's Home Morale Emergency Committee called for a 'sedative talk' by Anderson to calm public disquiet. Instead Sir Nevile Bland, former Minister to the Hague (who had escaped from Holland after witnessing the country being overrun by German forces), was allowed to broadcast to the nation about the threat posed by Germans and Austrians in Britain. All, he emphasized, 'ought to be interned at once'. Bland's Fifth Column broadcast, not surprisingly, increased public demands for mass internment.[34]

What is significant, however, is how the liberal desire to protect 'the liberty of the subject' melted away. The sponsors of the refugees, who had acted as their guarantors in British society, offered no resistance to the government's measures. One figure in Bloomsbury House was staggered to find her colleagues in the refugee organizations 'bending over backwards' to be of assistance to the government with the Jewish representatives 'afraid of increased antisemitsm'. She was not alone. A detailed memorandum was sent to the Central Council for Jewish Refugees calling for an end to mass internment which 'did not serve the real interests of this country, or the effective prosecution of the war.' It concluded that 'The only possible explanation of the action recently taken against the refugees must . . . be that the Government has yielded to the agitation of certain circles whose attitude to the victims of Nazi persecution has never been sympathetic'.

Such views and responses were not acceptable to those who controlled the refugee organizations. As we have seen, an attempt had already been made to anglicize the refugees so as to make them acceptable in British society. It now became essential in this crisis period to remove them totally from the public gaze – their very presence threatened the tentative status of all Jews in Britain.[35] Late in 1941, when the Home Office was faced with the possibility of parliamentary criticism of its internment policy, an internal briefing the Home Office pointed out that 'Scarcely a responsible voice was raised at the time to suggest that the policy was wrong'. It also suggested that 'public opinion was seriously perturbed at the possibility of many thousands of Germans and Italians remaining at liberty in this country'. The second point is debatable; the first is not – only in July 1940 was a serious popular challenge launched against government policy. By this time the implementation of internment, including the deportations abroad, was largely complete.[36]

To call the internees 'Anderson's Prisoners', as did one polemic in the summer of 1940, now appears grossly unfair. He found mass internment distasteful and also dangerous – Anderson feared a critical backlash once the panic was over. In their major study of internment published in 1980, Peter and Leni Gillman attempt to re-establish his reputation as a major figure opposed to the measures taken. It is perhaps now appropriate to complete the re-evaluation of his role, for whilst he was against the internment of 'C' category aliens, the lack of any meaningful resistance to the forces of intolerance by liberal circles (of which the Home Office was the most powerful element) allowed the balance of power to shift to those whose *weltanschauung* was largely informed by the exclusive world of English clubland.[37]

III. Clubland Takes Over

The Gillmans were the first to expose the major role played by the Home Defence (Security) Executive or Swinton Committee in the internment episode. Its activities in the summer of 1940 are still obscure (although the fourth volume of the official history of British intelligence in the Second World War has added a little to our knowledge of this secret committee which took over control of all crucial decisions regarding internment policy after its formation on 27 May 1940). The Swinton Committee was not subject to public scrutiny which it could be argued was hardly surprising given the immensity of the military crisis when it was formed. The issue is less reassuring, however, if we consider some of those who were members of the Swinton Committee or connected with it.[38]

There is still no definitive list of its membership. We do know, however, that Sir Joseph Ball was its deputy chairman and William Charles Crocker had attended one of its meetings.[39] Ball it has been noted had arranged the purchase of *Truth* in the late 1930s and apart from its extreme commitment to the appeasement cause he and Crocker had been responsible for the injection of its gutter and conspiratorial anti-Semitism. Later in the war its deputy editor was A.K. Chesterton, an ex-Mosleyite obsessed with the 'Jewish peril' who later formed the neo-Nazi National Front. *Truth* relished the alien internment episode. In an editorial it pointed out that before its attack on the refugees had been seen as mere anti-Semitism. Now its demands were being put into action (even if in the process many of its friends and writers were also being interned under Regulation 18B as a fascist or pro-Nazi threat to the security of the country).[40]

Those that excuse the internment of aliens as military necessity ignore the direction it took and the motives of those responsible. The whole episode can only be understood by examining the class and racial snobberies of those such as Ball and Crocker. Others were involved such as the chairman of the Joint Intelligence Committee, William Caventish-Bentinck, who distrusted Jews and even in the 1980s remarked that he thought that 'the Jewish people have a vivid imagination'. Here was a clear case of projection.[41] Alien internment gave those reared on the conspiratorial world of foreigners in inter-war fiction a chance to put their prejudices into action. Brigadier Harker, the new head of MI5 and a clubland friend of Ball, was convinced that an Italian Fascist organization was sabotaging the war effort.

Neville Bland, who it has been said symbolized 'the image of an era and of a style of life' saw the threat less in terms of the Mafia and more from the refugee domestic servant who 'not only can be, but generally is, a menace to the safety of the country'.[42] Italian restauranteers and shopkeepers might proclaim their loyalty to Britain as riots threatened, thus 'The Spaghetti House' in Soho became the 'British Food Shop'! A similar process had operated in the First World War when German and Russian shops were attacked and would be repeated in 1947 when the Jews of Britain were subject to violence after events in Palestine. Yet such attempts at proving Britishness at times of crisis were futile. Origins – national, ethnic or racial – were crucial. The club was shut and outsiders were to be excluded. In late May 1940 Mass-Observation reported that not only was anti-alienism now respectable – it was also 'quite the done thing'. Clubland, if only briefly, had its day.[43]

The move from a selective to a mass internment policy in a matter of weeks in May/June 1940 and the subsequent internment of roughly one third of the 'enemy alien' population and one sixth of the Italian community might suggest a random selection process. It is indeed true that for the individual refugee there was a large element of luck involved in whether one remained at liberty or not. A police swoop on Hampstead Public Library – a favourite haunt of refugees – was one of many less than professional attempts to find 'the enemy in our midst'. Yet there was a logic behind some of the apparently arbitrary and contradictory policies which can only be understood if the various ideological strands of the process are unravelled.[44]

One of the most blatant inconsistencies was over 'C' category aliens. The move from selective to mass internment was marked by the decision to intern those in this category, yet it never included 'C' category women. In the First World War only a tiny number of women were interned – a reflection of the patriarchal assumption that women could not be spies. The exemption of 'C' category women in the Second World War was a continuation of this patronizing approach. Nevile Bland and of others such as Viscount Elibank who remarked that

> Is it not well known that some of the greatest and most famous spies in the world were of the female sex? Is it not also not also well known that very often one female spy is better than ten men? . . . Today this country is ridden by domestic servants of alien origin . . . and many of them are not trustworthy.

are indicative that a reaction had set in against the gains made by women in the inter-war period – the female after Mata Hari could be the super-spy! Many refugee domestics, who represented both the enemy within and more explicitly the threat from below stairs, were given 'B' category and interned automatically in the panic period. Stereotyping of certain women was thus both responsible for more being placed in an uncertain loyalty category but also for the majority being exempt. Behind the muddle the rules of clubland operated yet again.[45]

Humanitarian considerations, however contradictory to general policy, did not totally disappear from May to July 1940. Those over 70 were exempt (no doubt on the same patronising grounds as 'C' category women). Lack of resources but also hundreds of local initiatives ensured that not all 'C' category men were interned. Similarly Brigadier Harker's desire to remove liberty from all of the Italian community was not acted upon. Luck, as well as friends in useful places played a major role. Yet the decision to physically remove the 'enemy alien' presence by the deportation measures, carried out as Louise Burletson points out in this volume in the absence of *any* public debate, reveals again that there were those determined to rid Britain of a presence that they perceived as a menace. Internment was thus not a 'minor blot . . . a result of momentary panic' in Britain's alien record – it represented the successful culmination of the campaign of those inside and outside of government who had never welcomed the presence of such outsiders.[46]

IV. The Rules of Fairness

> '[T]ell an Englishman that he is stupid – and he will
> smile benovelently; tell him that he is obstinate,
> insular, selfish, cruel, uneducated, ignorant and his
> neck is dirty to begin with – he will shrug his shoulders.
> But tell him that he isn't fair and he will be pained and
> angered.'[47]

> 'if you want to be really and truly British, you must
> become a hypocrite.'[48]

The stranglehold of 'clubland' on the internment episode was relatively short-lived. By early July 1940, as the threat of invasion receeded, the military and security forces no longer had the dominant influence on government policy. The security/military world could no longer demand the *extension* of internment although they were still influential in *delaying* the release of those behind barbed wire. The House of Commons debated the policy of internment on 10 July 1940 and liberal opinion revived and reasserted itself, particularly after news was released of the horrendous loss of life on the torpedoed *Arandora Star*. *Truth* responded to the outcry in its own inimitable way:

> Oh, isn't it appalling
> The cruelty to these
> Poor alien refugees . . .
> Surely the best solution
> Is – ship them home again?[49]

By then, however, its influence was once again limited to its own reactionary world. Internees were released under the guidelines proposed by a series of White Papers, although biases, including those of gender again, still operated in the system. One refugee wrote to Eleanor Rathbone from her internment camp in the Isle of Man pointing out that

> The 18 points of the White Paper [on release categories] chiefly refer to men and not to women and there does not seem to be any provision made for applications for their release. If men join the Pioneer Corps they show by this action that they are willing to help England. In such a case they are no longer regarded as enemy

aliens. Are there any similar possibilities for women? Most of us women came over to England on a domestic permit. If we were lucky we stayed in our positions until our internment. In many cases, however, we lost our work before because of the notorious classification in category 'B' or because the district had been declared as [a] protected area.

She suggested a 'female labour corps' as an alternative to the Pioneer Corps which would enable some releases, benefit the war effort and relieve the idle life of the 'so-called enemy aliens which is a great misapprehension for the majority of the women concerned.' Women were gradually released, if not through the proposed labour scheme. The Home Office was back in control of enemy alien policy by the autumn of 1940 and releases escalated at the end of that year and throughout 1941. With a remarkable flexibility, however, it managed to portray the *whole* episode as a success of liberalism. As Angus Calder suggests with regard to alien internment, it was vital to maintain the mythology of Britain fighting a clean and honest war. The Home Office did so by not only emphasising that the measures were necessary, but also by suggesting that once initiated the policies were carried out in the most humane way. As it put it, '[His Majesty's Government has] always had the position of these unfortunate individuals in the forefront of their mind'.[50]

To make sure that such an image was widely disseminated (for again it became essential not to provide propaganda for the Germans or to upset American opinion), a policy of censorship and more subtle manipulation of public debates took place. Direct censorship was only used in severe cases. In April 1941 the Jewish press in Britain printed several articles on the Isle of Man internment camps which a Home Office official regarded as unfair. It was decided not to respond because 'any action which savoured of an attempt to gag the Press would probably provoke a storm more embarrassing to us than [the articles themselves]'.[51]

It was more common as Burletson suggests, to ensure that debate about the internment episode took place in a restrained manner and that the press reported it in a 'balanced' way. What was essential in this process was that pro-alien activists and the media themselves co-operated. It was an immensely successful operation and meant that, as Philip Taylor has suggested with regard to freedom of information more generally in Britain during the war

censors and journalists became natural allies. By 1941, the M[inistry] o[f] I[information] had developed a censorship system which not only appeared more liberal than in fact it was but which also provided a sophisticated means of disseminating official news and views through the media without revealing that Fleet Street, Wardour Street and Broadcasting House had become agents for the distribution of official propaganda.[52]

The importance of British myths of decency were such that even pro-refugee campaigners such as the Bishop of Chichester, George Bell, concluded after a House of Lords debate on the deportations of 1940 that 'no other country would have behaved with such consideration and sense of fairness and desire to do the proper thing as our own country'.[53] It was essential (and very feasible, given the short duration of mass internment during the Second World War, unlike the First) for British society to reconstruct internment as a victory not for the prejudices of 'clubland' but the continued British sense of fairplay. Yet rather than a slip due to the pressures of war, the internment episode of 1940 should be seen as part of a tradition of anti-alienism where restrictive measures, whatever their intolerant impulses, have been and continue to be defended in the interests of all, including the aliens themselves.

Conclusion: Who or What was 'Totally unEnglish'?

Compared to the horrors of the Second World War, alien internment in Britain appears insignificant. It was not, as François Lafitte, who wrote the most devastating contemporary critique of internment, has put it 'at all how we saw matters in the summer of 1940'.[54] We need to ask now if the Holocaust, for example, is the context in which the British government's policies should be seen? The model of attempted genocide is surely irrelevant to our understanding of how a liberal democracy operated in war. The internment episode needs to be examined within a domestic context of what was and was not possible.

In the first debate on internment in the House of Commons, Major Cazalet, another leading pro-refugee campaigner, called the government's policies 'totally un-English'. Cazalet represented one long-standing but declining British tradition (and now, due to the likes of Norman Tebbit, nearly dead) – the freedom of asylum as an absolute right.[55] It is essential, however, to examine other, less savoury traditions – ones that got the upper hand in the military crisis of summer 1940. Moreover, the proponents of such traditions saw themselves as the staunch defenders of Englishness. It was an Englishness defined as an opposition to outsiders no better portrayed than in the clubland fiction of inter-war Britain. In 1940, if only briefly, that fiction and government policy melted together and became totally indistinguishable:

> 'He might have been French, equally he might have
> been Italian, or Spanish, or Hungarian, or for that
> matter anything else but an Englishman. But whatever
> he was or was not, he certainly looked one thing – bad
> all through.'

> '[The Italians were] filthy in their habits . . . cowards
> to a degree'

> '[The Austrian and German refugees were] harmless
> people who had suffered almost beyond belief for the
> greater part . . . But – and it was a very large 'but' –
> there were others, those ugly little black sheep who
> creep into every flock and indeed are there only for
> their own ulterior purposes. Gentry, and sad to say,
> ladies, who could do incalculable harm if their
> activities were not speedily checked.'

> '[The Austrian and German Jews were] subversive
> liars, demanding and arrogant'.

Which of these quotes came from an official government report on the alien internees and which from the hugely successful clubland novels of John G. Brandon (originator of that great Anglo-Saxon, Sexton Blake), published in this case in 1940 as *Murder in Soho* and *A Scream in Soho*?[56]

The internment of refugees from Nazism and the Italians of Britain in 1940 needs to be considered with regard to the clubs of Sir Joseph Ball and Brigadier Allen Harker and not Auschwitz-Birkenau or Treblinka. As Christopher Ricks has written with regard to attempts to minimize the importance of prejudice in liberal democracies: 'The scorn, contempt and humiliation bent upon Jews [and one could add in our context Italians and all others deemed 'unEnglish'] by those innocent anti-Semitic clubmen can be made light of only by those who do not live within a culture ruled by clubs'. In the summer of 1940 it was not only English culture that was ruled by clubs.[57]

NOTES

The author would like to thank the archivists of N.M. Rothschild for permission to quote material from their records.

1. Bernard Wasserstein, 'A Benign Bargain', *Times Literary Supplement*, 20 March 1992.
2. Philip Howard, 'Thanks Moses, you were a real Brit', *The Times*, 19 Oct. 1984.

3. Max Beloff, review of W. Mosse (ed.), *Second Chance: Two Centuries of German-speaking Jews in the United Kingdom* (Tubingen, 1991) in *The Jewish Journal of Sociology*, Vol.XXXIII No.2 (Dec. 1991), p.136.

4. Sir Gerald Hurst, *Closed Chapters* (Manchester, 1942), p.159. Hurst was in charge of an aliens tribunal in Kent at the start of the war. Thanks are due to Bill Williams for unearthing this autobiography.

5. George Mikes, *How to be an Alien* (London, 1946) reprinted in idem., *How to be a Brit* (Harmondsworth, 1987), pp.22, 52.

6. John Mills, secretary of 'Les Ambassadeurs Club' (Mayfair) to I.W. Baum, 19 Nov. 1943, refusing him membership. The National Council for Civil Liberties found that discrimination against Jews in gentlemen's clubs was common. See their archive at the University of Hull, 45/5 and 45/2.

7. Executive minutes of the Council of Christians and Jews, 23 June, 23 Sept. 1954 in CCJ archive 2/4, University of Southampton. For Tebbit, see *The Guardian*, 21 April 1990 and more generally K. Amin and R. Richardson, *Politics for All: Equality, Culture and the General Election 1992* (London, 1992), pp.48–9 and *Race and Immigration*, No.236 (June 1990).

8. *Truth*, 20 Oct. 1939. For its circulation and other details see memorandum, 1941, in Board of Deputies of British Jews archive (BDA) C15/3/33.

9. *Truth*, 2 Aug. 1940 and similarly 5 June 1942; Tony Kushner, *The Persistence of Prejudice: Antisemitism in British Society during the Second World War* (Manchester, 1989), pp.81–3.

10. See Kingsley Martin papers, Box 29 File 5, Horace Samuel to Martin, University of Sussex on *Truth* in the war. Richard Cockett, *Twilight of Truth: Chamberlain, Appeasement & The Manipulation of the Press* (London, 1989) passim on Ball and more specifically idem, 'Ball, Chamberlain and *Truth*', *Historical Journal*, Vol.33, No.1 (1990), pp.131–42. For the comments of the Conservative chairman, Sir Thomas Dugdale, see S. Koss, *The Rise and Fall of the Political Press in Britain*, Vol.2 (London, 1984), p.611.

11. *Truth*, 12 Jan. 1940; A.Trythall, 'The Downfall of Leslie Hore-Belisha', *Journal of Contemporary History*, XVI (July 1981), pp.391–412 and Samuel Rich diaries, 16 Jan. 1940, AJ 217 in University of Southampton archives for Belisha's reaction. Charlie Pottins, 'Cabinet Conspiracy', *Jewish Socialist*, No.19 (Spring 1990), pp.32–5 provides an interesting account of the affair and of the Ball/*Truth* connection.

12. Eugen Spier, *The Protecting Power* (London, 1951), p.23 and Ch. 2 *passim*; for Stern see PRO HO 283/10/3A; Sponza, contribution to this volume, p.127.

13. Anderson in *Hansard* (HC), Vol.354, col.367, 4 Sept. 1939 and *Hansard*, Vol.364, col.1542, 22 Aug. 1940. For contemporary criticism, see 'Judex', *Anderson's Prisoners* (London, 1940) and F. Lafitte, *The Internment of Aliens* (Harmondsworth, 1940).

14. For the range of experiences at the initial tribunals see the oral history project, 'Britain and the Refugee Crisis 1933–1947' at the Imperial War Museum Department of Sound Records (IWM Refugee Crisis); Harris House diary, 'We Went to the Police', Manchester Jewish Museum.

15. R.M. Urquhart, an official in the Foreign Office Consular Department quoted by Peter and Leni Gillman, *'Collar the Lot!': How Britain Interned and Expelled Its Wartime Refugees* (London, 1980), p.65; Maxwell to Anderson, 3 Jan. 1940 in PRO HO 213/460.

16. Simpson to Cooper, 28 Dec. 1939 in PRO HO 213/455 and HO 213/459, 1 Jan. 1940 for statistics.

17. For the press campaign see A. Sharf, *The British Press & Jews Under Nazi Rule* (London, 1964), Ch.6. TUC sympathy, but opposition to the refugees on economic grounds, is found in a 1939 survey in TUC archives, 910.4181, Modern Records Centre, University of Warwick. For continuing opposition to the refugees on *economic* as against security grounds as late as April 1940 see Mass-Observation's *Us*, 10 May 1940. See Louise London, 'Jewish Refugees, Anglo-Jewry and British Government Policy, 1930–1940', in David Cesarani (ed.), *The Making of Modern Anglo-Jewry* (Oxford,

1990), pp.163–90 for the role of the refugee bodies.
18. For examples of harsh treatment by the tribunals see IWM Refugee crisis, tapes 4300, 4497, 3963. In January 1940 the Home Office decided to review procedures because of 'divergences of practice owing to varying interpretations'; PRO HO 213/547.
19. A summary of its work can be found in Schonfeld papers, 593/1 in University of Southampton archive.
20. The whole episode can be followed in RAL 000/315C, Rothschild archive.
21. Ibid. For the role of Bloomsbury House see PRO HO 213/231.
22. See, for example, *Sunday Dispatch*, 7 Jan. 1940; *Sunday Express*, 21 Jan. 1940 and *Sunday Pictorial*, 28 Jan. 1940; Mass-Observation Archive (M-O A): FR84, 26 April 1940, University of Sussex and *Us*, 10 May 1940 on the lack of press impact.
23. Ward Price in the *Daily Mail*, 20 April 1940 and 9 Oct. 1939. For Ward Price's earlier views, see his *I Know These Dictators* (London, 1937).
24. *Daily Mail*, 24 May 1940; *Sunday Chronicle*, 26 May 1940; *Sunday Dispatch*, 14 April 1940.
25. *Sunday Dispatch*, 14 April 1940. See Richard Usborne, *Clubland Heroes* (London, 1953); Colin Watson, *Snobbery with Violence: Crime Stories and Their Audience* (London, 1971); C. Cockburn, *Bestseller: The Books that Everyone Read 1900–1939* (London, 1972) and Gina Mitchell, 'John Buchan's Popular Fiction: A Hierarchy of Race', *Patterns of Prejudice*, Vol.7, No.6 (Nov.–Dec. 1973), pp.24–30 and idem, 'Caricature of the Bulldog Spirit', *Patterns of Prejudice*, Vol.8, No.5 (Sept.–Oct. 1974), pp.25–30 for the importance of such literature in the formation of national identity; Mikes, op. cit., p.35.
26. Terri Colpi, *The Italian Factor: The Italian Community in Great Britain* (Edinburgh, 1991), p.97.
27. T. Benson and B. Askwith, *Foreigners or The World in a Nutshell* (London, 1935), pp.64–8, 137. The drawing was by Nicolas Bentley, later the illustrator for George Mikes.
28. The playing cards are in the Manchester Jewish Museum; *Daily Mirror*, 27 April 1940.
29. In October 1940 Mass-Observation carried out a survey on foreigners and 'different racial groups'. The response to the Italians was not totally negative – crude stereotypes survived (thus they were seen as by far the most cowardly group but, equal with the Jews, the most cultured and artistic). More significantly was a change in attitudes due to the war; the Italians were also now commonly perceived as a 'problem'; M-O A: FR 523B.
30. For the change in public opinion see M-O A: FR 107 and H. Cantril (ed.), *Public Opinion 1935–1946* (Princeton, NJ, 1951), p.12.
31. Peake in *Hansard* (HC) Vol.364, col.1579, 22 Aug. 1940 and similarly Anderson in PRO CAB 67/6 WP (G) (40) 131 and Churchill in CAB 65/7 WM (40) 123, 15 May 1940; F. Hinsley and C. Simkins, *British Intelligence in the Second World War* Vol.4 *Security and Counter-Intelligence* (London, 1990), Ch.3.
32. PRO HO 45/25754/863027/1, 10 Jan. 1940; Anderson in letter to his father, 2 March 1940, quoted by J. Bennett, *John Anderson: Viscount Waverley* (London, 1962), p.239.
33. See Hinsley and Simkins, op.cit. and Sponza's contribution in this volume for the development of policy and also PRO CAB 65/7 WM (40) 123, 137, 161, 15 and 24 May, 11 June 1940 for Cabinet discussion; Paul Foot, *Immigration and Race in British Politics* (Harmondsworth, 1965) and Ian Macdonald, *Immigration Law and Practice in the United Kingdom* (London, 1991).
34. Home Morale Emergency committee, 4 June 1940 in PRO INF 1/254; Bland in CAB 65/7 WM (40) 123, 15 May 1940. His broadcast was made on 30 May 1940. See 'Judex', op. cit., pp.26–7.
35. Esther Simpson, IWM Refugee Crisis, tape 4469; S. Adler-Rudel sent the memorandum to Anthony de Rothschild on 11 July 1940. See Rothschild archives, RAL XI/35/19. Correspondence in the papers of Joseph Cohen would seem to suggest that the memorandum was drawn up by the prominent British Zionist, Harry Sacher. Cohen wrote to Sacher on 5 Aug. 1940 explaining why no action had been taken on the

memorandum: 'I think it is apparent the the Government's policy of general internment can at least only be modified and not annulled.' In Central Zionist Archives, Jerusalem, A173/63.
36. Home Office briefing, 14 December 1941 in PRO HO 215/23.
37. 'Judex', op. cit; Peter and Leni Gillman, op. cit., pp.112–4 and 132. See also the comments by Lafitte in the republished version of his classic polemic *The Internment of Aliens* (London, 1988), p.xii.
38. Peter and Leni Gillman, op. cit., pp.141–4; Hinsley and Simkins, op. cit., pp.52–3, 58, 61 and *passim*.
39. Peter and Leni Gillman, op. cit., pp.143–4; Horace Samuel, memorandum on the Swinton Committee, 1941 in Kingsley Martin papers, Box 30/1.
40. For Ball and *Truth* see Cockett, *Twilight of Truth*, pp.11–2; *Truth*, 24 May 1940 and Kushner, *The Persistence of Prejudice*, pp.81–3; BDA C15/3/33 for its war activities and the diaries of Ernest Benn, a prominent contributor to *Truth*, at the Modern Record Centre, University of Warwick.
41. For Cavendish-Bentinck see PRO FO 371/34551 C9705, 27 Aug. 1943 and his later comments in Rex Bloomstein's 'Auschwitz and the Allies' broadcast in Sept. 1982. See *The Listener*, 16 Sept. 1982.
42. For Bland see Leni and Peter Gillman, op. cit., p.102 and note 34. For Harker see PRO FO 371/25193 and 25210 and Sponza's contribution to this volume.
43. See Colin Holmes, *John Bull's Island: Immigration & British Society, 1871–1971* (London, 1988), p.98 for attacks on German shops in the First World War and George Orwell's diary, 12 June 1940, reproduced in S. Orwell and I. Angus (Eds.), *The Collected Essays, Journalism and Letters of George Orwell*, Vol.2 *My Country Right or Left 1940–1943* (Harmondsworth, 1984), p.394 for Italian shops in the Second. Both indicate attempts by these shopkeepers to prove Britishness. For the same process with Jews in 1947 see *Daily Herald*, 4 Aug. 1947; M-O A: FR 107, 14 May 1940.
44. For the Hampstead incident see Lafitte, op. cit., p.76. Klaus Hinrichsen has beautifully described such happenings as 'the first great victories of the battle of Golders Green and Hampstead'. IWM Refugee Crisis, tape No.3789.
45. Panikos Panayi, *The Enemy in Our Midst: Germans in Britain during the First World War* (Oxford, 1991), Ch.3 and his contribution to this volume; Julie Wheelwright, 'The Tender Trappers', *The Guardian*, 15 Aug. 1990 for the change in attitudes brought about by Mata Hari and idem, *The Fatal Lover: Mata Hari and the Myth of Women in Espionage* (London, 1992); Bland in PRO FO 371/25189 W7984 and Elibank in *Hansard* (HL) Vol.116, cols. 411–5, 23 May 1940; Lafitte, op. cit., pp.36–9, 62–3 on domestics and categorisation. See also Tony Kushner, 'An Alien Occupation – Jewish Refugees and Domestic Service in Britain, 1933–1948', in W. Mosse, op. cit., pp.553–78.
46. Burletson, contribution to this volume; Howard Brotz, 'The Position of the Jews in English Society', *Jewish Journal of Sociology*, Vol.1, No.1 (1959), p.101.
47. George Mikes, *How to be Inimitable* (London, 1960), republished in *How to be a Brit*, p.170.
48. Mikes, *How to be an Alien*, p.51.
49. For the later interference of MI5 see Latham minute of 19 April 1941 in PRO FO 371/29176 W3503 and INF 1/264 No.56, 23 July 1940 for the outcry over *The Arandora Star*; *Truth*, 9 Aug. 1940.
50. See Cmd 6217 (July 1940); Cmd 6223 (August 1940) and Cmd 6233 (Nov. 1940) for the categories of release, Home Office briefing, 14 Dec. 1941 in PRO HO 215/23; letter from E. Behrmann to Eleanor Rathbone in Rathbone papers, University of Liverpool, XIV/2/17/20; A. Calder, *The Myth of the Blitz* (London, 1991), p.117.
51. J. Edmonds brief, April 1941 in PRO HO 215/24; Burletson, contribution to this volume.
52. Philip Taylor, 'Censorship in Britain in the Second World War: An Overview', in A. Duke and C. Tamse (eds.), *Too Mighty to be Free: Censorship and the Press in Britain and the Netherlands* (Zutphen, 1987), pp.173–4.
53. Bell in *Hansard* (HL), Vol.121, col.365, 17 Dec. 1941.
54. Lafitte in the introduction to *The Internment of Aliens* (1988), p.viii.

55. Cazalet in *Hansard* (HL), Vol.362, col.1209, 10 July 1940.
56. The first and third quotes are from Brandon. See his *Murder in Soho* (London, 1940), p.31 and *A Scream in Soho* (London, 1940), p.8. Donald Ireland provides a brief biography of Brandon in John Reilly (ed.), *Twentieth Century Crime and Mystery Writers* (London, 1980), pp.179–82. The second and fourth quotes are from Lieutenant-Colonel W. Scott's report on *The Dunera* reproduced in Peter and Leni Gillman, op. cit., p.254. The recently released Home Office file PRO HO 215/263, includes the diary of a refugee on board *The Dunera*, and gives an indication of the abuses that took place on the ship.
57. Christopher Ricks, *T.S. Eliot and Prejudice* (London, 1988), p.66.

The State, Internment and Public Criticism in the Second World War

LOUISE BURLETSON

As the phoney war ended and the military situation deteriorated with the collapse of Denmark and Norway, British right-wing newspapers ran an anti-alien campaign. When Holland collapsed, Sir Nevile Bland (British Minister to the Dutch government at the Hague) broadcast his conviction that 'Fifth Columnists' had been responsible for Holland's defeat. He claimed that no German, Austrian nor any person who had connections with them could be trusted. As Britain was threatened with invasion, the general public and the Security Services demanded mass internment. During May and June 1940 B and C category aliens were arrested and interned, and following Italy's entry into the war on 10 June, Italians were included.

The policy was executed by the War Office. But its other wartime commitments and the haste and numbers involved led to chaos and appalling conditions. Over 7,000 aliens were transported to the Dominions in an attempt to ease this pressure. At first only a liberal minority of the general public and the internees themselves criticized the official policy but, as the danger of invasion diminished and reports on the conditions of internment reached the public, there was an outcry at its injustices.

The official response to this criticism was constrained by many, often conflicting, considerations. The policy of internment became a political minefield culminating in the disastrous transportation policy.

Introduction

Since relevant government records began to be released in 1972 there has been a growing number of works on alien internment. Although much has been gained through this research, no professional historian has analyzed the study of internment in all its complexity. Ronald Stent and Miriam Kochan have concentrated on the positive aspects of internment.[1] Peter and Leni Gillman are journalists and their account suffers from a sensationalist tone[2] whilst Connery Chappell's work lacks detailed analysis and footnotes.[3] Writers such as François Lafitte and Neil Stammers have allowed their personal politics to colour their accounts.[4] Other studies which do not specifically deal with internment have covered important aspects of the subject. Tony Kushner has examined the role of anti-Semitism.[5] Thurlow's work on fascists in Britain includes a balanced evaluation of the internment of Regulation 18(b) cases, and Michael Seyfert has displayed a penetrating insight into the psychological aspects of internment.[6]

The newly released Home Office files HO214 and HO215 and oral history tapes, such as those held in the Imperial War Museum, reveal how external pressures affected official decisions. This can be seen on the level of camp life and on a wider scale with the transportation policy. The Home Office files HO45 and HO213 deal with general policy and procedures and provide background details whereas the contemporary Parliamentary Debates on internment display the government's presentation of its policies to the public.

I

In order to understand the factors which shaped the response of the camp administration, the grievances of the internees must first be put into the perspective of their unusual situation. The treatment of internees was particularly harsh during May and June 1940 and many of those arrested were innocent refugees. The large numbers involved in mass internment and the hasty nature of arrests resulted in disorganization and overcrowding in the camps. Few among the British public and camp administration perceived the psychological anxiety of the refugees. Many had experienced the Nazi atrocities: 'What was at stake was the refugees whole position, their status and acceptance in their country of refuge which many regarded as their new home.'[7]

They had been identified as a threat to national security and during this period were cut off completely from the outside world. Letters were subject to delays of six weeks while the postal censorship in Liverpool was organized. Newspapers and wireless sets were banned in all camps until July 1940. The lack of information led to wild rumours about the war situation and supposed German invasion. Until November the internees were: 'forbidden to write to members of Parliament or to make an appeal to the Home Secretary'.[8] They were arrested without trial and had no civil rights. When the Home Office took over on 5 August 1940, 100,000 letters to and from internees were caught in a bottleneck in Liverpool. The situation eased as the backlog of mail was sorted out, and by this time newspapers and radios were allowed into the camps. In this atmosphere camp life began to flourish.

The importance of camp life should not be underestimated. Feelings of uselessness, uncertainty and boredom were a potent danger which led to depression and sometimes suicide. The camps were run on the basis of self-government[9] and the administration was not instructed to organize daily life beyond the bare necessities, such as roll call and mealtimes. The organization initiated by internees did much to ease the trauma associated with loss of liberty. Gerhart Gary Kraus (a refugee interned in Onchan Camp) remembers how jobs and wages were organized on a supply and demand basis.[10] Michael Seyfert has paid tribute to the artistic, literary and educational activities in the camps.[11] Cabarets, concerts and art exhibitions eased tension while internal camp newspapers dispelled rumours surrounding the military situation and publicized the available activities. Camp universities were organized and libraries created. Internees pooled what books they had and this basic stock was: 'expanded by donations from emigrants' organizations, British institutions and individuals'.[12]

The text of books was however examined by the camp administration and those with unsuitable political content were withheld. Occasionally, a Commandant was unresponsive to complaints associated with literature and the availability of paper. This showed a lack of understanding of the importance of camp life. Disruption and obstacles unbalanced equilibrium and undermined morale. This dimension must be added to the more obvious problems caused by mixing fascists, anti-fascists and communists.

The mixing of fascists and Jewish refugees is indicative of the nature of mass internment. They were arrested by virtue of their nationality rather than their loyalty to the Allied cause. Whether Jewish or Nazi, German or Austrian they were perceived as enemy aliens and therefore dangerous. Pleas, letters and petitions to the camp administration indicate how important this issue was to the anti-fascist internees. Frank Pierre (interned on the Isle of Man) wrote in October 1941 how this situation: '. . . creates a continual strain of nerves, hearing of fascist songs, exchange of fascist salutes . . . you will easily imagine what I feel when I see people smiling when the radio announces the executions in France and other countries under the fascist yoke.'[13]

Even where a dozen Nazis occupied a camp with 1,500 anti-Nazis there were rumours that they were: '. . . giving Nazi salutes and having candlelit parties and swastikas.'[14] At worst the clash of such incompatible forces led to violence, at best they created a divisive atmosphere. The anti-fascist refugees were desperate to disassociate themselves from the enemy and demonstrate that their nationality was not synonymous with disloyalty.

Although the sacrifice of leaving their homeland was proof of the refugees' rejection of fascism, to the British public this was not evidence of any commitment to the United Kingdom. The Home Office files reveal the frequent attempts of internees to prove their loyalty to the allied cause. A petition signed by 22 Jewish internees of Peveril Camp on 19 December 1942 provides a typical example. They offered to work in factories, on the land, to join the fighting services or the pioneer corps 'to save or at least avenge our relations' in territories which have been overrun by the Nazis.[15] On a more subtle level: 'Often the decision to write (poetry and literature) in English was a means of disassociating oneself from fascist Germany or of demonstrating a commitment to Great Britain.'[16] Having placed the grievances of the refugees in the context of their vulnerable position it can be seen how even a seemingly petty complaint could assume great importance under these conditions.

Each camp was run by a 'Commandant' who was appointed by the War Office and, after 5 August 1940, by the Aliens Department of the Home Office. Apart from hearing grievances and requests, usually from the popularly elected camp leader, he or she was responsible for the day to day running of the camp. Regular reports on conditions, activities, morale and grievances were sent to the central government. Censored letters were seen by the Commandant and petitions to any government official always contained a covering letter with their views and, usually, a defence of their own position. The Commandants' perceptions of the internees' position shaped their responses and affected the whole atmosphere of the camp.

Many Commandants confused the concept of enemy aliens interned for preventive reasons with prisoners of war. This was encouraged by the use of the Geneva Convention as the reference for camp conditions, even though it was totally unsuitable for camps which included 'elderly, retired, professional gentlemen' who: 'had already had their constitution and their nervous system seriously undermined as a result of the privation through which many had gone in German concentration camps.'[17] Added to this, many officials had little or nothing in common with their 'prisoners'. Most spoke a different language, came from a different culture and often did not share the same religion. From this psychological distance and their position of authority, the Commandants' policies were subject to distortion, although it is not always easy to see where a lack of understanding ends and prejudice begins. Frank Pierre was a Trotskyite Jew interned in October 1940. In May 1942 he wrote to Colonel Wedgwood MP explaining that the Postmaster 'is the alleged Fuhrer of the fascists'.[18]

He feared that the addresses of his correspondents might be passed on to the enemy. Commandant Superintendent S.M. Ogden wrote in his covering letter that, as 75 per cent of the camp had fascist sympathies: 'it would be quite impossible to run the camp if all the administrative jobs . . . were allocated to the so-called anti-fascist section which consists largely of Jewish criminals.' He went on to comment that 'the issue is purely a political one. I have told (Pierre) that if he continues to raise political issues . . . disciplinary action will follow'.[19] Yet, as Pierre had written earlier, men were engaged in a fight to the death over these 'political issues'.

A lack of sympathy and feelings of prejudice bred a deep suspicion of the motives behind the internees' complaints. In some cases the Commandants seem to have interpreted the victim as the aggressor who was trying to undermine their position. In March 1943 the Onchan Camp Leader requested that the Home Office install an internee doctor and compensate the relatives for a recent death within the camp. Commandant Lieutenant-Colonel Scott added: 'I feel that demands based on this incident should not be immediately met and that the matter could be further explored at a later date when it would not appear that we have been forced into a decision by the camp supervisor's demands.'[20]

The idea of a conspiracy within the camp was made all the more potent as public opinion became increasingly sympathetic towards the internees from July 1940. The change was encouraged not only by the military situation but also by complaints from internees to outside representatives. Consequently, Commandants were further alienated from the internees and their position became increasingly vulnerable as attacks seemed to come from all sides. Frequently they were forced into a defensive position which could lead to misunderstandings. In February 1944 Commandant Chief Inspector Cuthbert requested that in future all complaints be made in front of the Commandant as well as any visiting delegate. In this way they could defend themselves from 'grossly exaggerated stories of hardship'.[21] It is understandable that Commandants should want to reply to criticism. Nevertheless it is equally understandable that the internees were loath to criticize the administration in front of the person responsible for the quality of their living.

If a camp leader was considered to be a troublemaker the Commandant did not consider it beyond his power to depose him.[22] In an article in the *Jewish Chronicle* on 4 April 1941 an ex-internee made 'grave charges' against the administration of Mooragh Camp, Ramsey. Colonel Baggalley (Commandant of the Men's Camps, Isle of Man) wrote to Sir John Moylan (Aliens Department): 'Some of my best officers have come to me and requested to be transferred to their own or other units because there is a growing feeling that to be connected with Internment Camps does one no good at present and might prejudice one's future after the war.'[23]

The Home Office was also sensitive to public opinion and was careful not to oppose it. Instead it attempted to diffuse criticism. Although a rigid distinction should not be made between the Commandants appointed by the War Office and those appointed after 5 August 1940, there is evidence that the Home Office tried to ascertain who was prejudiced or un-sympathetic and avoid their services. Dame Joanna Cruickshank was forcibly retired following allegations that she favoured Nazis. Chief Inspector Cuthbert and Miss Wilson (previously Commandant and Deputy Commandant of the Married Camp) were chosen to replace Cruickshank and her assistant because 'their knowledge and experience inspires confidence from the security point of view and *they are both very tactful*' (my italics).[24]

Furthermore, Chief Inspector Cuthbert successfully requested that Captain Johnson should not be appointed as Commandant of the Married Camp because he 'is very anti-alien, I know this from personal experience and from what I have heard from internees themselves'.[25] In this way the Home Office was responsive to public opinion and aware of the benefits of a sympathetic Commandant.

The essential injustice of mass internment underpinned the main grievances of the internees. Kurt Frankenschworth (an interned refugee) spoke for thousands like him when he said: 'I have no wish to feel happy and contented here, I want to get out.'[26]

The majority of Commandants do not seem to have fully perceived the plight of refugees. In most cases their response to requests would have been acceptable had the internees been Prisoners of War. Of course not every Commandant was unsympathetic or suffered from conspiracy paranoia. Nevertheless they were in a difficult position. Hostility had led to mass internment yet, since then, public opinion had changed drastically.

II

There were various channels through which criticism of internment was expressed, and many influences shaped the Home Office response. Public opinion towards the refugees was never uniform. Even at its most liberal, there were hostile undercurrents towards the aliens. This prejudice was heightened by jealousy. The Isle of Man, where most internees were held, was not subject to the same restrictions on food and drink as the mainland, nor was the bombing heavy. This created feelings of resentment against the aliens which were intensified by the press.[27] The

Home Office was careful not to incite these emotions any further. Consequently, it did not deny the German Consul's allegations of ill-treatment at the hands of the British – even though it knew them to be false.[28] Similarly, it tempered its response to the liberal demand for the release of the internees by releasing 'the aliens within a restrictive framework which catered for the prejudices of both the security forces and public opinion'.[29]

Public opinion was also influenced by the treatment of British subjects in Germany. If they were ill-treated, hostility towards the aliens increased at home. However, if the Home Office exacted reprisals, there was the danger of a swing of sympathy towards the internees. When the Foreign Office first suggested the use of reprisals, a Home Office official warned that public opinion would be strongly critical of the Secretary of State: 'if he limited the supply of blankets to internees, especially if the internees sent to Canada were included'. Nevertheless he accepted that it may become 'necessary to put the threat into operation'.[30] In the event the Foreign Office retracted its suggestion giving no reason. Similarly, there was no question of restoring privileges to the Japanese in Palace Camp once articles of the appalling treatment of British subjects in Japan had been printed.[31]

The Home Office also had to take into account German public opinion in its decision making. Liberal public opinion in Britain had to be weighed against the danger of there being reprisals against British subjects in Germany. For instance, Dame Joanna Cruickshank's sympathy for the fascists had resulted in an improvement in the British women's conditions in the German camps. Although the Home Office gave in to public demand for her removal as Commandant of the Women's Camp, they were aware of the dangers this involved.[32] The point is further illustrated by J.F. Moylan. He suggested that a troublemaker be removed from the Women's Camp to Holloway Prison but felt it was necessary 'to be on our guard against reprisals by the German Government against British women in their hands'.[33]

In fact the German government did not initiate reprisals against British subjects in Germany. However, it did use adverse publicity about Britain's treatment of the internees as ammunition in the form of propaganda. The Home Office was acutely aware of this. A diary containing 'a most distressing account of the ill-treatment and cruelty aboard *The SS Dunera*' was withheld by censors and submitted for decision: 'in view of the possible ill effects of this account if circulated elsewhere – especially at the present time when the enemy accuses England of ill-treating prisoners'.[34] The German government had no scruples in supplementing genuine grievances with imaginary ones. This was shown when they broadcast fabricated allegations made by the

German Ambassador for England about his harsh treatment.[35]

Added to all these considerations the Home Office had to remain permanently aware of the allied and neutral countries' attitude towards internment in Britain. An alienated American public could seriously affect Britain's military position. A series of press articles appeared in the United States condemning the conditions in British internment camps. One official subsequently minuted:

> In view of the vital importance of securing the sympathies of the United States and, to a lesser extent of the other American countries and the well-known susceptability of the American public to propaganda of a sentimentalist nature, I should imagine that this would fall within the sphere of National Policy.[36]

This leaves us in no doubt of the perceived importance of American goodwill.

All these forces were subject to change. They were constantly assessed and reassessed in order of priority as the military situation and public opinion fluctuated. These considerations provide the framework which guided the Home Office's reaction to criticism. Let us now turn to the main channels of criticism and examine the official response.

As a result of the conflicting opinion held both here and abroad the government was subject to many pressure groups. As a neutral Protecting Power, the Swiss government acted for the Nazis in Britain, sending representatives to inspect the camps, hear grievances and report to the main administration. Article 42 of the 'Prisoners of War Convention' assured the right of petition to the Protecting Powers and camp authorities and forbade punishment if the complaints proved groundless. François Lafitte commented: 'Although complaints must be transmitted immediately to the neutral Protecting Power, we know of telegrams to official bodies to which internees look for protection which were delayed for weeks or never arrived at all.'[37] This implies that telegrams were intercepted by government officials. There is no evidence of this and communications were poor during the war. Nevertheless it should not be ruled out as a possibility.

The International Red Cross represented the refugees and was supplemented by smaller organisations.[38] A Parliamentary Committee was also established with Miss Eleanor Rathbone MP as its secretary. Apart from visiting the camps these organizations received countless letters and petitions from the internees. Following these visits by the Protecting Powers and International Red Cross, the representatives met with members of the Internment Camps Division of the Home Office who, in turn, were briefed in advance on what was likely to be brought up in discussion.[39] Members of Parliament were involved in many of the refugee organizations and so brought their cases into the Parliamentary arena.

Individual cases were brought before the House. In addition, press issues such as the injustice of mass internment and the mixing of fascists and anti-fascists were kept alive by Mr G. Strauss and Miss Eleanor Rathbone, to name but two.[40] Their task was aided by letters from the refugees who were often articulate and intelligent. However, Defence Regulation 18b cases did not attract the same public sympathy as the refugees. Following a riot at Peveril Camp Peel, the Home Office faced a different form of criticism.

On Wednesday, 17 September 1941 three Nazi sympathizers escaped. The following day when Osbert Peake (Parliamentary Undersecretary for the Home Office) visited the Camp, as pre-arranged, he was abused and jostled by the detainees. On 19 September the escapees were captured and, following a misunderstanding over whether they had been fed, a riot broke out in the Camp. There were reverberations throughout the country. Parliament reflected the concern of the people over what was seen as lax administration in the fascist camps. In the Tynwald the members of the House of Keys condemned the conduct of the military in charge of the camps. Mr Bellinger MP (Labour, Bassetlaw, Nottingham) drew attention to these allegations in the House of Commons[41] while Mr Wedgwood MP (Labour, Newcastle-under-Lyme) asked Mr Morrison (Secretary of State for the Home Office) whether 'the Commandant of the fascist internment camp in the Isle of Man has been changed'.[42]

Parliament was the shop window for the government's policies and attitude. Here it attempted to create a feeling of democracy, openness and calm. Consequently in the ensuing debate Mr Morrison dismissed the 'published accounts' as 'very exaggerated and sometimes a little inventive'.[43] However the government was anxious not to appear confrontational. While not condemning the military it bowed to public pressure and removed it from camp administration.

When Parliament and the press were united in their criticism of the Home Office the pressure on the latter was considerable. The power of the press should not be underestimated; it both represented and created public opinion. There were means of curbing articles which undermined the administration, and information of value to the enemy was censored under Regulation 3 of the Censor's Charter. Authors of alarmist reports could be prosecuted under Defence Regulations 39B(A). This stated that: 'No person shall endeavour by means of any . . . false report to influence public opinion . . . in a manner likely to be prejudicial to . . . the official prosecution of war.'[44]

The Ministry of Information and the War Cabinet discussed the introduction of wider compulsory censorship in May 1940 as the military situation grew worse.[45] But the considerations explored earlier in this chapter limited the government's options. The public, it feared, would condemn any overt censorship. Government speakers had, since March 1940, been issuing propaganda 'on our traditional love of liberty and freedom'.[46] Also, Lord Granville (Governor of the Isle of Man) feared that any prosecution under Defence Regulation 39B(A) would make 'a cheap martyr and get a lot of public sympathy'.[47] The Ministry of Information argued it would not only shock public confidence but also the United States which valued freedom of speech highly. Sir Walter Monckton (Director of the Press and Censorship Bureau) summed up what became the official response when he observed: 'The Press is like a young horse to be ridden with good hands and a light curb'.[48]

Information of value to the enemy was loosely interpreted and informal letters were sent to the editors advising them on the content of their papers. It was 'an exercise in subtle moral blackmail'.[49] The government did not defend itself against specific allegations unless its position was unassailable. Instead it submitted complimentary articles from Refugee Organizations to the newspapers. Where possible it avoided all publicity which might prove awkward, such as the removal of Dame Joanna Cruickshank as the Commandant of the Women's Camp.[50]

The Home Office had to weigh various considerations against each other when responding to criticism. In practice, individual considerations fluctuated in importance; wide compulsory censorship was seriously considered when invasion seemed imminent. The danger of adverse publicity clearly coloured every official decision. But all these crises of publicity led to the development of new procedures. Following the alarmist press about the Peveril riot, Camp Commandants were supplied with official statements with which to contradict false statements in the local press.[51] Similarly, a procedure for dealing with hungerstrikers was formalized[52] and the use of firearms, buckshot, hosewater and truncheons in the case of riot was certainly discussed if not formalized into a procedure. This information was contained in a file which has subsequently been destroyed.[53] The internment machinery was constantly being modified as problems were overcome and their lesson learnt.

III

On the evening of 3 July 1940, the British public heard that *The Arandora Star* had been torpedoed. She had been carrying 479 A class Germans and seamen of whom 175 were killed, and 734 Italians of whom 486 lost their lives. At the time the death toll was not known but the impact on the public was still great. For many this was the first they had heard of the aliens' transportation overseas. All the considerations discussed earlier were applied to the formulation, execution and defence of the transportation policy.

The transportation policy was hatched in May 1940 when the threat of invasion was at its height: 'The concentration of enemy aliens in internment camps in a small country such as the United Kingdom was . . . a source of potential danger in the event of invasion or the landing of parachutists.'[54] Only 'the most dangerous characters of all'[55] were to be sent overseas and, on 30 May 1940, the Secretary of State for the Dominions asked the High Commissioner for Canada (Vincent Massey) to approach the Canadian government and ascertain if they would receive those internees who posed a threat to national security 'at the earliest possible moment'.[56] Telegrams making a similar request were sent by the Dominions Office to Australia, Newfoundland and South Africa on 14 June. This was kept secret from the general public. It was not even discussed in the Cabinet which was presented with a *fait accompli* on 11 June 1940. It was told that 3,000 prisoners of war and 4,000 internees were to be sent to Canada.

The perceived need for secrecy is difficult to justify and seems to go beyond the fear of reprisals in Germany. One Foreign Office official noted: 'steps are being taken to stop the Press from mentioning or commenting on the idea'.[57] The government seemed wary of an adverse reaction from the public, yet, when the transportation policy was later criticized, it was for the inclusion of category B and C Austrians and Germans and 'friendly' Italians, not for the removal of hostile aliens. Even when the policy of internment came under its severest attacks in June and July it was never suggested that 'the most dangerous characters' (category A aliens and fascist Italians) were unfairly treated, and they attracted no sympathy. This suggests that Lord Swinton and the Home Defence (Security) Executive, who formulated the policy, supported by the Prime Minister, foresaw the opportunity to include B and C aliens and 'friendly' Italians, and accurately predicted the likely reaction of the public.

The Swinton Committee[58] consisted of representatives from the War Office and the Security Services. It had executive responsibility for MI5 and was not responsible to Parliament or the Cabinet. During this period it had absolute power over the internees. Although mass transportation would not have been acceptable to the public, it would have been attractive to this Committee. The War Office, already overburdened, was unprepared for the huge numbers and haste of internment and the 'camps immobilised a considerable number of personnel'[59] while 'it seemed desirable both to husband our resources of food and get rid of useless mouths'.[60] Furthermore, if the less dangerous internees were released in the Dominions they might emigrate to the USA or be able to stay rather than return to Britain, where the War Office and Security Service considered all aliens a threat to national security.

This explains not only the inclusion of B, C and Italian internees but also 'that many of those who went to Australia on the "Dunera" were transmigrants to the USA and hoped to get there from Australia'.[61] The internees were therefore identified as a problem which could be greatly eased if shared with the Dominions.

When approached by the government, South Africa refused to accept aliens from England; Canada reluctantly agreed and set an upper limit of 7,000; Newfoundland restricted numbers to 1,000; and only Australia offered an open-ended commitment. In each case the understanding was that the Dominions would only receive those whose: 'continued presence . . . in (Britain) would constitute a most serious danger in the case of an attempted German invasion.'[62] Despite this, 2,290 category B and C Austrians and Germans and 407 civilian Italians were sent to Canada and only 2,108 category A internees.[63]

In order that the policy be executed smoothly and with as little publicity as possible, the government encouraged B, C and Italian internees to volunteer for the journey overseas. Gerhart Gary Kraus (a refugee interned during the war) remembers how the officers in the Camps: 'preferred to have volunteers or people who didn't object, than having people which might be a cause of difficulty all the way till they get to Canada.' Consequently, the Camp administration was happy to swap those on the list for volunteers.[64] The 1,000 internees at Huyton Camp, who knew that they were going overseas, were allegedly told that:

(1) they would have 'more personal freedom subject to certain restrictions, and possibilities for work in one's own sphere;
(2) their wives and children would follow shortly;
(3) any prospective transmigrants would not be placed in a worse position as regards their migration plans.

On being personally consulted, the officers in charge of the camp persuaded all inquirers to volunteer as there was a great future overseas for them'.[65] The government denied authorizing any such inducements. This may have been the case, nevertheless it does not conflict with the official attitude. Although the government later stressed that it only ever hoped to allow wives and children to accompany the men who went overseas, it gave the impression that it was only a matter of time before the arrangements were completed. 'In connection with these arrangements an opportunity was given to husbands and wives . . . interned in the Isle of Man to meet together and discuss the matter, so that the party might be confined to those willing to go to Australia together.'[66]

On 23 October 1940, R. Clare Martin wrote to Mr Jenyns referring to women who had given up their jobs and belongings in a hurry and whose 'destitution had arisen from their waiting nearly three months for the government to send them to Australia as had definitely been promised.' The letter addressed the question of whether or not to intern these women. It suggested that since it would lead to awkward questions in Parliament 'so long as the voluntary organizations maintain them under present conditions and provided there is a reasonable prospect that they will go to Australia shortly I should leave things as they are'.[67]

But it is unlikely that the British government ever believed that wives and children would later be accepted. The Dominions had only agreed to receive 'the most dangerous characters of all', and even then reluctantly. To accept the families of internees would: increase the workload, possibly excite public opinion that these friendly aliens should not be interned at all, cause complications of nationality in the event of births and encourage backdoor immigration. When the government was formally refused its request, the majority of overseas travellers had already left the country.

The British government had deliberately put Canada in a difficult position. When the first internees arrived the Canadians were expecting dangerous characters. Walter Wallich (a refugee schoolchild interned during the Second World War) remembers how a group of 14 Roman Catholic priests in black robes were singled out for the worst treatment by the Toronto Scottish; they assumed that these were German parachutists who had been captured and were still in disguise.[68] The British had clearly contravened an agreement. When Mr Silverman MP (Labour, Nelson and Colne) pointed this out in the House of Commons on 7 August 1941, Mr H. Morrison (Home Secretary) replied: 'My honourable friend is under a misapprehension', but in the face of evidence to the contrary, Morrison had to leave before the matter was raised in Adjournment.[69]

There is little doubt that the execution of the transportation policy was confused. As one official minuted: 'Practically all A internees were sent on the first ship to Canada. There was subsequently little or no discrimination as between B and C internees because information as to an internee's category was not available in the Camps.'[70] Despite Frank Newsam's (Assistant Under-Secretary, Home Office) specific instructions that no Defence Regulation 18b cases be sent overseas, he angrily minuted that thirteen such cases were sent on *The Arandora Star*, nine of which were British subjects.[71] One internee went further and wrote in his diary: 'When one considers the lack of forethought and organising ability compared with the Germans' systematic methods one has to wonder how the War can end in favour of England.'[72]

Although it was never an official policy agreed in the Cabinet, the evidence suggests that the Swinton Committee, supported by Winston Churchill (Prime Minister), always hoped to reduce the problem of internment in Britain by sending B, C and 'friendly' Italians as well as A category internees abroad. Aware of a possible unsympathetic reaction from the public that the Dominions would not agree to receive the former categories, the committee kept their aspirations secret and encouraged the internees to volunteer with inducements which they knew could not be fulfilled. Once these internees arrived in Canada and Australia, there was a possibility that the governments could be persuaded to allow them to stay or emigrate. The British public would not find out until the policy was underway and it would then be explained in terms of the Dominions being a safer place for the internees.[73] This might have worked had every ship not been plagued by scandal.

On 21 June 1940, *The Duchess of York* sailed for Canada with 2,108 German and Austrian A internees and 523 prisoners of war: two men were wounded and another shot dead by a British officer. *The Arandora Star* which sailed on 30 June was torpedoed and sank. *The SS Ettrick* sailed on 3 July carrying 1,307 B and C internees, 407 Italians and 880 Prisoners of War; the passengers were robbed on board and again on arrival. *The Sobrieski* left England on 4 July with 983 B and C internees and 545 Prisoners of War who were kept in cramped conditions and robbed on arrival.[74] Finally, *The SS Dunera* embarked for Australia on 10 July with 244 A class Germans, 200 Italians and 2,288 B and C Germans who were kept in appalling conditions and were robbed and beaten.[75] Beginning with the torpedoing of *The Arandora Star*, bad publicity quickly gained momentum. From the camps in Australia and Canada the internees sent letters back to England describing their treatment. They were referred to by Refugee Organizations and MP's along with reports submitted by internees.[76] The newspapers also took up the campaign with enthusiasm. The immediacy and emotive style of diaries lent weight to criticism. References to censored extracts contained in the Home Office file show that the government was sensitive on this issue. One German internee wrote of his 'inhuman treatment' on *The SS Dunera* which was likened to a 'slave ship'.[77] Another refugee who described the same 'hellish voyage' reflected: 'Having suffered in a German concentration camp it seems a terrible thing to receive the same treatment at the hands of the British.'[78]

Even with censorship there was no shortage of ammunition with which to attack the transportation policy. As the public reacted against mass internment, releases began to take place in Britain and tension increased as many eligible for release remained in Australia and Canada.

The government had allowed an autocratic element to rise from its ranks which formulated its own policy without adequate regard to the dangers of hostile public opinion. When the transportation policy went disastrously wrong it was in danger of losing the confidence of the public, offending the allied and neutral countries and feeding German propaganda. Let us now look at how the British government attempted to retain its credibility during this period.

IV

By the end of July 1940 the transportation policy lay in ruins and Parliament became the main battlefield where the government fought to retain its credibility in the face of strong criticism.

Under a barrage of challenging questions in the House of Commons the government stalled for time. When asked whether evidence would be taken from the Jewish internees on board *The Dunera* Captain Margesson (Joint Parliamentary Secretary, Treasury) replied: 'the court of inquiry will take evidence from wherever is necessary in order to arrive at a conclusion'.[79] The spokesman trod carefully. The government was innocent until proven guilty. On being asked whether there would be compensation for internees pending the court of inquiry, Mr Law (Financial Secretary of State for War) initially refused as this would be assuming that the allegations were well founded.[80] The situation was confused and the government needed time to establish a policy. On 6 February 1941 the Home Secretary, Herbert Morrison, told Mr Strauss (Labour MP, S.E. Southwark) that enquiries were being made into the theft from internees who arrived in Canada aboard *The Ettrick*. When, two months later, Mr Strauss enquired as to whether they were completed one official wrote: 'We are in the unfortunate position that as far as we can ascertain they were never set on foot.'[81]

In this confusion the Home Office was frequently unable to prepare the government speakers beyond supplying them in advance with one or two suggested answers to any questions submitted by an MP.[82] Beyond this the ministers had to use their own discretion and, as a result of inadequate background information, mistakes were made.[83]

MPs demanded that all the facts surrounding the policy be made public. Mr Wedgwood appealed to the British pride in her democracy. On 25 February 1941 he told the Commons: 'I believe publicity is possible in a democratic country . . . we must show the world that we are not afraid of people knowing what has happened and what steps the Government have actually taken.'[84] The issue was an emotive one and references were frequently made to friendly Jews and friendly aliens who never deserved to suffer.[85]

In the face of emotional argument the government spokesmen were careful neither to appear cold nor in opposition to the public. Mr Richard Law stated the government's position when he told Mr Wedgwood that he wished it had not been necessary to have a Debate 'upon this subject, because I would not like the idea to get about that there was a division between the views of my right Hon. Friend and the views of the Government if these allegations were proved to be true'.[86]

In an obvious gesture of generosity and understanding, the government decided to compensate the people from *The Dunera* prior to a court of inquiry. 'It may prove a little costly to the Exchequer but we have thought . . . that . . . it is better to clear our good name than to wait and have this business dragging on for months with quite unjustifiable reflections upon our good name and character in the meanwhile.'[87] It also promised justice. Disciplinary action would be meted out by the War Office 'in a way which will clear the good name of this country from any imputations that may have been put upon it'.[88]

But although it was prepared to appease the public, the government would not do so at any price. Publicity would not only give the Germans an opportunity for propaganda and cause for reprisals, it would also discredit the government at home. Law used the same technique as Wedgwood; he appealed to the British national pride. It was true that in a democracy 'the fullest publicity was required' but 'to publish every detail of any inquiry that could be made would be construed in enemy countries and in enemy propaganda as an admission of guilt, not applying to a particular case, but generally to the British character and the British way of waging a war'.[89]

Public knowledge of the undemocratic Swinton Committee and the part which it played in the transportation policy would have shaken confidence in the British government. This information was successfully kept secret as ministers insisted that the decision 'was taken by the government' thereby implying that it was unanimous.[90]

Let us turn now from the House of Commons to the House of Lords before drawing any conclusions. The first major debate on the issue of transportation took place in the House of Lords on 17 December 1941, significantly later than it had been raised in the Commons. During this period Mr Paterson and Major Layton represented the British government in Canada and Australia respectively and heard the grievances of internees. The government therefore had time for careful preparation and also the advantage that action was already being taken. Before looking at the debate it is worth studying the evidence of preparation, which reveals much about the technique of the Home Office and its major considerations.

Copious notes were made of the facts and figures relating to the transportation policy in theory and in practice, generally and specifically relating to the Bishop of Chichester's motion.[91] Further notes were made on considerations which must rule any answer made by the government spokesman. Various issues were listed that it would be preferable to avoid or, if this was not possible, to be brief. A defence of government actions was also given under listed topics. For example, if *The Arandora Star* was referred to: 'it might be pointed out that the proper view to take of that unhappy incident is not that it reflects any discredit on the government for sending out the internees . . . but the example it affords to the callousness and brutality of the German methods of submarine warfare.'[92] The frequent and emotive references to friendly refugee aliens had been used in the Commons and was anticipated in the Lords: 'It is important to correct the impression that any German classified as B or C was necessarily a refugee from Nazi occupation.'[93]

Apart from defensive ammunition, the Duke of Devonshire was armed for an offensive:

A point which might be specifically stressed in replying to the debate is the remark made to Mr Paterson by a Canadian official . . . to the effect that nothing was so typical of England as that when she was in imminent danger of invasion she should be so conscious of the possibility of injustice having been done to some enemy aliens.[94]

Furthermore, the Duke was given the emotive argument that 'If the problem had been dealt with by the German government it may be assumed that having once despatched the internees they would have been glad to forget all about them.'[95]

Eighteen possible questions and answers with references to specific paragraphs in the brief completed the preparation of the Duke of Devonshire. Even the Bishop of Chichester, who raised the debate, was not untouched by the government's preparation. Reference was made to the endeavours of the German government to exploit the transportation policy and the 'difficulties in making arrangements for the release of suitable cases'. The government spokesman was:

to have a word with the Bishop of Chichester before he speaks and warn him of the danger of ill considered observations. (He) might, in particular, be asked to use restrained language in commenting on the case of the *SS Dunera* and to confine himself to a request for information as to what progress has been made in dealing with claims for compensation.'[96]

The brief also suggested that the Press Department:

take steps through the Minstry of Information to see that the debate is properly handled by the Press and by the BBC so that proper prominence is given to the Government's case and no prominence is given to any exaggerated complaints which may be made in the course of the debate.[97]

Such careful preparation can leave us in no doubt of the importance which the government spokesman attached to the Debate. Behind one government spokesman there moved a huge, invisible and silent machine working to weight the debate in his favour. Neither the Press, the BBC nor the Bishop of Chichester acted entirely independently, though the government was at great pains to give the impression that this was the case. Now that the backstage work has been considered, let us look at the performance as it appeared to the public.

The Bishop of Chichester seems to have been sensitive to the request of the Home Office. In his speech he condemned the 'Nazi hatred and persecution' of refugees[98] and expressed an appreciation of the necessity to place National Security above all else. He did not elaborate on the treatment of passengers aboard *The Ettrick* and *The SS Dunera*. His questions were confined to the issues of compensating, releasing and easing the lot of those interned in Australia and Canada. He also paid tribute to the admirable work of the Home Office, Mr Paterson and Major Layton. This debate appears more restrained and structured than its counterpart in the Commons where the MPs adopted a more direct line of attack. Nevertheless there are themes common to both. The government spokesman disarmed criticism by expressing 'shame, disgust and anger' over the case of *The Dunera*.[99] Despite this, the Duke of Devonshire continued to justify the policy itself. The government had apparently only superseded the concept of British justice with mass internment because 'the Fifth Columnist is innocent until the crisis . . . has arisen and it is not possible for the police or anyone else to secure evidence against him'.[100]

He took great and calculated offence at the Prelate's term 'deportation'. It was used as a tenuous lever to deliver an emotive speech in which he favourably compared the transportation of the internees to the evacuation of children to Australia and Canada.[101] The concept of

'Britishness' dominated the debates in both the Commons and the Lords. Aware of its nationwide power, those representing all sides of the argument drew heavily on its resources. The British character was perceived as a combination of liberality, justice and free speech. The concept was particularly potent at this time. Propaganda portrayed the war as a fight for democracy, justice and liberality which was being threatened by the autocratic, repressive, Nazi regime. Upholding 'Britishness' was therefore part of the national war effort. The debate in the Commons on 25 February closed with a tribute to: 'the spirit in which the matter has been dealt with by the Government this afternoon'.[102]

Likewise the Bishop of Chichester ended the debate on 17 December 1941 in the Lords with the conviction that: 'no other country would have behaved with such considerations and sense of fairness and desire to do the proper thing as our own country'.[103] In the course of both debates the government succeeded in appearing open, democratic, able to accept criticism and keen to see justice done. In this way it contributed to morale at home while improving its tarnished image in democratic-minded America. It denied Germany more ammunition for propaganda purposes. But was this image no more than a facade?

Walter Fleiss, a refugee who travelled on *The Dunera*, described how he later read: 'to what lengths they went even in Parliament to talk about us bloody foreigners, so to speak . . . to do justice to us. How they tried to rectify it, how they tried to compensate us. And they did compensate us in money terms of course.'[104] Mr Wedgwood argued that financial compensation was not justice. The government courtmartialed three soldiers in relation to the treatment of the internees on *The Dunera*. Evidence was not taken from any victims and the sentences were light. Following their announcement Wedgwood retorted: 'As far as the Commanding Officer is concerned, is it that he is severely reprimanded and promoted from Captain to Major? . . . We asked for an inquiry but instead we have had a hushing-up court-martial'.[105] It is hard to evaluate whether the government did as much as it could under the circumstances. Adverse publicity was detrimental to the war effort, yet the matter was discussed, those involved were compensated, and Major Layton and Mr Paterson did much to set the record straight.

The government attempted to lighten the burden of internment by sharing it with the Dominions. The policy went disastrously wrong. Despite this it managed to appear as a liberal democratic administration able to take criticism and attempt to rectify its mistakes. Although a few, like Mr Wedgwood, were not so easily appeased they became lone voices, and it is significant that there are victims like Mr Fleiss who accepted that the government did everything it could to administer justice.

Conclusion

The members of the War Office, and, to a lesser extent, the members of the Home Office responsible for the operation of the internment policy between 1940 and 1942 were largely in accord over their attitude towards the internees. Regardless of the aliens' political views, they were seen as enemy nationals and therefore a threat to British security. They were an inconvenient burden on British resources when she could least afford it. Furthermore, the government desperately needed support at home and abroad and was painfully aware that it was partly judged by the way in which the enemy aliens were treated. In short, the internees were an unwelcome liability.

The government's sensitivity to public opinion did not serve to make it democratic (the very existence of the Swinton Committee is evidence of this). Instead, it increased the importance of *appearing* democratic. The Security Council appreciated that its decision to share the burden of internment with the Dominions would be unpopular with a significant proportion of the public, and was almost successful in keeping its indiscriminate transportation policy quiet. When the injustice of this ill-fated policy became known to the public, the government salvaged its credibility by compensating many of the victims and by projecting a liberal and democratic image in both the Houses of Parliament. The war-time conditions enabled the government to use methods unavailable in peace-time. Pressure was exerted on individual critics and the media in the form of an appeal to loyalty to their country during a time of national crisis; they were warned that severe criticism would undermine confidence in the government and fuel enemy propaganda.

The government's internment policy was criticized at all levels from every angle from most sections of the public. The official response to criticism had to please both the hard line and the more liberal attitudes which existed in a war time society with ambiguous feelings towards enemy nationals, many of whom were refugees. When the government lost its balance and offended a significant section of public opinion it realized the necessity to rectify its mistakes – even if it did not always admit to them.

NOTES

1. Ronald Stent, *A Bespattered Page? The Internment of 'His Majesty's Most Loyal Enemy Aliens'* (London, 1980).
2. Peter and Leni Gillman, *'Collar the Lot!' How Britain Interned and Expelled its War-time Refugees* (Tiptree, Colchester, 1980); Miriam Kochan, *British Internees in the Second World War* (London, 1983).

3. Connery Chappell, *Island of Barbed Wire, the Remarkable Story of World War Two Internment on the Isle of Man* (London, 1984).
4. François Lafitte, *The Internment of Aliens* (Harmondsworth, 1940).
    Neil Stammers, *Civil Liberties in Britain during the Second World War* (Beckenham, 1983).
5. Tony Kushner, *The Persistence of Prejudice, Anti-Semitism in British Society During the Second World War* (Manchester, 1989).
6. Michael Seyfert, 'His Majesty's Most Loyal Internees', in Gerhard Hirschfeld (ed.), *Exile in Great Britain. Refugees from Hitler's Germany* (Leamington Spa, 1984).
7. Ibid., p.171.
8. *Parliamentary Debates* (hereafter PD) *Hansard*, (Commons), Vol.367, col.391. Eleanor Rathbone MP (Independent, Combined English Universities) to Osbert Peake Parliamentary Under Sec. Home Office), 3 Dec. 1940.
9. Ibid., Vol.374, col.1928. Mr Morrison (Home Secretary), 23 Oct. 1941.
10. Imperial War Museum (hereafter IWM), Oral History Recordings, Britain and the Refugee Crisis. Gerhart Gary Kraus, 4420/06.
11. Michael Seyfert, 'His Majesty's most Loyal Internees' in Gerhard Hirschfeld (ed.), op. cit., sections VII and VIII.
12. Ibid., p.183.
13. Home Office file (hereafter HO) 214/39(IC), Frank Pierre to Colonel Wedgwood MP Labour, Newcastle under Lyme, 24 Oct. 1941.
14. IWM, Oral History Recordings, Britain and the Refugee Crisis. Gerhart Gary Kraus, 4420/06.
15. HO215/126. Petition from 22 Jews in Peveril Camp to the Commandant, 19 Nov. 1942.
16. Michael Seyfert 'His Majesty's Most Loyal Internees' in Gerhart Hirschfeld (ed.) op. cit., p.186.
17. HO214/10 Correspondence between Lynson-Hicks and Co. Solicitors and Sir Waldron Smithers MP (Cons., Chislehurst, Kent), 24 Aug. 1940.
18. HO214/39. (5a) Correspondence between Frank Pierre and Secretary of State for the Home Office, 11 May 1942.
19. Ibid. (10b) Correspondence between Commandant S.M. Ogden and M.G. Kirk (Private Secretary to J.F. Moylan: see note 18), 22 May 1942.
20. HO214/29 (9a) Correspondence between Commandant Lieutenant-Colonel Scott and M.G. Kirk, 18 March 1943.
21. HO215/106 (2A) Correspondence between Chief Inspector Cuthbert and M.G. Kirk, 19 Feb. 1944.
22. Ibid. (Minutes 9), 19 March 1944.
23. HO215/24 (18a) Correspondence between Colonel Baggallay and Sir John Moylan, 9 April 1941.
24. HO215/405 (Minutes 1), 21 May 1941.
25. Ibid. Correspondence between Chief Inspector Cuthbert and Sir John Moylan, 21 May 1941.
26. IWM, Oral History Recordings, Britain and the Refugee Crisis. Kurt Frankenschworth 004298/05.
27. Connery Chappell, op. cit., pp.104–5.
28. HO215/129, Nov. 1941.
29. Tony Kushner, op. cit. p.148.
30. HO215/395, Minutes, 29 Dec. 1941
31. HO215/38 (7a) Correspondence between W. St. Clair Roberts Esq. (Prisoners of War Dept, Foreign Office) and Mr Bluett (Internment Camps Division, Home Office) 26 Aug. 1942.
32. HO215/405 (5F), J.F. Moylan, 29 May 1941.
33. Ibid. (5F), J.F. Moylan, 29 May 1941.
34. HO215/263, Note by Censor to A.C. Press, 1942.
35. HO215/129, Nov. 1941.
36. HO215/21, Minutes (1) 1941.

37. François Lafitte, op. cit., p.122.
38. One of the smaller yet influential organizations was the 'Church of England Committee for Non Aryan Christians' chaired by George Bell, Bishop of Chichester.
39. HO215/106 (11a), Draft for Home Office discussions with International Red Cross, 1944.
40. Labour MP, S.E. Southwark; Independent MP, Combined English Universities respectively.
41. PD, Vol.374, col.1928, 23 Oct. 1941.
42. Ibid., col.1475, 16 Oct. 1941.
43. Ibid., col.717, 2 Oct. 1941.
44. Statutory Rules and Orders 1939, Vol.1, Administration of Explosive Substance.
45. Ian McLain, *Ministry of Morale: Home Front Morale and the Ministry of Information in World War II* (London, 1979), p.38.
46. Ibid., p.47, 'Notes for Speakers', 17 Sept. 1939.
47. HO215/19 (3a), Correspondence between Lord Granville (Governor of the Isle of Man) and Mr Osbert Peake, 7 Oct. 1941.
48. Ian McLain, op. cit., p.91, Sir Walter Monckton to Sir Horace Wilson, 3 Nov. 1939.
49. Ibid., p.92.
50. HO215/405 (3a), Correspondence between Sir John Hoyland and Dame Joanna Cruickshank, 20 May 1941.
51. HO215/303, Correspondence between G. Griffiths and Sir John Moylan, Sept. 1941.
52. HO215/414, Oct. 1943.
53. HO215/493 for cross-reference to an informal reference in GEN 31/6/5 which can no longer be traced by the Home Office.
54. HO215/265, Prisoners of War and Civilian Internees sent to Canada, Memorandum for the Information of the Canadian government, July 1940.
55. Peter and Leni Gillman, op. cit., p.164 (their source is not given).
56. HO215/265 (2D), Correspondence between Vincent Massey (Canada House) and Viscount Caldecote (Dominions Office), 22 July 1940.
57. Peter and Leni Gillman, op. cit., p.167 (their source is not given).
58. This refers to the Home Defence (Security) Executive chaired by Lord Swinton.
59. HO215/265, Prisoners of War and Civilian Internees sent to Canada. Memorandum for the information of the Canadian government, July 1940.
60. François Lafitte, op. cit., p.130, Statement by the Duke of Devonshire, House of Lords, 6 Aug. 1940.
61. HO215/262 (5b), Brief for reply to question posed in House of Commons, March 1942. See also reference to hopeful transmigrants by Bishop of Chichester, PD (Lords), Vol.121, col.342, 17 Dec. 1941.
62. HO215/265 (2D), Correspondence between Vincent Massey (Canada House) and Viscount Caldecote (Dominions Office), 22 July 1940.
63. Ibid. Prisoners of War and Civilian Internees sent to Canada. Memorandum for the information of the Canadian government, July 1940.
64. IWM, Oral History Recordings. Britain and the Refugee Crisis, Gerhart Gary Kraus 004420/06.
65. HO215/262 (4b), Memorandum submitted to His Excellency the High Commissioner of the United Kingdom in Austdralia by The Internees from England at No.7 Camp, Eastern Command, Hay, NSW, March 1942.
66. HO215/262 (5b), Brief for reply to question posed in House of Commons, March 1942.
67. HO215/258 (18), Correspondence between R. Clare Martin and Mr Jenyns 23.10.40. [Mr Jenyns is listed as an 'officer attached for special duties seconded from the British Museum'. Neither the file nor contemporary reference books give a title or job description of R. Clare Martin].
68. IWM, Oral History Recordings. Britain and Refugee Crisis, Walter Wallich, 004431/04.
69. PD (Commons), Vol.373, col.2074, 7 Aug. 1941.
70. HO215/254, Minutes, Aug. 1940.

71. HO215/255, Minutes, Aug. 1940.
72. HO215/210, (8a), Extract from Internee's diary sent by Postal Censorship Liverpool to B3 Division, Home Office, March 1941.
73. PD (Lords), Vol.121, col.355, Duke of Devonshire, 17 Dec. 1941.
74. The secondary literature gives varying figures for those on board ships which sailed for Canada. This study uses the figures given in HO215/265, Prisoners of War and Civilian Internees sent to Canada, Memorandum for the information of the Canadian government, July 1940.
75. For a description of the voyage of *The Duchess of York*, see Peter and Leni Gillman, op. cit., pp.170–71; *The Arandora Star*, pp.185–96; *The Sobrieski*, p.238. For *The SS Ettrick*, see Ronald Stent, op. cit., pp.109–11. For a description of the conditions aboard *The SS Dunera*, see IWM, Oral History Recordings, Britain and the Refugee Crisis, Johnson (Peter William) 003790/10/01–06.
76. For an example of a report submitted by a group of refugees returned from Canada to the Society for the Protection of Science and Learning, see HO215/210 (6a), March 1941.
77. HO215/21 (8a), March 1941.
78. HO215/263, censored extract of Internee's diary 10.10.42. For censored extract of diary referring to *The Ettrick*, see HO215/211 1941.
79. PD (Commons), Vol.368, col.14, Jan. 1941.
80. Ibid., Vol.369, col.296, 20 Feb. 1941.
81. HO215/211, Minutes, 1941.
82. For examples, see HO215/254, 1940; HO215/255, 1940.
83. For examples, see HO215/254, 1940; HO215/255, 1940.
84. PD (Commons), Vol.369, col.484, 25 Feb. 1941.
85. For examples see ibid., col.483 and col.485, 25 Feb. 1941.
86. Ibid., col.486, 25 Feb. 1941.
87. Ibid., col.488, 25 Feb. 1941.
88. Ibid., col.489, 25 Feb. 1941.
89. Ibid., col.487, 25 Feb. 1941.
90. HO215/214. Movement of internees abroad, Parliamentary question, 1940.
91. HO215/22 A and B respectively, Dec. 1941.
92. Ibid., (C) under 1 Publicity and Propaganda, Dec. 1941.
93. Ibid., (C) under 2 The Policy, Dec. 1941.
94. Ibid., (C) under 1 Publicity and Propaganda, Dec. 1941.
95. Ibid., (C) under 7 Conclusion, Dec. 1941.
96. Ibid., (C) under 1 Publicity and Propaganda, Dec. 1941.
97. Ibid., (C) under 1 Publicity and Propaganda, Dec. 1941.
98. PD (Lords), Vol.121, col.337, 17 Dec. 1941.
99. Ibid., col.356, 17 Dec. 1941.
100. Ibid., col.354–55, 17 Dec. 1941.
101. Ibid., col.355, 17 Dec. 1941.
102. PD (Commons), Vol.369, col.490, Mr Edmund Harvey, 25 Feb. 1941.
103. PD (Lords), Vol.121, col.365, 17 Dec. 1941.
104. IWM, Oral History Recordings, Britain and the Refugee Crisis, Walter Fleiss 003936/06.
105. PD (Commons), Vol.373, col.1779, 5 Aug. 1941.

The British Government and the Internment of Italians

LUCIO SPONZA

A survey of the differentiated, but equally muddled policies pursued by the government immediately after Italy's entry into the war, is followed by an inspection of the changes introduced after The Arandora Star *disaster; the problems faced by the special tribunal instituted to remedy the major faults of the previous policies are then considered. The conclusion argues that, in addition to the lack of coordination and agreement among different Departments, the internees' plight had also to do with their conditions as immigrants. The article is mainly based on PRO sources, most of them previously unused.*

I

At the War Cabinet meeting of 15 May 1940 Churchill informed his colleagues 'that the Germans had broken through at Sedan, and that the road to Paris was open'.[1] For nearly a month, after the German invasion of Denmark and Norway, the press had been ranting about the danger of a 'Fifth Column' in Britain. Now the issue was on the Cabinet's agenda. With the German and Austrian 'enemy aliens' already under control and even interned (if classified as Category A), Sir John Anderson, the Home Secretary, indicated the 'Italians and British subjects of Italian origin' at the top of the list of 'various bodies and groups of persons in this country against whom action would need to be taken'.[2]

As the development of events in the Continent got worse by the day, and Italy's imminent entry into the war on the side of Germany became a certainty, security measures had to be quickly devised. Any attempt at a proper screening of the Italians was out of the question. The War Office (led by Anthony Eden) and MI5 (headed by Brigadier Allen Harker) were impatient and pressed the Home Office to act more decisively.[3] On 29 May the War Cabinet agreed that:

- 'Italians employed as key men in industry and in electrical power stations should be stood off at once';
- an offer to Count Ciano (the Italian Foreign Secretary) be made to the effect of deporting 'all Italians in this country in exchange for

British subjects in Italy' (against some 2,000 Britons in Italy, there were over 18,000 Italians in Britain – not counting their children if born, respectively, in Italy and in Britain);
– 'Action should be deferred for the present in regard for the internment of Italians regarded as dangerous characters.' They were also described as 'desperate characters' and numbered about 1,000.[4]

At the War Cabinet meeting of the following day, however, the Home Secretary put the number of dangerous Italians scheduled to be arrested at 1,500, plus 300 British subjects of Italian origin (for whom Defence Regulation 18B would apply). The former would be repatriated 'as soon as practicable'.[5]

At the crucial Cabinet meeting of 11 June, the day after Italy's entry into war, it was announced that the Prime Minister had already instructed the Home Secretary to proceed to a 'general internment of male Italians'. No surprise is recorded in the minutes at Churchill's display of 'no regard for the elaborate arrangements the Cabinet had agonized over, and he issued the terse instruction: "Collar the lot!"'.[6] While the arrest of Italians was speedily being carried out, the following policy was being hammered out:

   (i) as an immediate step, the '1,500 desperate characters' were to be seized;
  (ii) subsequently, all male Italians aged between 16 and 70 had to be rounded up, unless they had been living in Britain for at least 20 years;
 (iii) exempted from arrest were those indicated in a special list supplied by the Italian Embassy, who were to be immediately evacuated and despatched to Italy;
 (iv) as many as possible of all the other Italians were also to be eventually sent back to Italy;
  (v) the '1,500 desperate characters', instead, were no longer destined for repatriation but either kept interned in Britain or deported to Canada – an option regarded particularly suitable for the most dangerous men of that 'desperate' group.[7]

Let us consider the implementation of those five directives.

(i) The figure of '1,500 desperate characters' (or 'professing Fascists') had been supplied by MI5. When asked to produce the names, MI5 could only find about 750, but the War Office came to its partial 'rescue'. Harold Farquhar, a diplomat recalled to the Foreign Office and a central figure in our story, explained how that was done: 'In an attempt to complete the quota which MI5 had failed to make up . . . the War Office had made an arbitrary selection of a further 400 which they had taken out of the 20/30 age group.[8] The basis upon which MI5 had arrived at the original figure was the number of Italians they knew to be members of the Italian Fascist Party, or other Fascist organizations based in Britain. MI5 was reluctant to disclose the sources of its information and to show any individual file.

Later, it became apparent that well-known anti-Fascists had been put on the ill-fated *Arandora Star* to be deported to Canada (among the 446 Italians who perished when the liner was sunk by a U-Boat torpedo, was Decio Anzani, the Secretary of the Italian League for the Rights of Man). William Gillies, of the International Department of the Labour Party, thought it was neither coincidence nor a result of a muddle, that of the five anti-Fascists he had written about to Sir Alexander Maxwell (of the Home Office), three had been included in the War Office list. Among the Italian anti-Fascists in Britain it was commonly believed that MI5 also pursued the 'subversives' indicated to them by the Italian secret service.[9]

(ii) The general rounding up of male Italians between 16 and 70 years of age was carried out fairly swiftly, but with unequal zeal and some confusion throughout the country. The top age limit was sometimes reduced to 60. Contrary to government instructions, embassy and consular officers and personnel were arrested (the Consul of the Republic of San Marino was also locked up). Terri Colpi has recently written:

> Outside London the 'round up' was a very much more detailed and thorough operation. This was particularly true for small towns with only a few Italian families where the local police knew the Italians and where to find them. Indeed, it appears that in the provinces 'the lot' were collared. Virtually all 'Italians' were arrested regardless of period of residence, political affiliation, or nationality – many British born and naturalized British subjects were arrested.[10]

4,100 Italians (only a few women among them) were quickly rounded up for internment, against an expected number of 10,000. The vast majority were immigrants who had been living in Britain for a long time. Most of them came from mountain villages of northern and central Italy; they had poor formal education and were politically indifferent, but strongly cared for religious orthodoxy and family values. They mainly consisted of waiters, shopkeepers, shop assistants, cooks and restaurant managers. Their sons, if British-born and of military age, were in the Forces (unless they had opted for Italian citizenship). Even if they had not, but belonged to a Fascist organization, they were detained under Defence Regulation 18B. These numbered about 400 (100 more than had been previously estimated). There was also another kind of immigrant, although these were not very numerous: doctors, technicians, company and bank managers. They were well-integrated into British society, although they probably nourished an ideological affinity for Fascism.

Around 500 merchant seamen had been captured when their ships were seized in British ports and waters, at the outbreak of war with Italy. They were regarded as 'rabid Fascists' and kept together in one of the camps on the Isle of Man (Metropole Camp). Conversely, some internees were anti-Fascists, either active political refugees or Jewish émigrés. We do not know how many there were – probably a fraction of the 300 or so refugees from Fascist Italy.[11]

(iii) The Italian Embassy supplied the British authorities with two lists of names. In addition to the diplomatic and consular staff and their families, several hundred prominent members of the Italian community were included – totalling 730. They were to be evacuated in *The SS Monarch of Bermuda*, sailing from Glasgow. It was an operation coordinated with the Italian government, so that the British opposite numbers and other British subjects would leave from Italy at the same time in an Italian ship. The meeting and ship switching-point was Lisbon. It seems that the Italian end of the operation was carried out smoothly. In Britain various problems arose – not all of them attributable to the very difficult conditions in which Britain found itself at that dramatic time.

MI5 struck 40 names out of the Embassy lists, but some of them slipped through the net (the most notable case was that of Sir Aldo Castellani, an expert in tropical diseases). Others were arrested before the police knew about the 730 names – and some eventually missed the boat. Admittedly, it was not only the lack of coordination that was responsible for *The Monarch of Bermuda* sailing off with the reduced number of 629 Italians on board. On the one hand, some who had a place on the liner did not want to leave Britain, either because they felt that this was their home or for other reasons. On the other hand, in at least one instance a person bribed his way into the evacuation party.[12]

(iv) The issue of the repatriation of Italians became more entangled and divisive the more it was discussed – and in the end it came to nothing. The reciprocal repatriation envisaged by the Cabinet on 29 May was discreetly dropped from official documents and replaced by a recommendation for 'compulsory deportation' to Italy.

The Foreign Secretary was keen on the idea of expelling 'the bulk of the Italian colony in this country' – even unilaterally. Apart from 'ridding ourselves of a threat to our security' – Halifax argued – 'by harbouring a large, potentially hostile, alien colony and at the same time avoid the necessity of feeding all these people, it is thought that such a step might seriously embarrass the Italian Government', mainly because many involuntarily deported people would soon become 'centres of disaffection'. Furthermore, it was thought that many wives and children of internees would become destitute, if allowed to remain in Britain.

Anderson dampened Halifax's enthusiasm by remarking that there were no ships available for that operation. Yet the Foreign Office continued to believe that 'at least one shipload' of Italians ought to be sent off – on a voluntary basis – so as to enable the return home of British subjects resident in Italy. For this purpose the Brazilian Embassy (which looked after the interests of Italians in Britain) had sent the Foreign Office a list of 574 names (including many young children) of people who wished to be repatriated. This confirmed the view expressed by the Aliens Advisory Committee of the Foreign Office, that relatively few Italians would volunteer to go back to their country of origin.[13]

(v) As the Gillmans noted, the suggestion that the '1,500 members of the Fascist Party' should be deported to Canada, was squeezed in by the War Office and MI5 representatives on the Aliens Advisory Committee when it met to discuss the repatriation of Italians.[14] We already know how MI5 arrived (or rather failed to arrive) at the compilation of the '1,500 dangerous characters'. Like those who in order to cover up their mistakes make further blunders, MI5 (abetted again by the War Office) repeated, with more tragic consequences, the same mess it had made in early June. Now it was asked by the Home Office to prepare a list of people to be deported to Canada, and 1,300 names were produced – apparently of Fascist Party members. Here is how Farquhar completed the story:

> This list [was] sent on to the Home Office, who in due course transmitted it to the War Office, who look after all internees, and I understand that the authorities in charge of the prisoners of war [sic] camps had only been able to find about 700 out of this list. What then happened they do not quite know, but they suspect that the military authorities just filled up the number haphazardly by picking out any Italian between the age of 16 and 70, whether members of the Fascio or not.

In conclusion, Farquhar noted, 'Once an enemy alien has become an internee he falls into the clutches of the War Office and we seem to be a little bit helpless in the matter'. Sir Orme Sargent, of the POW department of the Foreign Office, minuted the following additional comment:

There seems to be a fatality which at every stage prevents us from carrying out the policy of HM Government, which is to deport Italians as far as possible instead of interning them . . . I suspect that if we are ever to get various authorities into line the subject will have to be brought again before the Cabinet, who will have to be asked to give a further and this time a more definite ruling in the matter.[15]

II

A couple of weeks earlier the indefatigable Harold Farquhar had communicated to the Home Office the Foreign Secretary's impatience with 'the rather slow progress which MI5 appears to be making in regard to the classification and segregation of those Italians still remaining in this country'. It was then suggested that other means had to be explored 'of expediting this combing out process, such as, for instance, a small travelling commission who could tour the various internment camps'.[16]

This was the first hint at the setting up of a special tribunal for the sorting out of Italian internees. Consistently, it was the Foreign Office which took the initiative and tried to secure the support of the Home Office, against the inertia of MI5 and the War Office. A few days later, on the wake of *The Arandora Star* disaster, the government policy for internment and deportation was effectively questioned in Parliament. During the debate 'a sorry picture of muddle, ignorance and lack of responsibility was disclosed'.[17] It was now made known to the public that notorious anti-Fascists and Jewish refugees, naturalized British subjects and invalids had been interned – whereas, it was pointed out, equally notorious pro-Fascist characters had been left free. The next-of-kin of internees had not received news about their loved ones for weeks and some were in a condition of destitution and despair. As the administration of the internment camps was a responsibility of the War Office (to be transferred to the Home Office in August), Anthony Eden and his Minister, Sir Edward Grigg, continued with obvious discomfiture to hold on to the impossible official line that all the Italians enlisted in the doomed liner were members of the Fascist Party, and were therefore dangerous individuals. They did concede, under pressure, that 'a few mistakes' might have been made and that an inquiry ought to be held (under Lord Snell) to investigate the method of selection of persons embarked on *The Arandora Star*.

There was scepticism at the Foreign Office as to getting to the truth, even before Churchill stated, in a written answer to a question, that it was not proposed to publish the ensuing report. When the 'Summary of the *Arandora Star* Inquiry' was circulated within the Departments concerned (before its publication at the end of November), among the scathing remarks minuted at the Foreign Office, Farquhar's lugubrious comment was: 'The whitewash has been laid on very thick, but not enough to prevent one seeing a few of the bones still sticking out.'[18]

While in Parliament the debate on internment and deportation was taking place, 444 survivors of *The Arandora Star*, including 200 Italians, were reimbarked in *The SS Dunera* to be deported to Australia, together with nearly 2,300 Germans and Austrians who had been graded B and C. The infamous treatment these people received by their guards during the long voyage was to become known later. But extracts from a letter written by a young soldier who had been guarding the Italian survivors into *The Dunera*, in Liverpool, were passed to the Home Office from the Foreign Office. They revealed that the internees' belongings had been thrown 'into piles out in the rain'; that various people, 'including policemen!, started helping themselves to what had been left behind'; that the Italians were then 'hounded up the gangway, and pushed along with bayonets with people jeering at them'; that they were not allowed to see any of the telegrams their relatives had sent them when they heard that they had been rescued from the sea earlier that month.[19] An exchange of letters between Halifax and Anderson followed. Neither the Foreign Office nor the Home Office were consulted about the re-embarkation of the survivors. Sir John Anderson wrote to Lord Halifax that:

> The decision to send these people to Australia was taken by the War Office authorities who, no doubt, regarded themselves as covered by previous Cabinet decisions that Italian Fascists should be sent overseas . . . I agree with your view that the arrangements for dealing with these Italian Fascists have been most unsatisfactory . . . In order to avoid any further muddle, I have taken, or am taking, the following steps, namely:
>
> (1) I have given orders that no more Italians should be sent overseas except with my express concurrence;
> (2) I propose to take steps at an early date to appoint a small Committee of Enquiry to visit the Camps in which Italians are detained and to classify them on some systematic basis.

Halifax replied that he was 'only too happy' to give Anderson any support in his power in implementing his proposals, and suggested Sir Percy Loraine as the possible representative of the Foreign Office within the constituent Committee. The former Ambassador to Rome was eventually asked to chair it.[20]

The extracts from the young soldier's letter – the Gillmans argue –

'helped towards the forming of an alliance between the Home and Foreign Office that was to prove decisive in the course of internment in Britain'.[21] By the end of July, in addition to the abandonment of any further deportation, the Home Office laid down a policy and the procedures for the release of internees. New advisory bodies were set up: one chaired by Justice Sir Cyril Asquith, to advise the Home Office; one chaired by Lord Lytton, to advise the Foreign Office. For the purpose of releasing internees, 18 categories were indicated in a White Paper (Command Paper No.6217). Those who could apply for release ranged from the old to the invalid, from doctors and dentists to scientists, academics and – in fact – anybody who could contribute to 'work of national importance'. 'The exempted categories . . . were conceived in a very niggardly and narrow-minded spirit' – wrote François Lafitte – 'With one or two exceptions the whole attitude to internees which inspired [the White Paper] is the attitude of a farmer to his horses or cows – "use them or lock them up"'.[22]

The White Paper only applied to 'German and Austrian Civilian Internees', because it was addressing the issue raised by MPs and certain sections of public opinion – that is, the issue of *refugees*, rather than the more general but less pressing question of civil liberties concerning shopkeepers and waiters (whose forced return to Italy, incidentally, was still considered by the Home Office officials as a distinct and even desirable possibility). As Anderson put it clearly, but simplistically, in a Parliamentary answer on 23 July: 'So far, I have dealt mainly with the problems of aliens of German and Austrian nationality. The same arrangements will, however, extend so far as applicable to Italians, among whom there are of course few or no refugees.'[23]

At the end of August a second White Paper was issued (Command Paper No.6223), which added another Category, 19 (referring to those who had opposed the Nazi system and had been 'actively friendly towards the Allied cause'), and also indicated that the same categories of eligibility for release applied to Italian internees, whose appeal was to be referred 'to an Advisory Committee appointed by the Secretary of State [Home Office] for the purpose of advising him whether any such applicant can be released without prejudice to the interests of national security'.

Finally, a new revised White Paper was published in October (Command Paper No.6233), with the addition of three more categories and the indication that Category 19 'will, in the case of Italians, be applied to opponents of the Fascist system'. By the beginning of September the Home Office Advisory Committee (Italian) was set up under the Chairmanship of Sir Percy Loraine. It began to examine applicants' cases at the end of that month.

III

The Loraine Committee, as it was normally called, consisted at first of one secretary, one legal expert and one representative of the Foreign Office – under Sir Percy. The first secretary had served for many years in the British Consulate General in Naples. Although, therefore, three out of four members were or had been related to the Foreign Office, and shared its views, Sir Percy was under the authority of the Home Office. This anomaly was not redressed when the Committee was expanded to enable the formation of three Panels – two of them to deal with the cases of 'dual nationality' (that is, British subjects of Italian origin) which were regarded as more urgent; one of them to consider the cases of the Italians proper.

The different interpretations of the terms of reference indicated in the August White Paper, the various degrees of misconceptions about the Italians' loyalties and the uncongenial balancing act Sir Percy had to perform between the Foreign Office, the Home Office and the Security Services (notably MI5), made sure that the Committee soon ran into difficulties. Furthermore, the pride of a distinguished former Ambassador (who had been accustomed to communicate directly with the Foreign Secretary) was hurt when the Home Secretary instructed one of his subordinates to reply to Sir Percy's letters. It was also unfortunate that Herbert Morrison (who became Home Secretary almost at the inception of the Loraine Committee) did not always have the cultivated manners of an accomplished top administrator – as had been the case with Sir John Anderson.

In fact, the problems began even before the Committee was appointed. The Foreign Office, along the lines suggested by the newly established Council of Aliens (under Lord Lytton), would have liked to see the distinction between 'friendly' and 'unfriendly' Italians as guidance to the working of the Committee. It would have also let it have the final word on this. The Home Office wanted the judgement to be firmly based on the specific categories indicated in the White Papers, with the additional reservation that since the plan for the forced repatriation of Italians had not been formally abandoned, it would have been inappropriate to release any Italian whom the government might subsequently desire to send back to his country. The legacy of previous muddle was still there. Moreover, and with some justification, the Home Office stressed that the Committee's role was to advise their Secretary of State, with whom the final decision rested.

However, Harold Farquhar for the Foreign Office and Frank Newsam for the Home Office engineered a compromise which was set out in a

'Memorandum for the Guidance of the Advisory Committee' at the end of August. It stated that:

> Membership of a Fascist organization raises the presumption of enemy sympathies or loyalty on the part of every alien . . . At the same time it is important to remember that membership of the Fascist Party is not necessarily conclusive proof of an Italian's unreliability. Many Italians have been forced to join the Fascist Party under pressure, through fear of the consequences which might result from refusal, or because membership of the party is a condition precedent on their ability to return to Italy. Membership of the Party may accordingly mean much or little, and it follows that membership must be considered in relation to all other relevant factors of the particular case.[24]

'Unfortunately' – as Farquhar later admitted – the Memorandum had to be submitted to the Security Executive Committee (chaired by Lord Swinton) and both Farquhar and Newsam 'had reluctantly to agree' to the deletion of the middle sentence of the above quotation ('Many Italians have been forced . . . on the ability to return to Italy'). The obsession of MI5 with the formal membership to the Fascist Party was even stronger in the cases of British-born sons of Italians who had joined the Party. Lord Swinton himself made it clear that 'membership of the Fascio would automatically classify an Italian as dangerous'.[25] Nor was he moved from his position by the so-called 'Foa Memorandum' which was promptly sent to him by the Foreign Office.

This Memorandum was a long testimony that Professor Bruno Foa, an Italian refugee, had written in response to Anderson's statement of 23 July already mentioned, in which he referred to 'few or no refugees' among the Italian internees. The main purpose of the document was to attract the attention to the plight of Italian Jews who had come to Britain, and to minimize the importance of their possible membership to the *fascio* (before 1938). But there were also persuading comments to the effect that membership of some Fascist organizations was often necessary for the people who had to live and work in Italy. 'The possession of a membership card is, in every day life' – he added – 'as much a necessity as, say, a birth or citizenship certificate in a democratic country'.[26]

What Foa argued for, in fact, used to be put in an ironic nutshell in Italy with reference to the acronym PNF (Partito Nazionale Fascista) – which it was said really stood for 'Per Necessità Familiare' (for family necessity). P.J. Dixon, of the Foreign Office (POW Department), would have appreciated it, since his minuted comment was: 'Professor Foa's paper seems to me to give a fair and accurate account, and to demonstrate, what was already known in the Foreign Office, of course, that membership of the Fascist Party does not necessarily imply pro-Fascist sympathies'.[27] Lord Swinton, on the other hand, denied the efficacy of Foa's argument with reference to the Italians in Britain. He had a point, in theory: in practice his opinion showed the depth of ignorance about the life of Italian immigrats in Britain (of which, I will return briefly in the conclusion).

When the Loraine Committee began to function, problems took a more concrete form. First, Sir Percy was frustrated by the lengthy procedure imposed on the Committee's operations, and by the unreliability of some sources of intelligence on the cases to be examined. Individual dossiers on the appellants were supplied by the Home Office through MI5; they consisted mainly of police reports. Sometimes there was such a delay in receiving the new dossiers that the Committee was forced to suspend its sittings for days, since only after consulting the documentation would the interviews take place. After interviewing the appellants, Sir Percy would recommend whether or not they could be released without danger to national security. Such recommendations were then vetted by MI5 before proceeding to the Home Secretary's desk.

As for the reliability of the dossiers, at the end of October, after having dealt with nearly one hundred cases, Sir Percy lamented to Harker (the head of MI5) that:

> In many cases these police reports have been drawn up carelessly, and have often been found to bear little relation to the facts. This is particularly true of the Manchester police, whose reports have been found to be particularly tendentious. So far we have had to deal with four female appellants. They have all come from Manchester, and in all cases we have recommended release for the simple reason that they were said to belong to an organization – the Fascio Femminile – which, in fact, is non-existent in Manchester.[28]

Yet, there was a more substantial cause for Loraine's grievance, directly involving MI5, on the issue of formal membership of the Fascist Party. Early in October, one Romolo Antonelli was recommended for release by the Committee, but MI5 objected on the grounds that 'the case against Antonelli was the case against the Italian Fascist Party', (with which Antonelli was associated), and that if the recommendation was accepted, it would open the gate to a 'wholesale, or 70% release of members of a Fascio'. Sir Percy found this suggestion, 'illogical, unjust, and lacking in relation of facts', because each case – he argued – was heard strictly on its own merits. 'If membership of a Fascio is to be taken as the sole criterion' – he wrote in a subsequent letter – 'and if no other circumstances in any given case is to be taken into account, this will render the Committee's functions so abortive as to defeat the object with which it was brought into being'.[29]

At the end of November, Sir Percy hoped that the Foreign Office might take up the question with MI5. But if anybody could do something to ease the strained relationship between the Committee and MI5, it was the Home Office – which had been itself stuck for some time on the issue of membership of the Fascist Party. As R.H. Heppel, of the Foreign Office, put it in his hand-written comment on Sir Percy's plea:

> The Home Office ought to be able to see for themselves that it is time they adjudicated between the C'tee and MI5 and put a stop to this argument which has been going on for nearly six months. We have already taken the greatest pains to make it clear to the Home Office that we do not attach much weight to membership of the Fascio. We cannot very well press the matter unless (a) it can be put on the plane of Foreign Policy (e.g. as affecting our future relations with Italy); or (b) Sir P. Loraine feels that his position is impossible because his advice is not taken, in which case we should have every right to protest.[30]

Sir Percy Loraine had no hope to have the Home Office effectively on his side. He actually resented the intervention of that Department so much that at the end of November he threatened to resign. It was a new twist to the sorrowful story of the government and the internment of Italians. Herbert Morrison removed George Worth, the newly appointed Secretary of the Committee, because of his alleged sympathies towards Fascism. Loraine knew the man, had recommended him for the post and was supporting him; he regarded the acceptance of an honorary membership of the Italian Fascist Party – back in 1932 – as irrelevant: at that time Worth was a businessman in Italy and there was no political meaning in that acceptance. Sir Percy was also stung by the fact that the accusation came from an Italian internee, Filippo del Giudice (the subsequently successful film producer),-who had been released on health grounds. There had been 'a view held by certain people that the Government in its treatment of Italians has shown partiality for Fascists and against anti-Fascists', Loraine was told,[31] and it seemed to him that the Home Secretary's dismissal of Worth revealed an anodyne reaction to those rumours. It must have irritated Sir Percy further to read a 'Memorandum on Filippo del Giudice', in which the alleged accuser of George Worth was himself censured – on apparently stronger grounds – for being pro-Fascist, and also for having a criminal past and a murky present. The document had been written by an acknowledged anti-Fascist, also released, and was circulated by George Martelli, of the Political Intelligence Department (Foreign Office).

Actually, Martelli had caused more direct grievance to Sir Percy's pride when, after visiting unannounced the internee camps on the Isle of Man, he recommended the release of three anti-Fascists who were required 'for special work of national importance' (that is to set up a propaganda network among Italians in Britain, which was to be called Free Italy Committee). The Loraine Committee advised against the release of two of them (one was A. Magri, the President of the Italian League for the Rights of Man) – but their recommendation was bypassed. Officials at the Foreign Office wondered under whose authority Martelli had accomplished his mission, to discover with some embrarrassment that it had all started with an agreement between the Under-Secretary of the Foreign Office and the Home Secretary himself, who was – ultimately – the authority under which the Loraine Committee operated. No wonder, therefore, that when Sir Percy met Herbert Morrison at the beginning of December, to see whether that bundle of entangled issues could be sorted out with a degree of mutual satisfaction (or whether he would hold firm on his threat to resign), he commented that the very authority of his Committee was at stake for the following reasons:

> Lack of cooperation, which we on our side had continuously sought, on the part of MI5; overlapping between the numerous departmental organizations connected with the work of the Committee, and the apparent lack of any clear definition of where the responsibilities of one or other began and ended; we felt indeed that there was a general lack of coordination, and that close coordination between the various services concerned was very necessary in the public interest; absence of information about how, why and when internees were released without their cases being referred to the Committee, or by whose orders.[32]

Morrison broadly agreed that there were inadequacies but was rather evasive when he said that 'remedial measures . . . were desirable and ought to be studied'. In the end, however, a compromise solution was reached on the other bone of contention: the dismissal of George Worth. He was now to be moved to a post in the Home Office, carrying equal status and salary. Sir Percy then withdrew his threat to resign.

The following March, Sir Percy Loraine was again disappointed by the negative reaction to what he considered to be an important proposal. He was concerned by the surprisingly small number of Italians who had availed themselves of the opportunity to volunteer for the Pioneer Corps (which, as Category 12 of the White Paper, would have entailed their release from internment), and wrote:

> In the course of a long series of interrogations of Italian appellants, it has become apparent that many [of them] who credibly profess their loyalty to this country . . . are deterred from volunteering for the Pioneer Corps by the fear of penal reprisals being taken on them by their national authorities after the end of hostilities and the re-establishment of peace.

Sir Percy regarded these fears 'not necessarily ill-founded' and suggested that assurance be given to volunteers for service that after the war they would be granted British citizenship.[33] But the suggestion was not well received at the Home Office, where the view prevailed as was expressed by the expert consulted on this matter (one Professor Chorley). In his draft paper, he made several points of which the following two are worth noting: the first was based on a misunderstanding of Loraine's letter, and on a somewhat twisted logic. He pointed out that:

> The proposal of the Loraine Committee is directed specifically to the Italians, very few of whom are refugees. While it might be administratively possible to make a distinction between refugees and others for this purpose, I do not think it would be desirable to do so, as it would be considered unfair to give a refugee who had been here five years an advantage over a non-refugee who had been here twenty. It would lead to heart burning.

The second point reveals a notable measure of prejudice:

> I am inclined to doubt whether such a promise [as suggested by Sir Percy] would have any great effect from a recruiting point of view . . My impression is that many of these Italians are quite content to be kept at the expense of the State doing nothing in internment camps, while others who would gladly return to their shops would not be prepared to undertake hard manual labour in the Auxiliary Military Pioneer Corps.[34]

A similar view of the Italians was expressed by Alexander Paterson, the Home Office Commissioner who was sent to Canada in November 1940 to inspect the internment camps there and make recommendations for releases and the return to Britain. With reference to young internees, he wrote that 'the majority would have been eligible for release under Category 22 of the White Paper,[35] but prefer to spend the rest of the war in a Canadian Camp, rather than face the chance of an Atlantic crossing'.

Was there also some reluctance to help Britain in her war effort?

Paterson knew the Memorandum written by an Italian refugee who had been himself deported to Canada but had been released and returned to Britain (to work for the BBC propaganda towards Italy, as several other Italian refugees did – including a survivor of *The Arandora Star* disaster). He had claimed that only 30 out of the 400 internees were openly pro-British. The remaining 370 were in his opinion 'either Fascists or silent sympathisers with them'.[36] Paterson did not agree. He thought the Italians' (or British-Italians') loyalty was rather elastic, depending on the fluctuations of the war. He wrote:

> Personally I incline to think that the Italian prefers a safe war and a safe sea . . . I came to the rough conclusion that about 100 were at heart pro-British, though not all of them 'openly' so in black times, another 100 were blatantly Fascist, including the leader of the camp and his pugilistic brother, and that the remaining 200 had no fixed political convictions, but were desperately anxious to be on the winning side at the end of the war. The new Commissioner of Refugee Camps is going to improve conditions at this Camp, and probably most of those who are now there will remain there until the end of the war. They will then go and sell ice-cream to the winners.[37]

IV

The question of loyalties needs to be addressed in our conclusion. For this it is necessary to revisit the two opposing arguments put forward on the issue of sorting out the anti-Fascist (or pro-British) sheep from the pro-Fascist (or anti-British) goats.

The Security Services, namely MI5, maintained the view that membership of the Fascist Party and/or any other Fascist organization was the clear-cut dividing line. The War Office and the Military tended to agree with this almost by instinct. When it was suggested in Parliament that the release of Italians should be speeded up, Captain A.S. Cunningham-Reid, MP, is on record as saying: 'As to the best of my knowledge there is no scientific apparatus to tell whether a Fascist is still a Fascist, would it not be far more prudent to leave things as they are?'[38]

The Foreign Office, though not dismissing altogether the importance of membership, recognized that it was a poor indicator of loyalties. To this view even William Cavendish-Bentinck concurred. Despite the fact that as the Chairman of the Joint Intelligence Committee he had been one of the architects of internment, he was also aware of the essentially emotional and social, rather than ideological and political, character of the Italians' membership of Fascist organizations in Britain. He once commented that 'the local Fascio . . . is, in fact, nothing more than the equivalent of the British Society in a South American capital'.[39]

Paradoxically, both contrasting views are inadequate. The crudity of MI5's opinion was abundantly, if unsuccessfully exposed by the Foreign Office people (and especially, of course, by Sir Percy Loraine). The shortcoming of the Foreign Office's perception was in its misunderstanding of the nature of loyalty within the Italian community in Britain. There are three considerations to make here.

First, although traditionally the allegiance of that immigrant community was with its family network and hometown, rather than with an abstract idea of the 'Italian nation', the reality and the mythology of the First World War laid down the basis for widespread, if vague, patriotism. In the 1920s and 1930s, Fascist activists (mainly professionals, intellectuals and Embassy and Consulate officials) to a large extent succeeded in making Fascism synonymous with Italian patriotism. In this they were helped by the fact that, until 1935, British authorities and public opinion had shown warm appreciation of Mussolini's achievements, especially his apparent success in inculcating some sense of order on the unruly and feckless Italians. The respect shown towards their country induced a sense of self-respect. The cooling off of Anglo-Italian relations as a consequence of the Fascists aggression on Ethiopia did not undermine the patriotic sentiments of most immigrants. Indeed, the Italian authorities in Britain, through the highly popular (in British as well as Italian circles) Ambassador in London, Count Dino Grandi, did show an interest in the welfare of the community which no previous Government had manifested.

Second, a major cohesive force within the Italian community was religion. The Roman Catholic Church had fully supported Mussolini's regime (until 1938, anyhow). In fact, some traditional Catholic holidays became major occasions for religious, political and above all social events. A case in point was 15 August, the Feast of the Day of the Assumption (chosen by the Italian Fascists in Britain for their annual reunion). Here is how an Italian in Scotland described it many years later.

> There always used to be a big picnic to celebrate the 15th of August and it was really a good day. Every year the Glasgow Italians, the Dundee Italians, the Edinburgh Italians all got together at some place, some big park, maybe it would be Alva or Stirling or somewhere. We used to have great fun – lots of food and games, tug-of-war and races and things like that. It was really good.[40]

Lastly, if Fascism, together with religion, gave the Italians some sense of national identity and patriotism, a third – negative – element contributed to their complex loyalties. The fathers and mothers who had left Italy either as young adults or as children, taken to Britain by their own parents, were grateful to this country for the opportunity it had offered them to settle, raise a family, run a small autonomous business, or – in any case – live a decent life. But there was also a degree of detachment because, as humble immigrants who kept to themselves, they had been all too often at the receiving end of a long story of contempt and abuse.[41] For their British-born children, who were less prepared to accept a degree of prejudice and intolerance, probably less intense but equally pervasive, there could be a sense of bitter resentment. The spiteful reaction by some of them could bedevil Zeno-Zencovich, who was a young and intelligent Italian refugee, a student at Cambridge with little knowledge of his immigrant compatriots. In his already mentioned 'Brief Report' he wrote:

> It is hard to say how painful an impression it produced to hear these people cursing Britain and everything British in that very language they had learnt in a country which had offered them hospitality, opportunity to earn and a standard of life absolutely unknown in their poor regions of Italy they or their fathers have left to seek fortune abroad . . . Only a few, when questioned about their hatred against the only country they had ever known answered that 'they felt to be Italians'. In the majority anti-British feeling was the result of a repressed social envy towards the so-called privileged English classes. Their animosity was fostered by the secret hope that, England defeated, they would enter the country as masters and conquerors.[42]

Such mass of distorted sentiments and imagined loyalties (and disloyalties) was easy to castigate. It was more difficult to understand it – let alone to remedy it. It was a sad statement on the dislocated condition of immigrants in general and embittered internees in particular.

NOTES

Abbreviations
CAB   War Cabinet Papers, Public Records Office
FO   Foreign Office Papers, Public Records Office
HO   Home Office Papers, Public Records Office

 1. CAB/65/7/123 (15 May).
 2. Ibid. The official history of Security and Counter-Intelligence during the Second World War deals with 'The Fifth Column Panic' in Ch.3; see F.H. Hinsley and C.A.G. Simkins, *British Intelligence in the Second World War* Vol.IV (London, 1990).

3. The story of the doomed resistance by Sir John Anderson to avoid the general internment of 'enemy aliens' has been exemplary told by Peter and Leni Gillman, *'Collar the
   Lot!': How Britain Interned and Expelled Its Wartime Refugees* (London, 1980).
4. CAB/65/7/146 (29 May).
5. CAB/65/7/148 (30 May).
6. P. and L. Gillman, op. cit., p.153. It was argued at the time that 'public opinion' had
   demanded the general internment of enemy aliens. Such argument was immediately
   and effectively dismissed (see François Lafitte, *The Internment of Aliens*, London,
   1988 [Reprint of the original book published in 1940], pp.165–7), although one cannot
   say that such policy was simply pushed from the top down either. The relationship
   between State policy and British popular opinion had a circular, rather than a linear
   character. What was written by Mass-Observation on the 'Attitude to Italy' also applies
   here: 'Before Italy declared war' – it was pointed out – 'there already existed a large
   contempt for the Italians . . . Leadership had actually increased and augmented this
   contempt, with the ready response of mass rationalization' (*Mass-Observation* Report
   No.194, on 'Attitude to Italy', 12 June 1940, p.1).
7. CAB/65/7/161 (11 June). Churchill added that 'as a general principle, we should
   endeavour to round up all enemy aliens as quickly as possible . . . and subsequently
   examine individual cases and release those who were found to be well-disposed to this
   country'.
8. FO/371/25192/221, 'Minutes on Memorandum by Mr Ronald' (28 June 1940).
9. Testimony by Ruggero Orlando, in M. Piccialuti Caprioli (ed.), *Radio Londra, 1939–
   45* (Rome–Bari, 1979), p.vi.
10. T. Colpi, *The Italian Factor: The Italian Community in Great Britain* (Edinburgh, 1991),
    p.109.
11. Only around 200–250 Italian Jews came to Britain, some of them with the intention
    of crossing the Atlantic. They fled from Italy between the end of 1938 and the first
    months of 1939, when anti-Semitic legislation was introduced there, affecting especially
    academics and members of the legal profession. The exodus was on a small scale in
    absolute, if not in relative terms: out of about 50,000 Italian Jews, some 6,000 emi-
    grated between 1938 and 1941. The countries and places of their main destination were:
    Spain and Portugal (2,000), the United States of America (800), Latin America (800).
    Merely about 100 went to Palestine.
12. The 'Independent Milk Supplies Ltd.' made enquiries about the disappearance of
    O. Vaglio, the proprietor of a small restaurant, who owed them some money. It was
    discovered that Mr and Mrs Vaglio 'by paying a considerable sum of money [£500]
    to a person unknown, had obtained a set of false papers to enable [them] to return
    to Italy on *The SS Monarch of Bermuda*, where he was described as an employee
    of the Italian Embassy'. FO/371/25192/371. The story of the evacuation of the Italian
    Embassy has been recently told by E. Ortona: 'L'esodo da Londra dell'Ambasciata
    italiana nel 1940', *Storia Contemporanea*, Vol.XXI (Feb. 1990), pp.173–82. The
    author, who was at the time a young diplomat, praises Farquhar and another
    Foreign Office official for their understanding and co-operation in those unhappy
    circumstances.
13. HO/213/492. This slim file contains the correspondence between Sir John Anderson
    and Lord Halifax. The Report by the Aliens Advisory Committee ('Disposal of Italians
    in this Country') was attached to Anderson's letter of 19 June. Halifax's idea had been
    put forward at the Cabinet meeting of 11 June. In a minuted comment on the copies of
    the same correspondence in FO files, Nigel Ronald (an official very critical of MI5)
    added that 'Italian women and children . . . were also potential spreaders of panic in
    air etc. raids from the Latin temperament' (FO/371/25192/110).
14. P. and L. Gillman, op. cit., p.165.
15. FO/371/25192/223–7, 'Treatment of Italians in this Country – Memorandum by Mr
    Farquhar and Minutes thereon. July 10–12, 1940', *passim*. About 400 Italians were
    embarked on *The SS Ettrick*, which sailed on 27 June. Some 710 to 730 Italians were
    embarked on *The SS Arandora Star*, which left Liverpool on 1 July.

16. FO/371/25192/235–6. Letter to Sir John Moylan (Home Office), 30 June 1940.
17. F. Lafitte, op. cit., p.75. See also P. and L. Gillman, op. cit., pp.220–23. The debate took place on 10 July, see *Hansard* (Commons), 5th ser., CCCLXII, 1229–30, 1244, 1250–53, 1287.
18. FO/371/25210/312 (12 Nov.).
19. The 'young soldier' – the Gillmans tell us – was Merlin Scott, the son of a Foreign Office official who decided to circulate extracts among his colleagues. The young man was subsequently posted to Africa, where 'he distinguished himself in action . . . before being killed at the age of twenty-one', P. and L. Gillman, op. cit., p.216.
20. FO/371/25192/256–7. The previous correspondence between Halifax and Anderson on this issue is in folios 246–51.
21. P. and L. Gillman, op. cit., p.216.
22. F. Lafitte, op. cit., p.194.
23. *Hansard* (Commons), 5th ser., CCCLXIII, 588–9.
24. FO/371/25210/90.
25. FO/371/25210/145.
26. FO/371/25210/209. Bruno Foa was an Italian refugee of Jewish origin; he had been for many years a legal adviser to the British Consulate General in Naples (and therefore was well acquainted with the then Secretary of the Loraine Committee), and the Secretary to the British Chamber of Commerce there; he had been a University professor of Law and had been in employment with the BBC for the previous 18 months. By the time his document was circulated, he had left for the USA.
    Prior to the anti-Semitic laws of 1938, no discrimination existed in Italy and several Jews were members of the Fascist Party. On the relationship between Jews and Italian Fascism see: R. De Felice, *Storia degli ebrei italiani sotto il fascismo* (Turin, 1988; original edition 1961); S. Zuccotti, *The Italians and the Holocaust* (London, 1987); J. Steinberg, *All or Nothing: The Axis and the Holocaust, 1941–43* (London, 1990); A. Stille, *Benevolence and Betrayal: Five Italian Jewish Families under Fascism* (London, 1991).
27. FO/371/25210/146.
28. FO/371/25210/303. Letter of 29 Oct.
29. FO/371/25210/307 and 303. Letters of 23 and 29 Oct., respectively.
30. FO/371/25210/338.
31. FO/371/25210/350. Copy of a letter to Sir Percy Loraine by Sir Alexander Maxwell (23 Nov.).
32. FO/371/25210/348. Minute of the meeting between Sir Percy Loraine and Herbert Morrison, sent to Sir Orme Sargent, Foreign Office.
33. HO/213/47. Letter of 13 March 1941.
34. HO/213/47. 'Draft' of 28 March 1941.
35. Category 22 read: 'Any person . . . [that] has, since his early childhood, or for at least 20 years lived continuously or almost continuously in the United Kingdom; [that] has long severed connection with his country of nationality; [whose] interests and associations are British; and [who] is friendly towards this country'. This became the major category of release from the beginning of 1941; until then the highest number of releases were on account of Category 3: 'The invalid or infirm . . .'. These were followed by the already mentioned Category 12: 'Internees who are accepted for enlistment in the Auxiliary Military Pioneer Corps . . .'. The Loraine Committee concluded its operations in the summer of 1941. Applications for release were afterwards to be made directly to the Home Office. By June 1941 the number of Italians who had been released amounted to almost 1,800, with nearly 2,900 still in internment (of whom 330 in Canada and 200 in Australia). By September 1943 about 1,000 were still interned and at the end of the war there remained 364 – the majority of them were merchant seamen.
36. HO/215/28/1B. 'Brief Report on the Conditions in an Internment Camp for Italians in Canada, January 1941', by Livio Zeno-Zencovich, p.2.
37. HO/215/30. 'Conditions in (Internment) Camps. Report by Alexander Paterson. Canada', pp.27–8.

38. *Hansard* (Commons), 5th ser., CCCXCII, 1498, 21 Oct. 1943.
39. Quoted by P. and L. Gillman, op. cit., p.158.
40. M. Rodgers, 'Italiani in Scoz[z]ia', in B. Kay (ed.), *Odyssey – The Second Collection: Voices from Scotland's Recent Past* (Edinburgh, 1982), p.17.
41. See L. Sponza, *Italian Immigrants in Nineteenth Century Britain: Realities and Images* (Leicester, 1988), especially Part 2.
42. HO/215/28/1B. 'Brief Report', op. cit., p.3.

III. THE EXPERIENCE OF INTERNMENT

Women's Experience of Internment

MIRIAM KOCHAN

The British government interned some 4,000 women in the panic situation of May–June 1940. The tribunals had graded nearly all of them 'B' and a large proportion were in actual fact refugees from Nazi Germany. Most of them were eventually taken to Rushen camp on the Isle of Man. Here they were treated relatively easily and quickly organized self-help groups and activities, as is seen from the many personal reminiscences quoted. As irrationally as they had been interned, so the women were released from July 1940 onwards.

Only a relatively small number of women were interned by the British government during the nightmare days of 1940: approximately 4,000 as compared with 23,000 men.

This itself is an index of the distinction that was made between male and female enemy aliens. It is not the only difference. Not only were considerably fewer women interned, but those women who were placed in camps were handled more leniently (and no woman was ever sent overseas). True, the myth of the weaker sex was more prevalent then than it is today, but did this make women less of a threat to the safety of the realm? Were they regarded as less likely to be sympathizers with the Nazi cause? Did their femininity diminish the possibility that they were spying for the Germans? Surely not, when espionage had always been a favoured female occupation. The rationale for this discrimination is hard to determine, particularly in view of the fact that it is possible that a larger proportion of women than men were not refugees from Nazi oppression but German and Austrian girls who had been working in England as domestic servants at the outbreak of war and had chosen not to return to their homes. But perhaps this absence of logic is not surprising in an episode characterized throughout by irrationality.

The distinction between the sexes did not appear so strongly in the early stages of government wartime policy towards aliens. In 1939 both men and women alike were asked to appear before the tribunals headed

Many of the interviews contained in this contribution, including those with the late Marie Neurath, Edith Jacobus, Mrs Ehrhardt, Freda and Dr H., were conducted in connection with the author's book, *Britain's Internees in the Second World War* (London, 1983) and are quoted more fully in it.

by 'men of legal experience' which graded them 'A', 'B' or 'C' according to their supposed degree of trustworthiness. What it would be interesting to know, and nothing suggests that the information is available, is how many women were accorded different status from their husbands. It is, of course, impossible to judge from one or two examples, but it is suggestive that Edith Jacobus was graded 'B' when, as the result of an administrative muddle, her husband received that grade. Equally, both Mrs Ehrhardt and her husband Pastor Ehrhardt were graded 'C'.

The privilege of sharing as equals in the tribunal process was a mixed blessing. To be graded 'A' meant immediate internment for either sex and, in the case of the men, later culminated in deportation. Four hundred men and 200 women received this grade; the women were at first consigned to Holloway prison[1] and later sent to the Isle of Man. But whilst all male 'B's lost their liberty and 'C's were more or less indiscriminately interned in the course of the May, June and July weeks when a general internment policy was pursued, for the women the gradings were of even greater importance. By and large, only grade 'B' women and those who for some reason or another had not passed through the tribunal process were interned. This made the classification they were given crucial to the women in the event. It also throws a remorseless spotlight on the lack of logical explanation of who was and who was not given the dubious 'B' grade – originally only intended for doubtful cases lying between the definitely suspect and the genuine refugee – and the haphazard manner in which the grades in general were allocated. According to François Lafitte, 'a few suspicious tribunals took the line of putting all 'enemy aliens' whom they did not intern into B class. Several tribunals adopted the practice of placing all domestic servants in this class . . . Others put all unemployed refugees or all living in refugee hostels in B class'.[2]

A couple of examples of this process in action will suffice: 'I went to a tribunal', one refugee said, 'and he asked me "Have you any relations in Germany?" I said "Yes". So I was graded "B"'. 'There was a Jewish nurse in Cardiff who worked in a hospital and who typed letters to her mother in German', said another. 'Some of the nurses heard her typing and asked "Why should a nurse type?". She was made "A"'. 'In Stamford Hill, everyone knew that the judge was anti-German and antisemite', stated the then 19-year-old Miss Friedler. 'Straight away he told me I was an enemy alien, class "B"'. Even the government implicitly recognized the inadequacy of the grading process when it introduced a review system to reconsider dubious ratings. The 17 Advisory Committees set up in the spring of 1940 began their re-examination of all female German and Austrian 'B's on 20 May. Their work was interrupted by sweeping internment measures before it had barely begun.

However, when general internment began on 12 May 1940, there was no doubt that it was the men who were considered to constitute the danger. The Home Office order which appeared on that Whit Sunday ordered the internment of all male German and Austrians over 16 and under 60, regardless of their rating, living on the coastal strip from Hampshire to Inverness – the part of the country likely to be affected if the expected German invasion materialized.

This does not indicate that there was any lack of early intimations that women too might give cause for fear. Colonel Henry Walter Burton, Member of Parliament for Sudbury, West Suffolk, for example, suggested to the House of Commons that enemy aliens living on the east coast were passing on information to the enemy. Their signals to aircraft, if only by means of hanging out their washing, had led to the destruction of British shipping. One assumes that dealing with the laundry was seen as a female occupation. In a similar vein at the end of March the *Sunday Dispatch* noted that English 'Servant girls in country districts have supplied valuable information about German girls in their own job who seemed to spend a good deal of time near important military and Air Force centres'.[3]

On 14 May a memorandum by Sir Nevile Bland, British minister at the Hague, crystallized this concern on the basis of his experience in conquered Holland. It contained the much quoted passage:

> The paltriest kitchen maid, with German connections, not only can be but generally is, a menace to the safety of the country . . . I have not the least doubt that, when the signal is given . . . there will be satellites of the monster all over the country who will at once embark on widespread sabotage and attacks on civilians and the military indiscriminately. We cannot afford to take the risk. *All* Germans and Austrians at least ought to be interned at once.

On 16 May 1940 the Joint Intelligence Committee took the same view, recommending that internment be extended to all enemy aliens, male and female alike, between the ages of 16 and 70.[4] Even then no government order to intern women was made. Instead, the government responded by ordering the internment of all category 'B' male aliens aged between 16 and 60. Not until 27 May, in the panic of the disastrous international situation and the mounting xenophobia at home, was the first official order for the arrest of women issued. A letter was sent to Chief Constables all over the country instructing them to prepare to arrest all German and Austrian category 'B' women between the ages of 16 and 60. Only the invalid and infirm and those in an advanced state of pregnancy were to be excluded. Mothers could take any children under the age of 16 with them – but if the child were dangerously ill the mother was exempt.

Arrests, the letter instructed, should be carried out as a general rule in the early morning. The police were to enlist female assistance in the performance of this delicate task from a policewoman, a police matron, or perhaps a member of the Women's Voluntary Service. The arrested women should be allowed to take one suitcase each and anything else they could carry, such as a rug. In fact they were to be advised to take as much warm clothing as possible. 'Women should be given reasonable time to pack their requirements for the journey', the letter stated. 'They should be informed that it might be two or more days before they reach their destination.' The police were also ordered to search the houses of these women and inform MI5 of 'any information suggesting the existence of plans for assisting the enemy'.[5]

All in all some 3,500 women were interned as a result of this measure, 1,500 from the London area. 'In some instances in London', *The Times* reported on 28 May, 'the police had to wait at houses until the women had dressed. By noon several hundreds had been taken to special centres. The great majority seemed to be under thirty, and most of them appeared to be of the domestic-servant class.' Paltry kitchen maids in fact? This observation was probably correct, as domestic service permits were one of the few means available to enable female refugees to enter Britain. Each of the women, *The Times* continued,

> carried a small, tightly packed suitcase, and some also had paper parcels. Many mothers took their children with them. At one of the London receiving centres there were young nuns, babies only a few weeks old, and boys and girls. One group of young women were fashionably dressed, and each had a fur coat. Several of the older women were in tears. All carried gas masks.[6]

By the end of May 3,200 women had been interned. Almost all of them were taken to the Isle of Man. Contingents of female internees from other places of detention joined them there over the ensuing weeks, including those graded 'A' and interned immediately in Holloway, and also Italian women swept up in the internment machine when Italy entered the war on 10 June.

Before following their progress on the Isle of Man, it is important to examine these half-way houses for the enemy aliens. We get an early glimpse of their inmates from a complaint by a released 'genuine' prisoner published in the *Sunday Dispatch*:

> The alien women, Germans, Austrians, some of them Jewesses, used to march round the exercise yard singing German songs, accompanied by mouth organs. The day I went into Holloway, I was

kept waiting from ten in the morning until nearly ten at night while a
big batch of them had their baggage examined before being allowed
to take it into prison.[7]

The descriptions all the internees give of life in Holloway are very
similar, varying only according to the period when they were taken there
and the circumstances of their arrest. Paula Fichtl, Austrian maid in the
household of Sigmund Freud, like so many others, was shocked by the
sign on her cell door reading 'enemy alien'. She was brought to Holloway
in May. As she left Maresfield Gardens, Hampstead, between two
policemen, Anna Freud half laughingly said: 'You see, Paula, this is what
happens to a Christian girl who helps Jews.' Throughout her life, Paula
remained convinced that this was the reason for her internment. She was
taken away in a Black Maria.[8]

Prison was an unusual and humiliating experience for many of the
German and Austrian refugees whose integrity had never before been
questioned in Britain and who now found themselves behind bars. One
such was Marie Neurath who had escaped to 'freedom' with her fiancé
Otto from occupied Holland. She was taken into custody the moment she
set foot on British soil. After a night at Fulham Institute ('a Dickensian
poorhouse – we had blankets on the floor'), she was taken to Holloway.
She recalls:

At first we were put into little boxes like chicken boxes . . . We were
allowed to use the toilet but had to keep the door open. Then we
were stripped and investigated and given a bath and also a
toothbrush and a nightshirt. Then we were asked what our religion
was and were given the appropriate form of Bible. Then we were
taken to our cells – we each had separate cells . . . We got enough to
eat and were never hungry there. We had exercise in the prison
court, where there was grass and we were told to move about and
not just sit. We walked and talked with each other. Later, they
allowed us to leave our doors open and visit each other. We were
given books and wool. We had to knit stockings for soldiers. We
heard from another wing the Horst Wessel song, so we knew there
were Nazi people there. We met them at church services. There was
a chaplain who came from cell to cell.

Livia Laurent, who was taken to Holloway at the end of July 1940, was
impressed by the diplomatic skills of the chaplain. He had the rare ability
to preach a sermon acceptable to the whole congregation who met
together to attend the church service, whether they were real prisoners,
people interned under 18b or aliens, she reports. She also obtained a

certain amount of comfort from the great camaraderie and friendship prevailing amongst the internees who moved freely between the cells to share meals and troubles. On the other hand, a new hazard at that juncture was the air raids which spread panic amongst those confined helpless in cells.[9]

This horror was shared by 20-year-old Hannah W., locked up in a high cell in Glasgow prison in the late summer of 1940 after being picked up in the depths of the Scottish countryside. She says:

> It was an old, old building . . . I was locked up and all I had was a cot, a wooden table, a chair, a very hard bed with one blanket and a pot. I had my black fur coat with me and I curled up in that, otherwise I would have been very cold. The blanket was not enough. The food was unbelievable. All we had for our last meal at five o'clock was a slice of mildewed white bread. The tea tasted so awful I asked the guard what was wrong with it. He said they put some stuff in it so that the women wouldn't think about men. We exercised in the yard every day but you couldn't see anything from it. I asked for a copy of Sir Walter Scott to take my mind off things. I was there for three weeks before I was taken to the Isle of Man.

Paula Fichtl had never heard of the Isle of Man. She had no idea of her eventual destination when the Holloway contingent was loaded on to a bus and then a train to Liverpool. There they were marched through the streets of the town to the accompaniment of cat-calls and whistles. 'We asked the policeman who was escorting us where we were going', one internee reports. 'The answer was the inevitable: "I don't know; there's a war on"'. The transfer took place at night. After a brief sojourn in a Liverpool sailors' hostel, which Livia Laurent remembers as the worst night of her life, the women were taken aboard a steamer to Douglas, Isle of Man.

The first contingent disembarked after a stormy crossing on 29 May. 'When we arrived on the Isle of Man, the inhabitants stood watching us refugees arrive', said Edith Jacobus. 'And do you know what they did? They spat on us as nasty Germans. We were taken by train and bus together with real Nazis to Port Erin. Amongst us were non-Jewish maids and things who were employed in Britain.' Complaints about the presence and proximity of Nazis was a recurring factor in all internment experiences, and especially perhaps at the women's camp. 'Since the women were mostly in the "A" and "B" classes, the proportion of Nazis and Nazi-sympathisers was "higher" than in the men's camps', Lafitte notes.[10]

The Edwardian seaside resort of Port Erin on the south-west tip of the island was the end of the journey. Together with Port St. Mary, it formed Rushen camp, with Dame Joanna Cruickshank as commandant. The Home Office, which decided all government internment policy, also assumed responsibility for the administration of the women's internment camps. This was distinct from the men's camps where the custody of the internees was arranged by the War Office until the end of July. The women, in the somewhat gentler hands of the Home Office, were spared the pistols, rifles, bayonets, and roll calls which dominated life in the men's camps. The only barbed wire at Rushen cordoned off the two villages. Within it, the internees could wander freely. Even so, Miss Friedler felt a prisoner. 'Once I walked to Douglas', she says. 'I had to get permission'.

Thus it was the Home Office which in May asked proprietors of hotels and boarding houses at Port Erin if they would be prepared to accommodate internees in return for a payment of three shillings per person per day. Here again we find a contrast to War Office policy in respect of the men's camps on the Isle of Man where hotel owners were requested to vacate their premises completely, leaving behind their entire stock in trade: furniture, bedding, linen, cutlery, crockery and utensils. It must be presumed that the male prisoners were considered too dangerous to be in contact with civilian hotel owners. The result was a bizarre reversal of roles. The men were left completely uninstructed to manage their own domestic affairs, such as laundry, cooking, catering; the women had some of the services and supervision of professionals. They also had some slight contact with normal island life and in some cases, friendships, sometimes even warmer relationships, were formed. Marie Neurath, for example, continued to correspond with her landlord long after her release.

The women who arrived at Port Erin on 29 May had first to be distributed amongst the available accommodation. Paula Fichtl says that she was taken to St. Catherine's Church, where a small note was pressed into her hand saying 'Imperial Hotel'. She was left to make her own way there through a square filled with groups of women clutching similar pieces of paper trying to find their respective addresses. Once there, Paula was given a double bedroom on the first floor. At the large Hydro Hotel, one Dr H. found scope for her administrative skills. She herself admits:

> I was a good organizer . . . I said, 'Give me a list of rooms', and I looked at them all. Next day, I was sitting downstairs, allocating rooms. I tried to give the refugees with children the best rooms. I kept the very best two rooms for an emergency. There was a lady in

the hall with two children. She was crying. I rushed down and gave her a beautiful corner room with three windows.

Most of the internees were not so lucky. Some had to share a room with as many as three other women and the majority a double bed with one other – often complete strangers and sometimes alleged Nazis. Groups from the same homeland tried to avoid being separated. 'There were a lot of German girls of my age', says Miss Friedler. 'We were in the same boat and we kept together.' She was billeted in the kosher Breakwater Hotel. 'It was not a very good hotel', adds her young brother Ya'akov, who joined her there later. 'It was on two or three floors.' Marie Neurath found herself with 24 other women, mainly from Holland, in a boarding house, Ailsa Craig, run by a Scottish couple from Glasgow. Sixteen-year-old Ursula Mittwoch, taken from her London school, still in panama hat and uniform, shared a room with a girl from her school but from a different class. She had celebrated her birthday in March and had not yet been graded by a tribunal.

The need for organization did not stop there. Many of the women, including Marie and her pregnant friend Freda, whom she had met on the boat fleeing Holland, had no clothes other than those they stood up in. Clothes collections were made: 'I dressed them from top to bottom', says Dr H. 'I got quite nice dresses', Marie Neurath confirms. On one of the first days, Dr H. says:

> when the whole road had come down to the hotel and all the women wanted to talk to the commandant, I had a brainwave. I said, 'The commandant cannot talk to all of you. Elect a representative from every house. Tell her all your worries and then she will come with all your worries and we will have a meeting.' And we had meetings. I had a very efficient secretary next to me and she had to write down everything. Then we asked the commandant to come to meet us and we read our report out to her in English.

Marie Neurath, elected representative of Ailsa Craig, found one of her major duties was organizing the work routine. Ursula Mittwoch remembers that her hotel was run by the owner and there was a cook. The rest of the work was done by the inmates according to a rota. 'The system ran well', she writes, 'and the place seemed in no danger of sinking into sordid neglect. The food was simple and adequate.' 'It was easy to get cooks', Dr H. stated:

> because our hotel was a big house and you just had to ask. We had a lot of domestics. One of the Austrian girls was head cook. I used to say, 'Who wants to do the cleaning? Who wants to clean the

commandant's room?' The commandant had a maid of her own. Later, everyone received sixpence a day real money for work they did. I had an excellent woman for the laundry; she gave out the laundry and collected it. One had to do the lavatories. I insisted that people took turns. In the morning, I had to make announcements: 'Such and such a thing has been reported missing – has anyone found it?' Then I had a complaints box. It was anonymous. I had to sort this out: stealing, neighbours making too much noise, etc. They also put suggestions in it. I had to see that all the lights were out at nine in the evening.

Hannah W. volunteered to help in the kitchens through sheer boredom. Paula Fichtl's housekeeping abilities quickly gained recognition. She was placed in the kitchen, serving food to her fellow internees and feeding the hotel cats. When payment for the work done by the internees was introduced, Paula deposited her earnings in the bank and was eventually able to buy herself a black fur jacket. The authorities had allowed a branch of the Isle of Man bank to open in Port Erin, she records. The women used to bring their fur coats and jewellery there for safe-keeping. Dr H.'s duties were not solely administrative. Her medical services were almost immediately required. In this respect she had the care of all the 190 adults and 30 children in the Hydro Hotel. She found a lot of anxiety and depression and passed these cases on to a psychologist in the camp. 'We started a hospital in a little house off the main road', she says.

> It was only a surgery with a very nice nurse. We got the equipment. If I needed something medical, I just had to ask. The diseases depended on the places where they were living and the food they were getting. There was a little bit of vitamin deficiency in the small houses. Some of them used nettles as vegetables. The owners of the small houses got an allowance and it was their decision how they used it.

Many of the internees complained about the quality and quantity of the food served. The young boy Ya'akov Friedler remembers that the diet in the Breakwater consisted of two things: either macaroni with tomato sauce or kippers. 'They kept on making these Manx kippers even though it was wartime. We had them sometimes two or three times a day', he says. 'There were a lot of complaints about the food by the women who shouted at the waitresses, themselves internees, and fights nearly broke out. It was a very tense situation. Then they had an idea: let the boys do the waiting. And to us they did not complain. We had to get up a bit earlier in the morning, but we didn't mind.' 'We lived mainly on bread',

Edith Jacobus remembers. 'There was plenty of bread to eat and starchy food, with the result that we got styes in our eyes and eczemas. We never saw butter or eggs; people who had money bought their own.' Women in the camp who had money were not allowed to keep it. They had to deposit it with the commandant, who rationed it out to them at a rate of five shillings a week. If they needed to make a large expenditure, they had to present an invoice. The camp also contained a midwife from the interned German Deaconess order who cared for the pregnant women there and delivered some babies at the Hydro. Ursula Mittwoch recalls 'some Protestant nurses interned with us, and I remember one of them saying that if it saved Britain one spy, the exercise of internment had been worth it'. However, when the time came for Marie's friend Freda to give birth, she was taken to the relative luxury of the hospital in Douglas – but by then it was already October 1940.

An early concern was for the children in the camp because, as we have seen, the women had been allowed to bring children under the age of 16 with them when they were interned. Here again talent among the internees was forthcoming. They included a highly qualified teacher who set up a successful school for the small children. The situation was not as satisfactory for the older ones. Eleven-year-old Ya'akov Friedler remembers little by the way of education. 'There was some sort of school with one or two teachers', he states. 'It was more play than lessons. We had a lot of handicrafts and we dissected seagulls; there were a lot of them around. The United Synagogue sent us a reverend and on my twelfth birthday, he started teaching me for my barmitzvah.'

It was not long before the women in the Rushen camp began to organize their own activities. The main incentive was the boredom complained of by all. 'We had nothing to do', Marie Neurath explains. Paula Fichtl crocheted endless shopping bags which she sent back to Maresfield Gardens. 'The women didn't know what to do with themselves', says Ya'akov Friedler. 'They knitted and made things with sea-shells. They played a lot of bridge and taught us boys to play in order to keep the tension low.' But other women wanted more sophisticated occupations. 'There were two women from Hamburg and one of them had studied economics', Marie recalls:

> She had an idea: 'Let's start a service exchange'. So many people there could do different things; one could cut hair, one could teach languages, some made ornaments from shells on the beach. We organized paper money to buy and sell with. We got support from the official administration: they allowed us real money to buy materials with – wood, leather, etc.

Paula Fichtl attended the language courses opened under this scheme. Gradually her knowledge of English improved and she was able to read the letters sent her by the Freud family and eventually to answer them in English. She hoped that this might make them arrive more quickly. This was a fairly vain hope; the delays in the mail were lengendary. Many of the houses put on dramatic and musical productions. 'We had performances', remembers Ya'akov Friedler.

> They were variety acts in German. The women wrote the songs, mainly about men. One of them went:

> My man is in Onchan [a men's camp on the Isle of Man]
> He is cooking cutlets
> And I am alone in Port Erin
> And when I go to bed I press the pillow instead of him.

> The hotel next door to us was full of real Nazis. The women in it used to greet each other with 'Heil Hitler' in the street. We put on a big show once and those women asked if they could come.

With more concern for intellectual matter, Marie Neurath wrote a musical play.

> Several plays were put on, Schubert's *Drei Madel*, for example. In our house there was a girl who knew Persian and Persian literature. She told me exactly the story of *Turandot* in every detail. She gave me the backbone. She was also most interested in making the costumes, and she selected beautiful gramophone records for the music. We learned something about play-acting, and it gave us great pleasure. We chose the heroine because she was the only girl with a beautiful evening dress with her. We did it in our house, then in the great hotel.

That specific production was an explicit plea for a mixed camp where the women and their menfolk could live together.

Most evidence we have collected comes from Port Erin, where the majority of female internees were housed: approximately 3,000 as compared with 1,000 at Port St. Mary, according to Livia Laurent. Notwithstanding the discrepancy in numbers, Port St. Mary at its peak contained groups of teachers and intellectuals, had a good school, excellent lectures, a warm club room, and was able to stage a production of *Everyman*, she records.

Not everyone engaged in productive or creative activity. It was a good summer and, as long as they observed the dusk to dawn curfew, the women had complete freedom to wander through the two villages, stroll along the promenade or swim in the sea. As they had not thought to include swimming costumes amongst the necessities in their small suitcases, Paula Fichtl remembers that some bathed in their underclothes. The local inhabitants found this quite shocking, she says, and held their hands up in horror, exclaiming at 'these immoral Europeans!'. Hannah W. recalls nearly drowning on a day when the sea was very rough and the waves 'were as big as horses'. Another internee says: 'In the beginning, there was a golf course. My parents sent us our golf clubs and we played golf every day.'

It may have been reports of such goings on that caused Sir Annesley Somerville, MP for Windsor, to ask the Home Secretary on 6 June 1940 whether he considered it right that 'these persons should be kept in luxurious idleness at this time . . . and is he also aware that there is a very great deal of feeling on this matter in the country . . .?' or Sir J. Wardlaw-Milne, MP for Kidderminster, Worcestershire, to draw his attention to

> considerable public resentment at the fact that the alien women interned in the Isle of Man were fully provided for by the government in hotels and boarding houses at a payment of twenty-one shillings a week and are to be provided with swimming baths, tennis courts and golf links, while the wife of a private soldier in the army gets an allowance of seventeen shillings a week plus seven shillings deducted from her husband's pay?

Sir John Anderson replied that

> The place chosen for their internment was selected . . . not because of its amenities, but because it is most suitable for purposes of security. Payment must be made by the government to those persons whose premises are being used for the internment of these women and for the provision of food and the rates fixed are the minimum required for these purposes.[11]

Reports of the high life at Rushen camp appeared in the British press, causing Anna Freud to write to Paula expressing her pleasure that living conditions were so good, telling her to enjoy her holiday and offering to send her a bathing costume. Instead Paula opted for knitting materials to make presents for the Freud family.[12] But all was not rosy in Rushen. In the opinion of François Lafitte, 'Apart from the usual complaints about communications and information, the main difficulties in the women's camps seem to be due to lack of organization, understaffing and the lack of sympathy and understanding shown by the commandant'.[13]

Impressions of Dame Joanna Cruickshank vary considerably. She had served as a nursing sister with officer rank during the First World War and by 1938 had risen to the rank of matron-in-charge of the British Red Cross Society. She earned the reputation of being a harsh disciplinarian who applied the rules rigorously. Hannah W. liked her. 'Maybe she seemed very cool on the outside. She asked me to go to a Quaker meeting.' 'She was exactly dressed like my own headmistress', says Miss Friedler. 'She had this white collar right up to her neck. I went to her every day and cried because I had heard that my two younger brothers had arrived in England. We were the only ones left and I wanted to have them at the camp with me.' In the event, as we have seen, Ya'akov Friedler and his brother were brought to Rushen. At one point it would appear that some inmates became so incensed by Dame Joanna's stringent routine that they wrote letters to the mainland complaining. It was assumed that these eventually reached the Home Office because their authors were summoned to the commandant's presence and accused of 'betraying' her. 'I doubt whether she had any idea of the background of her charges', writes Ursula Mittwoch, 'any more than we had any understanding of the workings of the British Establishment'. Miss Friedler is voicing approximately the same sentiment when she says 'England didn't have much feeling for anything. It couldn't understand how we were feeling.' Dame Joanna left the camp in May 1941 to be replaced by Mr Cuthbert, who had been the secretary of the Bow Street tribunal which, incidentally, had interned Livia Laurent.

There were endless problems involving personal relationships. There were the inevitable conflicts between Nazis and non-Nazis. 'At our house, Marie Neurath tells, 'one table was more or less all Nazis who made antisemitic remarks. One day they were in the room and everyone was talking at the same time and they said, "Mein Gott, we are in a Judenschule!". They had been domestics and had had the choice of whether to stay in England or to go back to Germany.'

In essence, however, conflict was not just based on Nazis against anti-Nazis. 'If people hadn't bickered so much', Freda says, 'it would have been fantastic. People complained and fought. Every day there were about twenty people fighting. There were fights, verbal and physical, between the women all the time, about nothing or about house-duties – because we all had to do house-duties every day, like waiting at table.' 'Women together are always terrible', one internee concludes. 'There was always jealousy; it was quite a natural phenomenon.'

These were, of course, women who were separated from their menfolk. The children in the camp represented an outlet for unsatisfied emotions. 'Everyone in the house was a mother to us', Ya'akov Friedler remembers. 'They lavished all their affection on us boys, sometimes embarrassingly so.' Freda recalls that:

No man was safe on the island. In our hotel there was an old man of seventy-five; he was the owner of the hotel. He was watched over by his daughter. When she went off one day the women rushed in to rape him. The women went on the fishing boats to get men. The men there, the native inhabitants, had the time of their lives. The women fought over men like hyenas.

Conversely, Marie Neurath discreetly states, 'The whole situation created a rather Lesbian atmosphere'. Miss Friedler remembers that 'One of the girls from the Nazi house next door used to come over and talk to our girls. I think she was a Lesbian. She almost hypnotized us with her eyes.' But this was nothing in comparison with the very real agonies of separation from their loved ones, intensified frequently by complete ignorance of their whereabouts. Freda explains:

> We didn't know where our men were. We had such a tough old commandant. When we asked about them she said, 'There's a war on. Our soldiers' wives don't know where their men are, why should you?' Then, of course, there were the rumours: the men had gone, the men had been deported, the men had to go into the army. I was expecting a child. I was frantic.

Marie Neurath puts it more into perspective: 'Separation from family of course often meant suffering. But how can one compare this to the humiliation, torture, slave work, killing, in the concentration camps. Even in prison, I felt safe, escaped from the Gestapo.'

Communication with the outside world was minimal in the early days, heightening anxiety. For the first few weeks, no letters arrived at the women's camps at the Isle of Man. After a time, Marie says, 'blackboards were set up on which the names were written of those for whom letters had arrived. There was at first no postal connection from camp to camp' – even between the women's camps and the men's camps that had been set up in other locations on the same island. Notwithstanding, Ursula Mittwoch remembers receiving at least two packets of sweets from her form mistress at her old school and letters from some of her classmates.

There was also a great shortage of news of the progress of the war, giving rise to further worries. Ya'akov Friedler remembers:

> There was only one radio in our house . . . and that was in the landlady's room. She was an old spinster. I was the official reporter there. I used to stand outside her room and listen to the news and report back to the women. I also used to go to the local newsagent's and read the paper in the shop – I couldn't afford to buy one. It was always a day late, but that didn't matter; it was the only one we had.

Ursula Mittwoch does not recall reading a newspaper or listening to the radio while on the Isle of Man. 'News seemed to travel by rumour', she says.

10 July 1940 marked the turning point in government internment policy. On that day, despite the first of the series of air attacks by Germany on the British Isles which heralded the Battle of Britain, a major debate on internment policy took place in the House of Commons during which strong views on the evils of the scheme emerged. The swing in public attitude which then became apparent was to some extent influenced by the sinking, with considerable loss of life, of the ship *The Arandora Star*, carrying male internees to Canada. To Dr H. fell the unhappy task of telling internees that their husbands had been drowned. One such was the widow of Karl Olbrisch, former Reichstag deputy.

Deportation of male internees continued notwithstanding. On 9 July Dame Joanna Cruickshank informed the women that if their husbands elected to go to Australia, they and their children would shortly follow. At the end of the month a formal meeting between interned husbands and wives was arranged at the Balaqueeney hotel, Port St Mary, to decide if they wished to take advantage of this offer. For the couples, it was a highly emotional occasion. Many had not seen one another for several months. 'They marched in in alphabetical order', says Marie Neurath. 'He came in beaming with delight. We spent a wonderful afternoon on the beach. The object of the meeting was to decide whether we would go overseas. We quickly decided "no". The As, Bs, Cs and Ds had a long talk from Joanna Cruickshank about why they should go. We, the Ns, were spared.' In the event, their decision was irrelevant; as has been mentioned, no women were deported overseas, but Port Erin thereafter was known to the men as Port Erinnerung – Port Remembrance.

At a later stage meetings were put on a regular basis. 'The married women were finally allowed to meet their husbands', says Edith Jacobus. 'We were taken by train to Onchan where there was a big dance-hall. We were watched like prisoners by soldiers with rifles.' The unmarried men looking on at these events, found them moving and funny: 'We had access to a meadow', says one male internee, 'and they used to go and pick these incredible bunches of flowers to take to their wives. They picked dandelions and things.' The boy Ya'akov Friedler also noted the humour behind the tragedy at the women's camp: 'You should have seen the women before the meetings. They were making dresses, putting up hems, taking down hems, turning dresses into skirts. The men would have preferred them without dresses!' The women began making feverish preparations days before, Livia Laurent wrote, having their hair done and putting it in curlers. Dame Joanna Cruickshank did her best to dampen the excitement. On the day that the couples were to meet, she posted up a notice forbidding the women to wear trousers.

The meetings were quickly extended to cover blood and other relationships. 'The married men came back with photographs and handed them round. Then the young man would suddenly discover that he had an "aunt". The number of people who went on arranged visits grew and grew . . .', a male internee recalls. 'Later', Marie Neurath says, 'engaged people were allowed to meet and then everyone was engaged.' The meetings first took place at Collinson's cafe in Port Erin. 'An architectural nightmare, a mixture of early Asiatic, late Gothic and Ealing Broadway', according to Livia Laurent, it was also a major social and educational centre. Here it was that adult education classes were held, lectures given, handicraft and gymnastics, elocution and languages taught. 'In the afternoon', Laurent wrote, 'you could have coffee there and dance.' The venue for the monthly meetings was again transferred, this time to Derby castle, Onchan, where the couples could spend some two hours together, almost unsupervised.

Following the July debate, a move was made to release the interned children of 'C' grade parents who had not been interned themselves. Ursula Mittwoch fell into this category. She left the Isle of Man some nine weeks after she had arrived. 'In view of the fact that refugees were obviously not the country's first priority', she writes, 'it didn't seem too bad.'

Also in the light of the July debate, on 31 July the government issued a White Paper announcing that the Secretary of State was prepared to consider the question of releasing from internment 'C' grade Germans and Austrians falling within one of 18 categories. This was hardly relevant to the women most of whom were, as we have said, rated 'B'. For the women, the real hope came on 22 August when the Asquith Committee (set up by Sir John Anderson in July to help him deal with the enemy alien question) recommended that the 'B's should be given the opportunity to apply for release from internment if they were eligible under any of the categories in the White Paper. Their cases would then be referred to a tribunal which would decide which grade they should be given; if 'C' they would, security considerations permitting, be released. The Committee also recommended that when a category 'C' male alien was released, special consideration should be given to the question of releasing his wife.

Marie and Otto Neurath appeared before such a tribunal.

> They took our promise of marriage very seriously. When we had a
> tribunal at Douglas we were asked together, not only at the same

day but at the same meeting. The nice thing was that they even tested me about this promise. What would I do if Dr Neurath went to America? I would go to America. What would I do if Dr Neurath stayed in England? I would stay. When had I been in Germany for the last time? 1932. We both got 'C'.

They were released on 8 February 1941. Freda and her husband Kurt were put into the same category. Kurt recalled:

I was called to a tribunal and asked, 'Why did you leave Holland when Hitler came?' I told them my views. They agreed. There were half a dozen people there. 'What about Freda?' they asked, because they thought she was a Christian. There was no 'J' in her passport and she does not look Jewish. But we convinced them. They gave us 'C' then. Hurray! We were declared 'friendly aliens'.

Miss Friedler went to her tribunal. 'As automatically as she had been designed "Enemy" in the spy-scare days of 1940, she was now declared "Friendly"', her brother, Ya'akov Friedler writes.[14] The family returned to England to make a new life. Paula Fichtl was not so fortunate. She was summoned to appear before the tribunal in December 1940. She could not go because she was looking after children sick with scarlet fever and was therefore in quarantine. Paula left Port Erin in spring 1941.

Hannah W.'s experience was disastrous.

The tribunal was a real farce. They never gave you a chance. They asked me some questions and I could see they didn't believe me. I found out afterwards that my employers had told the police that I was a Nazi. I was given 'A'. Hannah was released after one and a half years internment. 'It was a waste of my young life', she says, 'I really resented that.'

September 1940 marked another landmark: children left behind on the mainland when their mothers were interned were brought to Port Erin. Mothers wept with delight, recorded the *News Chronicle*, as youngsters flung themselves into their arms. Freda too had her child. Her daughter was born in Douglas in what her husband, Kurt, describes as 'the finest nursing home you have ever seen', where she was looked after wonderfully. Kurt was allowed to come over from Onchan to visit her, bearing chocolates and escorted by a soldier with a rifle. When, after a fortnight, she was sent back to her hotel, her fellow residents showered her with gifts. 'Each one of the seventy women', she relates, 'had knitted or bought something, and they had also collected money to buy a little fire for my room.'

There were not only births in the internment camps, but also a wedding, as Miss Friedler recalls.

> Of course, it was by proxy as the bridegroom was not allowed to come over from the mainland. The bride, Lily, was a very beautiful, talented and religious girl from Breslau in our house. She was very small and slim. She was very excited. We had a party for the wedding and Lily wore a white veil made from net or something.

Releases took place at a slow but steady rate. Those remaining at Rushen in December 1940 celebrated a happy Christmas. 'We at the Hydro had good food', says Dr H., 'and everybody received a little present, which the commandant allowed me to buy at Douglas with another internee. We did our shopping, as far as I can remember, at Woolworth's and returned with a large sack of small presents.' Livia Laurent remembers a Christmas play at Port St Mary which endeavoured, not over-successfully, to combine Chanukah and Christmas celebrations. The first part was taken from the Old Testament; the second was based on the Nativity.

The idea of a mixed camp for couples held apart on the Isle of Man was already mooted during the debate on 10 July. In the improved atmosphere and the ensuing releases which took place at a steady but slow rate (facilitated to some extent by the recruiting activities of a representative of the ATS at Rushen), agitation for such a camp gathered strength. On 21 January 1941 Osbert Peake, Under-Secretary at the Home Office, gave the first practical details of a scheme for the mixed camp. Enquiries he had been conducting showed that the best means of carrying out the project was to assign married couples accommodation in one of the two villages used for the women's camp. The committee reviewing the cases of female internees had made such good progress, and so many women had in consequence been released, that it should soon be possible to house the remaining women in one village and utilize the other for husbands and wives whose release could not be authorized.[15] Livia Laurent recalls having to leave her billet in Port St Mary and move to Port Erin as part of the preliminary measures for the establishment of the mixed camp. It finally opened in the Balaqueeney Hotel in April 1941. 'It was perfection', one internee says. 'I had no worries: I had my husband; the food was very good. It was an absolute holiday, paid for by His Majesty's Government'. Freda remembers that:

> We each had a room in this big hotel. We earned 7s. 6d. a week for washing up 760 dishes after meals. There were about four or five hundred people in the hotel. One side of the dining-room was

kosher and one side liberal. Naturally, there were problems which had to be solved amicably in such a mixed assembly, thrown together by such tragic events. And, of course, they were heated at times. They accused us of using their cloths and mixing up their things. There were separate washing-up arrangements for the kosher. One of our people took over the cooking.

There were several professional theatre people there, producers and so on. We produced a revue, plays, Shakespeare. I took part in the theatrical productions. I was a photographer in the revue. It was most beautifully done and there were some lovely tunes. Everything was composed and written there. It was all in German. There was a lot of cultural life going on. We really got going with the classes.

We made string bags; the camp commandant sold them. You got about sixpence a dozen. We were allowed to go to the cinema and to go shopping, but we were always accompanied by a guard. We could use the beach and we went swimming in the summer – in fact practically all the year round. Every morning we had gym from seven to eight o'clock – a woman took that – and after it we went swimming. We were all very fit.

When the news was on every night, everyone was shouting 'Quiet! Quiet!'. We heard the news about deportations from Holland and Germany. We had Red Cross letters from Holland and they received one or two letters from us. There was tension all the time: 'Will my case come up for release?' We felt we were wasting time there. We wanted to make a start. We would have enjoyed it more if it had not been for this feeling. And also not knowing what was happening in Holland.

Freda and Kurt left the Isle of Man in August 1942. By that time, fewer than 5,000 enemy aliens of either sex remained on the Isle of Man. Of these, according to the Board of Deputies of British Jews, only 300 to 400 were refugees from Nazi oppression.

Ostensibly, therefore, the incident was over, some two-and-a-quarter years after it had begun. But the war was still on in summer 1942 and Nazi Germany far from defeated. Did the women no longer constitute a threat? Had they, in fact, ever been considered a threat? Or had they been imprisoned for their own safety in the face of the public xenophobia created by the invasion scare in May 1940? In which case, were not the 'C' grade women left at large equally at risk? Was the internment of women the result of government xenophobia, even anti-Semitism, as some suggest, or was it purely a panic measure taken at a time of immeasurable danger to the state? There is no hard and fast, no sensible explanation of why some 4,000 women, many of whom had fled the Nazi terror, were treated as suspect and lost a period of their lives behind barbed wire.

NOTES

1. François Lafitte, *The Internment of Aliens* (Penguin Special, Harmondsworth, 1940; repr. Libris, London 1988), p.63.
2. Ibid.
3. *Sunday Dispatch*, 31 March 1940.
4. PRO FO 371/25189.
5. PRO FO 371/25244. Quoted in Peter and Leni Gilman, *'Collar the Lot': How Britain Interned and Expelled Its Wartime Refugees* (London/Melbourne, 1980), p.133.
6. *The Times*, 28 May 1940.
7. *Sunday Dispatch*, 1 Jan. 1940.
8. Detlef Berthelsen, *Alltag bei Familie Freud: Die Erinnerungen der Paula Fichtl*, (Munich, 1987), pp.96–8.
9. Livia Laurent, *A Tale of Internment* (London, 1942).
10. Lafitte, op. cit., p.117.
11. *Hansard* (Commons), Vol.31, cols.981 and 1005, 6 June 1940.
12. Berthelsen, op. cit., p.101.
13. Lafitte, op. cit., p.117.
14. Bertha Leverton and Shmuel Lowensohn (eds.), *I Came Alone: The Story of the Kindertransports* (Lewes, Sussex, 1990), p.98.
15. *Hansard* (Commons), Vol.36, col.368, 21 Jan. 1941.

The Impact of the Second World War on the British Italian Community

TERRI COLPI

The impact of the Second World War on the British Italian Community was devastating. Despite generations of settlement, increasing economic prosperity and social acceptability, Italy's declaration of war on the Allies, on 10 June 1940, led to a night of widespread anti-Italian rioting. No prior security assessment had been undertaken and across-the-board internment of adult male British Italians followed. The arrests and subsequent processing were marked by chaotic muddle with tragic loss of life on The Arandora Star. *The war and internment destroyed the family and business structure of the Community; reconstruction and the regaining of respectability within British society took decades after the war.*

Introduction

The long and diversified history of the Italian Community in Great Britain has, in recent years, been a topic of much research and study. The student of ethnic minorites in Britain can now read and learn much of the Italian presence past and present.[1] Naturally, an immigrant group with well over a century's settlement provides many interesting and individualistic avenues for study. Increasingly, however, one area, more than any other, is generating interest at all levels: the experience of British Italians during the Second World War. As we confront a succession of Second World War fiftieth year anniversaries, this interest not only from within the British Italian Community itself, but from scholars of several disciplines, from the media and press – both in Britain and in Italy – and from the general population of both countries, on the effects of the war on Italians resident in Britain, has reached a high point. It is causing light to be shed on a facet of Second World War history which, for too long, has remained largely unresearched and undocumented, undiscussed and unknown.

This article offers the opportunity to discuss the impact of the war on

---

The material presented at the 1990 'Internment Remembered Conference' and found in this article formed the basis for the coverage of the Second World War in *The Italian Factor* (Mainstream, 1991).

the Italian Community. The material and historical interpretation is presented from an insider's perspective, the ideological starting point being the sentiment expressed by Lafitte in his study of internment, 'I cannot claim to be objective as well as impartial'. As a writer and commentator on the British Italian Community, I hope to maintain objectivity but as a person who grew up within the Scottish Italian Community, I cannot profess to remain impartial. To say that the effect of the Second World War on the Italians in Britain was devastating would not be an overstatement. The events and consequences of the war, particularly the loss of life with the sinking of *The Arandora Star*, affected the psyche and identity of the 'old' Italian Community[2] in a deep and fundamental way. In global terms, because of the war, the history of the Italian Community in Britain is unique and has no parallel.

Before turning to this main focus of the chapter, a few brief comments on the history and 1930s contemporary situation are necessary to set the scene *ante-bellum*.

I. Pre-War

Although skilled Italian craftsmen had been present in British cities from the late eighteenth century, it was not until the early middle of the nineteenth century that 'poor' Italian immigrants began to arrive and settle in any significant numbers, mainly in London. With the establishment in Clerkenwell of the first British Italian ghetto, the foundations of the Italian Community as we know it today were laid and the strong connection with catering developed.

By the 1880s, Italian street vendors of food had become an accepted facet of urban life and by the First World War Italian families had spread throughout the entire country, setting up their little businesses selling basic food, drinks and confectionary. Apart from in the large cities, particularly London, Manchester, Liverpool and Glasgow, where 'colonies', or residential clusters, of Italians were still identifiable even in the 1920s and 1930s, the inevitable business competition between Italians required a continual geographic dispersal. Many small towns in the north of England, in Scotland and Wales hosted therefore only a few Italian families. However, almost without exception, these families, settled and established often for more than a generation at the outbreak of the Second World War, were well integrated into local society. They were well-respected and even important members of their local communities. In Britain, they had identified and secured an economic niche and prospered accordingly through hard work and entrepreneurial drive. The 1920s and 1930s were something of a 'golden era' for the Italians in Britain.

Although the Italians were well 'integrated' into British society there was little 'assimilation'. Italians continued to live in a traditional family-centred way, with birth, death and marriage ceremonies, conducted through the church, forming the corner-stones of life. Italian or Italian dialect was spoken at home and the food consumed Italian in style. Where a family was in business all members were involved and this activity further united them as a socio-economic unit. Although the immigrants and their offspring were well-settled they preserved and cherished a love of, and nostalgia for, Italy. Many hoped to return, and indeed succeeded in returning, 'home' after years of work in Britain. People kept in touch with their family and village in Italy. For the majority, when they spoke and thought of Italy, reference was to their place of origin and birth: few knew much of Italy beyond their native village.

The rise of Fascism in Italy in the 1920s and especially 1930s, however, touched upon the lives of the expatriate emigrant Communities in an unprecedented way, bringing them into contact, ideologically at least, with a larger Italy. One of the aims of Fascism was to reunite into a brotherhood the many sons of Italy living abroad under the Italian flag. The emigrants were therefore increasingly considered as part of an expanded Italy in a moral, political and economic sense. The Fascist movement began to politicize emigration and the existence of many Italians abroad, seeking to play on, and exploit the nostalgia and simple patriotism of the expatriates. In the words of Mack Smith [*1959: 399*] 'Italians abroad were wheedled, at great cost to the Exchequer, into becoming Mussolini's greatest fans and propagandists'.

Gradually, the Italian Community in Britain embraced Fascism in a whole-hearted manner. The basic principle of Fascism – *Onore, Famiglia e Patria* (Honour, Family and Fatherland) – was, after all, the very principle by which most lived their lives anyway. It was therefore a slogan and sentiment with which they could readily identify. British Italians who lived through this period explain that Fascism to them was a form of patriotism. They were not political and their involvement with the party was primarily due to an attachment to their country and their involvement in the Italian Community.

Fascism became strongest and most prolific in the larger Italian Communities where it was able to reinforce itself by association amongst large numbers of Italians. Membership of the *Fasci*, Fascist clubs, which were established in the cities, consisted of two groups of people: the activists within their Communities – organizers and leaders – who were in the minority; and the vast majority who were members taking advantage of all the social and cultural activities that the *Fasci* offered. In general terms, the Italians saw only the benefits of Fascism – the clubs, the schools which taught Italian and the free holidays to Italy for children. People who were not actually *tesserati*, or members, also frequented the club houses and made use of the facilities. Also, it must be appreciated that it became increasingly difficult, in a bureaucratic sense, to conduct one's affairs in Italy, which were administered through the Italian Consulates, if one was not a member of the Fascist movement. By the late 1930s the Italians in Britain were, for the most part, at least nominal members and supporters of Fascism.

The vast majority of these people were harmless and simple patriots feeling a sense of pride in and belonging to their country which, it now seemed, valued highly their commitment and participation. This is not to say, however, that there were not some hard-core supporters of Mussolini within the ranks of the British Italian Community, indeed a number had gone off to fight for Italy in the Abyssinian War of 1935–36. There were, however, also a handful of notable anti-Fascists. Against this backdrop, the definition of a 'professing Fascist' was to prove subsequently a challenging one for the British government.

II. Build-Up to War

Between 1939 and 1940 there had been much speculation by the British government concerning the fate of the Italian Community should Mussolini declare allegiance to the enemy. No clear plan, however, emerged from the many proposals discussed and the tide of public and government opinion for blanket internment grew as events in Europe turned against the allies.

Throughout 1939 and early 1940 the German and Austrian Jewish refugees, who were flooding into Britain in an attempt to escape Hitler's Nazism, were 'classified' by tribunals into 'A', 'B' or 'C' categories depending on the perceived level of threat to security, with 'A' being the most 'dangerous' group. Administratively, the point of entry provided a relatively straightforward opportunity for the British authorities to monitor and assess the refugees. This was not possible with the Italians, many of whom had been settled in Britain since the nineteenth century. And indeed, before June 1940 and the declaration of war by Italy, no screening process had been inaugurated for the Italians. No attempt had been made to separate the 'professing Fascists' from the anti-Fascists and, more importantly, from the innocuous or non-Fascists, who, it is suggested, were in the majority.

Despite the fact that the authorities took no action to assess the Italian population resident in Britain, there was nevertheless concern about spies and fifth columnists. It was feared Italy would attempt to use the

Fascist organization for attacks on key individuals and key points in this country. MI5 was given the task of compiling a list of 'known suspects' described as 'desperate' and 'dangerous characters' who would not hesitate to commit acts of sabotage and who were to be arrested immediately if Italy declared war. It is interesting to speculate how such a list, earmarking 1,500 'desperate' Italians, was drawn up, especially in the absence of any interviews or questioning of individuals.

In 1933 a census of all Italians resident in Britain had been carried out by the Italian government, administered through its Consulates in London, Glasgow, Liverpool and Cardiff. Could MI5 have gained access to this census, which included one question asking if respondents held *Fascio* membership? A second source of information on Italians almost certainly utilized would have been the *Guida Generale degli Italiani in Gran Bretagna*, first published in 1933, and then, in a more extended volume, in 1939. This directory listed the majority of Italian households and businesses in Britain, with accurate names and addresses. Since the guide was compiled and published through the Fascist Party, it can be assumed that the British authorities equated inclusion with Fascist involvement. Finally, MI5 most certainly procured the membership lists of the various *Fasci*. To MI5, *Fasci* membership became synonymous with 'professing Fascism' and being 'dangerous'. It would later, after tragic consequences, become apparent to the Home Office and Foreign Office alike that the MI5 list of 1,500 names was fundamentlly flawed and included not only many ordinary Italians but also several well-known anti-Fascists.

In Cabinet meetings throughout May 1940, the discussion of internment, not only of Italians but also of the refugee Jews, continued. By this time only category 'A' of the German and Austrian Jews had been interned and debate centred around the Italians and categories 'B' and 'C' of the refugees. As far as the Italians were concerned, Cabinet decided to approve a scheme involving the immediate internment of all Italians on the MI5 list as soon as Italy declared war, followed by the selective internment of all males between 17 and 60 years of age who had been resident in Britain for less than 20 years.

As the government debated these issues, and the different ministries, Home Office, Foreign Office and War Office, tried to agree briefs and responsibilities, life in the Italian Community continued under increasing stress. With the outbreak of war in 1939, many entire families (mostly more recent arrivals, and who were therefore less settled), returned to Italy. The period between autumn 1939 and summer 1940 was a worrying time. It was generally sensed that Italy would not remain neutral but there was hope, until the last moment that she would, as in the First World War, become an ally of Britain. The Italian Community dreaded war, but its consequences and effects were more devastating and longer lasting than envisaged. The immediate consequences of Mussolini's declaration of war against the allies on 10 June 1940 were, for the Italians resident in Britain, anti-Italian rioting and arrest.

III. Anti-Italian Riots

As darkness fell on the evening of 10 June, mounting xenophobia among large elements of the British population reached fever pitch. A night of terror lay ahead for the Italian Community. Ransacking mobs attacked Italian property, mainly businesses, from Soho in London to Stonehaven in the north-east of Scotland. The fervour of hatred unleashed astonished most Italians and also many British people. Italian families in small towns who considered themselves well integrated into the local society, and who had been there for decades, often generations, could not comprehend this violent reaction against them. Certainly in many cases the mobs were comprised of the local hooligan element, but this was not always the case. Across the country, and most especially in Scotland, there was a night of smashing, burning and looting.

A survey of the press, both local and national, for 11 and 12 June 1940 revealed the extent and location of these riots. On 11 June *The Times*, in an article headed 'Anti-Italian Demonstrations', mentioned trouble in Soho, Liverpool, Cardiff, Belfast and considerable damage in Glasgow and Edinburgh. According to *The Times*, Edinburgh appeared to have been the most affected city and the *Edinburgh Evening News* (11 June 1940) reported these scenes in detail. An angry crowd of over a thousand people congregated in Leith Street and apparently, by the end of a night of smashing and looting, this main thoroughfare looked as if a series of heavy bombs had fallen. *The Glasgow Herald* (11 June 1940) described similar scenes which occurred from dusk onwards, especially in the Govan, Tradeston and Maryhill areas of the city. Again, ransacking mobs of several hundred people worked along the main routes systematically storming all the Italian premises. On the Clyde coast, in Port Glasgow, Greenock and Gourock, the scale of violence and damage paralleled the level reached in Edinburgh. The *Greenock Telegraph* (11 June 1940) reported unprecedented scenes of violence with which the police had difficulty in coping. All 17 of the Italian shops in the 'Port' were badly damaged and in one or two cases only the bare walls were left intact.

In the newspapers for 12 June 1940, the Italians continued to be headline news. However, the reports focused that day on the arrest of Italian men for internment. Only in the *Greenock Telegraph* is evidence found of a second night of serious rioting against the Italians, especially in Gourock. However, this was no spontaneous gathering – its intent was clear. Apparently the police were able to keep this mob 'on the move' but nevertheless the image of such a large crowd, presumably making a considerable noise chanting anti-Italian slogans, moving through the streets of this small coastal town was undoubteldy terrifying for the town's long-standing resident Italians. Indeed, as we shall see, the majority of the men had been removed by 11 June, only women were left at home. Since their shops had been destroyed on the night of 10 June and their husbands and sons already removed, it is difficult indeed not to sympathize with those women huddled behind closed doors. Fortunately, the ensuing violence did, however, seem to be focused against property rather than individuals. Extreme physical violence against persons rather than property was rare, although not unknown.

Of course one of the difficulties in maintaining law and order on the night of 10 June 1940 was that the police had been asked at exactly this time to conduct the arrest of Italian males. Eloquently put by Cesarani: 'The ingredients of popular xenophobia, racism, political cynicism and press hysteria had together culminated in Churchill's edict to "Collar the Lot!"'[3]

IV. Round-Up

The arrest of Italian males began a long catalogue of muddle and confusion. Differences, anomalies and idiosyncrasies abounded in the methods used, and the interpretation given to the hastily compiled instructions. Full explanation of the discretionary elements which inevitably crept into procedures at this and every subsequent stage in the episode of internment will require access to sensitive government files held closed for 75 years after the events involved.

Police were instructed to arrest the 'dangerous characters' on the MI5 list, which we must assume had reached all the provincial Chief Constables, and all male 'known Italians' with less than 20 years' residence in the age group 17 to 60. However, many men were arrested who should not have been and vice versa. Once in custody it proved enormously difficult for anti-Fascists, British subjects, sympathizers, innocuous Fascists, and men over 60 years of age alike to obtain release. Hundreds of entirely innocent civilians would soon perish as a result.

The first raids were made on the *Fasci* in London, Glasgow and Edinburgh at 6.00 p.m. on 10 June. Any Italians present were automatically arrested; in London 80 men had been arrested in this way within the first two hours of Mussolini's declaration. The main arrests followed different patterns across the country; arrests took place during darkness in Scotland and provincial England, but in London the majority were arrested between dawn and 8.00 a.m. on 11 June. Outside London the 'round-up' was a very much more detailed and thorough operation. This was particularly true for small towns with only a few Italian families where local police knew them and where to find them. Indeed, it appears that in the provinces all those of Italian origin were 'collared' regardless of period of residence, political affiliations or whether they were still Italian citizens.

In the cities, particularly London, from the point of view of the British authorities, the operation was much more difficult. Press articles for 10, 11 and 12 June confirm this and the words 'comb-out' of Italians appear more than once with reference to the Italian colonies of Soho and Clerkenwell. Police were not simply picking up 'known Italians' but were in addition looking for the 'dangerous characters' on the MI5 list, over half of whom lived in London. As there were just under 10,000 Italians in London according to the 1931 census, the difficulty of such a scale of operation is obvious. Many slipped through the net, possibly because the authorities, unable to cope with the large numbers, were therefore more lenient. Protestations about sons in the British Army and on length of residence seemed to hold more sway with the police.

The procedure for the arrests is something which still rankles with many 'old' Italians today. Often the process was amicable enough with the police politely explaining their orders and asking the Italians quickly and quietly to accompany them to the local police station. In other cases, however, in the middle of the night and witnessed by the entire family which had naturally been aroused, fairly unpleasant scenes occurred with police aggressively searching for 'enemy propaganda' and evidence. This sort of behaviour was especially difficult for the Italians to understand where the arresting officers were local bobbies, well-known men, who for years had frequented shops and cafés on a daily basis when on their beat. Not all arrests were conducted in an unpleasant way – and assuredly the circumstances would vary according to the reaction of the Italians involved. Certainly, in the vast majority of cases the Italians went quietly and with no trouble.

The grief and fear of wives and especially children who watched their fathers, elder brothers and uncles being taken away should not be underestimated. Owing to the black-out, sometimes the whole ghastly affair was conducted in darkness, adding to the drama of the situation. For children who were old enough to remember that night, and their fear and confusion for their fathers and themselves, the effect was traumatic. The next morning, the children faced agonizing taunting at school.

'Your father's been taken to a concentration camp', and so on. Mothers tried to explain what they imagined the differences would be between internment and concentration camps. Children, particularly boys, were regularly beaten at school and picked upon as 'Tally Bastards', 'Wops' and 'Ay-ties'. It was in this way a generation of British Italians learned it was not good to be Italian and how it was better to 'assimilate' or de-Italianize themselves.

Many adult British-born second generation or naturalized British members of the Italian Community who had escaped internment found that they too were considered the 'enemy' and treated as such by local populations. They too tried to de-Italianize themselves in order to survive – this was especially necessary for those in business. Italian restaurants and shops in Soho put up notices declaring themselves to be British. One well known restaurant put up a sign declaring itself Swiss; others stressed that they had sons in the British forces. A similar plea for peace was being made nationwide with shopkeepers flying Union Jacks.

There were, however, many other British-born Italian men who were determined to be interned with their fathers and to remain united with their roots and their Community. These young men were often *Fascio* members and were classified under defence regulation 18(b). As well as the difficulties of internment which followed, the family-based structure of the Community was severely tested. There were numerous cases where fathers were interned and sons served in the British forces. Brothers too were often split with older brothers being interned while younger brothers, born in Britain, served in either the armed forces or the non-active '270 Alien' or 'Pioneer Corps'. The anti-Italian riots, the arrests, internment and the day-to-day struggle to survive during the war, left an indelible mark on the minds and psyche of the 'old' British Italian Community.

V. Internment

(i) The Initial Phase

The men who were arrested on 10 June usually spent the first few nights at a local police station with subsequent transferral to 'collecting points' throughout the country. It was soon obvious to the authorities that they were not dealing with 'professing Fascists' but harmless caterers. In each of these locations varying periods, normally of up to two weeks, were spent before transferral to Warth Mills, a disused cotton mill near Bury, Lancashire. This was the final gathering station for all Italians from throughout Britain. Conditions were abysmal: only a few taps of cold water, minimal sanitation, straw palliasses to sleep on and appalling food rations, irregularly dished out. It was here, for the first time, that all geographical and socio-economic sections of the British Italian Community met: the young, the old, the Fascists, the innocuous or non-Fascists, the anti-Fascists, the upper-crust from London, the shop-keepers, the artists, the musicians, those from the north of Italy and those from the south of Italy. It was a most extraordinary gathering of 'Scottish', 'English' and 'Welsh Italians'. Around 4,200 British Italians had been arrested in two weeks, 600 of whom were British-born.

During this period, the British government attempted to finalize its plans for the internees and selections began amidst the abominable conditions. Officially, the 'professing Fascists' on the MI5 list were to be deported and after much persuasion Canada had reluctantly agreed to take them. By the end of June the Foreign Office had become suspicious of the Security Services assumptions and tactics. This is revealed in a Foreign Office Memo of 22 June 1940

> MI5's criteria for judging whether or not a person was a 'desperate character' more often than not resolved itself into mere membership of the *Fascio*. On it being pointed out that membership of the *Fascio* was to all intents and purposes obligatory on any Italian resident abroad who desired to have any sort of claim to diplomatic or consular protection, they relented somewhat and limited their objection to Fascists of military age and special ardour . . . As the discussion with MI5 proceeded there grew up a strong suspicion that in actual fact they had little or no information, let alone evidence, in regard to more than a fraction of the persons they had led the Home Secretary to describe to the Cabinet as 'desperate characters'.[4]

Nevertheless, by 21 June 'the list' had been sent to Warth Mills and to five other smaller camps around the country where Italians were still being held. Commandants were instructed to mark for deportation any persons named on the list. Only 700 of the 1,500 could be identified. A rather pathetic range of excuses was given by MI5 for this including the complete inexactitude that Italian names have a number of alternative spellings. The majority of the internees not on the list were destined for internment on the Isle of Man. To the Italians it seemed as if the selections for different destinations were made on an entirely random basis. Many old Italians describe being lined up and simply divided on the basis of 'You, this side. You, that side', and so on. The men found it difficult to comprehend or accept the separation of fathers, sons and brothers. Bearing in mind many old men in their 60s and 70s had been arrested, sons were extremely reticent to be separated from their fathers. Thus it happened that people began to swop papers if they were nominated for a batch that would have separated them from their kin.

The first groups of men departed and word filtered back to Warth Mills that they had been shipped to the Isle of Man. On 30 June another selection was transported to Liverpool docks. When the men saw the size of the ship that they were to board, some began to realize that they were destined for considerably further afield than the Isle of Man. The ship was *The SS Arandora Star*, destined for Canada.

(ii) The Arandora Star

The 1,500 ton *Arandora Star* set sail from Liverpool bound for Canada on 1 July 1940. On 2 July at 7.00 a.m. the ship was torpedoed 125 miles west of Ireland by the German U Boat, *U47*, under the command of Gunther Prien – a man known in Germany as the 'Bull of Scapa Flow'. *The Arandora Star* sank within 30 minutes, with a loss of over 700 lives, two thirds of whom were Italians. When news of the event came out and families tried to find out if they had lost a loved one, the shock and horror within the Italian Community was beyond all preconceived fears of the impact of internment. How could such a tragedy have occurred?

The Arandora Star sailed unescorted and was an easy target for the enemy. The flying of a swastika, indicating that the ship carried German PoWs, did not dissuade Captain Prien from taking a shot with his last torpedo. Perhaps this was because the ship also carried British soldiers and had anti-submarine guns visible on the decks. However, as well as the German PoWs there were German and Austrian Jewish refugees, and the Italian civilian internees. Should such an incompatible mixture have been crammed onto the same ship? *The Arandora Star* sustained a direct hit on her starboard side which wrecked the engine room. Both she and many of her passengers had little chance of survival. Many of the Italians had been allocated to the bottom deck cabins. This group experienced the highest casualty level. The ship was immediatley plunged into darkness and the possibility of finding a route up to safety in the pitch black through a maze of narrow corridors was virtually nil. Others who had been quartered in the ballroom and mess decks were more fortunate and stood a better chance of survival. A number of factors, however, such as barbed wire at strategic points on the ship, an insufficient number of life boats, the unsuccessful launch of several of those, and chaos exacerbated by the absence of any emergency drill, all contributed to the horrendously high death rate.

Uberto Limentani, a prominent anti-Fascist survivor, sent a report of his experience to the Foreign Office. In it he stated

The ship was shaken by the bursting of the torpedo, but did not look like sinking immediately. People went on decks, and lifeboats were launched, but those who could get into them were not comparatively numerous. I did not hear any directions given by the officers or men of the ship. I heard only eight blasts of the siren . . . Many people had jumped into the sea and a good deal of them had already died. When I realised (about 20 minutes after the torpedoing) that there was not much time left, I got down calmly into the sea and swam away from the ship which was quickly sinking. She had turned on the right side, her bow was submerged, people who were on the decks poured into the sea, and all of a sudden, she sank with a terrible noise.[5]

When news broke of the sinking of *The Arandora Star*, the British press tried to blame the high death toll on fighting and panic amongst the internees. Increasingly, however, the true nature of the tragedy came to the attention of Members of Parliament who raised questions in the House of Commons especially with regard to some of the individuals who were on board. No government department knew the correct story and journalists and relatives alike were being referred from the Home Office to the War Office and then to the Ministry of Information.

As a result of the muddle in which the selection of men had taken place and the rushed nature of the ship's departure, it has never been conclusively established exactly how many men were on board *The Arandora Star*. No proper embarkation list appears to have been compiled. If there was one, it probably went down with the ship and no record was left with the Port Authority. Today, documentation on numbers aboard and numbers lost, available at the Public Record Office, Kew – Foreign Office, Home Office and War Office files – all give differing figures.[6]

The best estimate is that 1,564 men were on board. Of these, between 712 and 734 were Italians. The rest were either German or Austrian (Jewish refugees as well as Nazis) and British servicemen. For the Italians, only two figures can be established. First, the number who lost their lives was 446. Second, the group of survivors fit enough to be subsequently shipped to internment in Australia numbered 200 men. A further group of survivors between 66 and 88 men, were injured and sent to Mearnskirk Emergency Hospital in Scotland, of whom around 40 later joined their compatriots interned on the Isle of Man. Others were released directly from hospital. The Italian survivors of *The Arandora Star* therefore numbered between 266 and 288. In summary, around 60 per cent of all Italians on board lost their lives.

The confusion of the disaster was compounded by the swopping of allocation papers mentioned above. In addition to the fact that the authorities had no embarkation list, the consequence of this action was that, when the ship went down, it took months before it was conclusively established who had been lost and who had been saved. A survivors list compiled by the Foreign Office was published after the tragedy. Many people who had been saved were reported as drowned and vice versa, obviously causing much anguish within the Italian Community. The Home Office list of the missing, which was compiled between November 1940 and April 1941, and was more accurate, was the final account of those who lost their lives – 446 men.[7] Most of the bodies were never recovered although many were washed up on the shores of Ireland and western Scotland, where they were buried in local cemeteries.

The average age of the 446 men who died was just under 50 and 10 per cent of the men (44) were over 60 years of age. Survivors of *The Arandora Star* dismayingly tell how many elderly men simply stood on the decks as the ship went down, resigned to their fate. Old and unable to swim (many originated from mountain communities in Italy where they had no contact with the sea), they knew their chances of survival were next to nil as they witnessed the harrowing scenes of struggle and squabble for the all too few places in the lifeboats. Why were so many old men chosen for deportation?

Mostly the men who died came from London, Glasgow, Edinburgh or Manchester. Arguably, these men were from the large Italian Communities where there was Fascist activity. However, over one-third of the total who were lost came from small towns throughout the country where there were only one or two Italian families. Some small but tightly knit Italian Communities were therefore very badly affected by the loss of life. This was particularly true for the Welsh Valley Italian Communities where the proportionate loss of life was colossal. In addition, bearing in mind the notion of chain migration[8] and that most of the Italians in Wales originated in the Bardi area of Parma, two sets of relatives in fact were devastated by this loss of life: those in Wales, and those at home in Italy. A total of 48 men from Bardi were lost on *The Arandora Star*. Not only does a street in the village – *Via Vittime Arandora Star* – bear testimony to the disaster, but a chapel was erected to the memory of the men in 1969. Another example of high loss of life from a small Italian Community was Ayr on the west coast of Scotland, from where ten men were lost, almost one from every Italian family resident in the town.

A number of cases soon came to light of men who were probably utterly harmless and certainly by no means 'dangerous' , and who should not have been on board *The Arandora Star*. Padre Gaetano Fracassi from

Manchester was an example. He was 64 years of age and had dedicated his life to the Manchester Italian Community. The Bishop of Salford had tried to expedite his release but to no avail. His loss is still talked about today amongst the 'old' Italian group of the city. Gaetano Pacitto, a naturalized British subject from Hull, 65 years of age, was another clear example.

The case of Francesco D'Ambrosio, confectioner and restauranteur from Hamilton, who had lived in Scotland for 42 years, had applied for naturalization and had two sons serving in the British Army was first cited by Professor Françoise Lafitte in 1940. D'Ambrosio was also the oldest Italian on board *The Arandora Star*: born in Picinisco, high in the Abruzzi mountains in 1872, he was 68 years of age.

Decio Anzani was perhaps the best-known example of an anti-Fascist from London who lost his life. He had lived in Britain for 31 years and was secretary to the anti-Fascist organization, the League for the Rights of Man. Other well-known anti-Fascists such as Uberto Limentani, mentioned above, and his cousin Paolo Treves had also been on board but both had saved themselves.

As early as 19 July 1940, Sir John Anderson, the Home Secretary, wrote the following letter to Lord Halifax, the Foreign Secretary, in which he made it clear that he realized mistakes has been made in selecting Italians for *The Arandora Star*.

> . . . it appears that the 734 Italians who were sent to Canada on the *Arandora Star* were selected by MI5 as persons they wished to get rid of from this country on the grounds that they were potentially dangerous . . . I agree with your views that the arrangements for dealing with these Italian Fascists have been most unsatisfactory. I am inclined to think that one, and possibly the main source of the trouble is that there has been no sifting of the Italians resident in this country such as has taken place in the case of Germans and Austrians.[9]

Despite all the evidence and individual cases coming to light, however, the Secretary of State for War, Anthony Eden, was still maintaining at the end of July 1940 that all the people on board *The Arandora Star* had been Italian Fascists and German Nazis. Eventually, Lord Snell was charged with conducting a government inquiry into the tragedy.[10] He recognized that the method for selecting 'dangerous' Italians had not been satisfactory with the result that among those earmarked for deportation were a number of harmless Fascists and people whose true sympathies lay with Britain. He admitted that there were mistakes in the compilation of the MI5 list. The report was a whitewash, however, in its conclusion that there were only about a dozen errors in selection and that Lord Snell did not consider this number of errors to be cause for serious criticism. The report was never published.

Perhaps as deplorable as the mismanagement of *The Arandora Star* was the treatment given to the survivors of the tragedy.

(iii) The Dunera

The survivors of *The Arandora Star* were picked up on the afternoon of 2 July by the Canadian destroyer *St Laurent* and taken to Greenock. The men were not given the opportunity to contact relatives. The able-bodied 200 survivors were at sea again on 10 July, this time on board the *HMT Dunera*, and bound for internment in Australia. One might expect that, given the traumatic episode of *The Arandora Star*, the passengers of *The Dunera* would have been treated at least to Geneva Convention standards for PoWs. Not only were conditions gruesome and deteriorating as the journey proceeded, but there were continual beatings meted out by the guards, constant threats and frequent searches. According to Stent [*1980*] nothing else occurred during the internment period which remotely touched the stark, almost unreal, horror of the 55-day journey of *The Dunera* from Liverpool to Australia. It was some considerable time before news of *The Dunera* began to leak out in Britain. Letters about the atrocities of the journey filtered through towards the end of the year. It was not until the beginning of 1941 that *The Dunera* began to attract attention in Parliament along with claims for compensation from the internees. Eventually, several members of the crew were court martialed but no enquiry was ever held and the affair was hushed up.

The men who were interned in Australia passed the war years in relative tranquility. Despite permission to return to England after tribunals conducted by a Major Layton, most were too scared to risk another sea voyage. From 1940 until December 1941 they were imprisoned at Tatura Internment Camp in Victoria. When Japan entered the War in 1941, they were transferred to Loveday Camp in South Australia, near the Murray River, where many worked as lumberjacks. From 1942 until the end of the War they again spent their internment at Tatura. Most took up work within the camp itself running their own facilities or helped the war effort on the outside. There was, however, a group of hard-core Fascists who made life difficult for the more apathetic, but generally a process of self-selection operated where the men organized themselves into 'like' groups. The younger men played football, built a chapel and were taught in a school set up by the more educated and intellectual internees. Although there were several deaths during the period of internment, the vast majority returned home to Britain in 1945 although a few remained and married local Australian Italian girls.

Of the original *Arandora Star* survivors, only 19 men are still alive (1992). On 2 July 1990, the fiftieth anniversary of the sinking of *The Arandora Star*, 21 men were awarded the prestigious civic title of *Cavaliere al Merito della Repubblica Italiana* by the then President Francesco Cossiga of Italy.

(iv) The Ettrick

On 3 July 1940, another ship, *The SS Ettrick*, had set sail from Liverpool also bound for Canada. There were 407 Italians on board and, this time, after a voyage of ten days, *The Ettrick*, which was accompanied by a destroyer escort, safely reached its destination. Similar to the voyage *Dunera*, this was a thoroughly unpleasant experience for the internees who were badly treated by the British soldiers in overcrowded and sordid conditions. The real trouble began, however, when the ship docked at Quebec and the men were kept aboard ship, on deck, for twelve hours before receiving any food. They were then taken ashore where they stood around on the quayside for a further six hours. During this time they were systematically robbed of their possessions.

The Italians were interned at a camp near Montreal on St Helen's Isle, where an old fort had been sited. Like the internees in Australia, virtually all spent the next five years in the same place, with some taking up jobs in lumber-jacking from 1943. Unlike in Australia, the main problems for the men to contend with were due to intense cold and snow rather than extreme heat and dust. During this time a certain Home Office Commissioner, Alexander Paterson, was sent to review cases and assess whether individuals could be released. In his reports he stated that he was surprised to find that many of the internees had strong Scottish accents and concluded that the Scottish police had interpreted their instructions more vigorously than in England. He found that the majority of men were eligible to return – many under a clause introduced subsequent to internment which applied to internees who had lived continuously, or almost continuously, in the United Kingdom since childhood. Very few men chose to return; many who had lost fathers and brothers on *The Arandora Star* were implored by their families to remain in safety until the war was over.

(v) The Isle of Man

The internment camps on the Isle of Man consisted mainly of terraced streets of peace-time boarding houses and mansion blocks, which had been commandeered by the War Office and fenced-in with barbed wire. Conditions here were, on the whole, better than in the purpose-built camps in the Dominions.

The main camps at which the Italians were held were: Metropole for the

Fascists and PoWs who were mainly merchant seamen;[11] Onchan where the 'aristocracts' – the wholesalers, hotel and restaurant proprietors and other 'Sohoites' were held; and Ramsey which accommodated the ice-cream men and fish and chip shop proprietors, owners of small cafés, shops etc. There was another large camp at Palace and a smaller one at Granville.

In July of 1940 Sir Percy Loraine, an ex-British Ambassador to Rome, was appointed by the Home Office to head a committee which would conduct tribunals to assess and classify the Italians. It had by then been recognized by both the Home Office and the Foreign Office that mistakes had been made in the internment and deportation of Italians. In his letter of 19 July to the Foreign Secretary, Sir John Anderson stated that he proposed to 'appoint a Committee of enquiry to visit the camps in which Italians are detained and to classify them on some systematic basis'.[12] The Loraine Committee had enormous difficulty in defining what constituted a 'true Fascist' and MI5 were reluctantly forced to accept that membership of a *Fascio* did not automatically disqualify individuals for release. Length of imprisonment in the camps depended upon willingness to help the British war effort, assessment tribunals being held at regular intrevals. Monsignor Gaetano Rossi [*1991: 59*] described the dilemma for the Italians at their tribunals. The Italians

. . . were asked if they were prepared to collaborate with the British authorities. Some of them agreed, but they did not say so openly, because such a declaration could have caused problems for them in the camp; many internees were not disposed to go against their own country; this refusal was not a proof of supporting the Fascist movement but simply a question of national feelings, but this aspect was continually ignored by the authorities.

By November 1940, the first group of 410 internees had been released. Even after 1943 and Italy's capitulation, many men could not agree to dis-owning Italy and helping the British war effort, and they therefore remained behind barbed wire until 1945. It was a wrenchingly difficult decision for many, especially those who had fought for Italy during the First World War. Group pressure amongst the internees encouraged the individual to remain a 'good Italian', which meant to stay in. However, often families on the mainland were experiencing enormous hardships and many men felt that their place was at home with their wives and children.

VI. Family and Business

The wives, mothers and sisters of the internees at home tried to carry on as best they could. With the bread winners removed and no social security for aliens many were reduced to relying on charity from the Italian Community as well as the population at large. In general, families who were in business fared better, but this was not always the case. If a business was in a 'restricted zone', which meant one of particular military significance, relatives were not allowed to continue trading and in some cases mothers with children were forced to move out of an area altogether, with little alternative means of making a living. Women who were suddenly thrust into the throes of 'running a business' rather than just serving behind the counter, had never really been involved in the management and organization or staffing of a shop, café or restaurant before. Linguistic and business skills often fell short of the mark and many businesses closed. Many Italian women, however, determinedly worked together and fought to keep their shops open for fear of losing them. Sisters, wives, sisters-in-law, mothers as well as uninterned men worked in cooperation during this period in an unprecedented way for the competitive Italian small business environment.

Although the majority of men had been released from internment before the end of the war, unless their business activity was classified as being 'useful to the nation', they were required to take up other occupations, either in agriculture or industry. This naturally proved enormously difficult for men who, in the majority, were not used to heavy labour. In the initial phase of release they were still geographically separated from their families, particularly if they were allocated to land work. Later, useful jobs were often identified closer to home which at least allowed the men to live with their families, although they were not allowed to work in their businesses. Large Italian manufacturing operations, particularly in the ice-cream wafer industry, fared well since they were able to switch their operations quickly to making biscuits for national food consumption. Bakeries too were of course able to carry on providing their staple products. The majority of small shops, owned and run by individual proprietors, struggled badly to maintain a foothold in the local economy. This applied for several years after the war since both rationing and local resentment did not end with the cessation of hostilities.

VII. Post-War and Conclusion

The major challenge faced by Italian families in the late 1940s and early 1950s was restructuring their lives after the war. The older generation, men and women alike, tried in the post-war period to recreate their family lives and social patterns as they had been in the 'golden era' of the 1920s and 1930s. In fact the old generation turned in on itself and felt most secure within the ranks of the 'Community'. As far as family was concerned, there was a restrengthening of old values, ties and bonds. Links with relatives in Italy were re-opened. Although splits had often occurred within both family and Community because of different choices made during the war, this generation understood and valued the 'Community' and the importance of solidarity.

Much discrimination towards Italians still existed in the post-war period and in fact, in the 1950s, much of the strong anti-Italianism expressed by the British population during the war continued. Garigue and Firth [*1956: 69*] found that the majority of Italians in London were 'convinced that having an Italian name may be basis enough for some discrimination to be directed against them, even if they are of British nationality and speak English as their mother tongue'. In the face of this ongoing prejudice, however, the younger generations of Italians, people who had been children and young adults during the war, often adopted a different approach to the older generation in reorienting themselves in the post-war era. Children who had grown up without their fathers and who had learned to live with their 'tally bastard' status were often tainted by their experience. They internalized their 'Italianness' and tried to camouflage their true identity. This generation often Anglicized their names, refused to speak or learn Italian, married local spouses and tried in every way possible for an alien ethnic minority to 'assimilate' into British society: in short to become invisible. Through education, many Scots, Welsh and Anglo-Italians of the 1950s 'escaped' from the traditional occupations in which they were so visibly tied to their ethnicity. In the professions and in white collar positions, it was easier to mask their ethnicity and become accepted. Also, the slightly older group of men, now in their 70s, who served in the fiercely anti-Italian British Armed Forces during the war, perhaps more than any other sector of the Italian population, were forced to throw off their heritage and shake themselves adrift from their roots.

In addition to these social difficulties, the post-war economic restructuring of the Community to regain the position of strength and economic well-being of the 'golden era' was, for many, an uphill battle. Many small-time entrepreneurs had been 'broken' by the experience of the war. They lost not only the will but the confidence to rebuild their little empires and live the good life in this country. They indeed felt as, and perhaps behaved as, 'enemy aliens' for the rest of their lives. In the 1950s many Italians of the 'old' Communities became naturalized British subjects since they were fearful of drawing further attention to themselves as aliens. In business, many men who dreamed of, and perhaps succeeded in, expanding in the 'golden era', became content to lead a quiet life, scared of petty officialdom. Looking through trade directories for the pre- and post-war periods, one is immediately struck by the number of Italian businesses which simply disappeared during the war. Although new outlets did open up in profusion as the 1950s progressed, the immediate impression gained is of the number which simply did not survive the war years. However, not all businessmen were ruined or debilitated as a result of the war. Several of the grand old restaurants of Soho which had been established in the 1920s and 1930s reopened after the war when their owners claimed them back from the Custodian of Enemy Property. Many younger men were able to make good progress again after the war and indeed many new business empires were founded in this period.

The single biggest change in the British Italian Community in the post-war era, however, was the mass influx of 'new' Italian immigrants who came to work in British industry. From 1950 to 1960 the numbers of Italians in Britain quadrupled, building up to a Community today of some 250,000 people. Although there are marked differences between the 'old' and the 'new' Italian Communities founded by this post-war immigration, it was this injection of new blood which ensured the survival of the British Italian Community. With European integration ever closer, the future for the Italians in this country is again stable and bright, but for some old British Italians their wartime experience is difficult to forget; at least now its documentation has begun.

NOTES

1. See Colpi, Hughes and Sponza in bibliography.
2. The 'old' Italian Community refers to Italian immigrants and their descendants who settled in Britain during the nineteenth and early twentieth centuries until the 1930s. British Italians today who owe their origins to this era, and whose families lived through the Second World War, can be contrasted not only historically, but also sociologically and occupationally, with the 'new' Italian immigrants who arrived in the post-war era and who were responsible for founding entirely 'new' Italian Communities, especially in England.
3. *The Guardian*, 2 July 1990. 'Collar the lot' referred to 60,000 Category 'C' Jews as well as all Italians.
4. FO 371 25192, folio 131, 22 June 1940.
5. FO 371 25210 167357.
6. FO 371 25210 includes a printed but undated 'Embarkation List' which gives a total of 712 Italians on board *The Arandora Star* – 486 lost and 226 saved. HO 215 429 1942 'List of Missing' lists 446 lost. In his report on *The Arandora Star* to Cabinet in October 1940, Lord Snell said there were 717 Italians on board and sidestepped the more difficult question of how many died. The War Office gives 734 Italians on board and 486 lost (FO 916 2581, folio 499). *The St Laurent* claimed to have picked up 246 Italian survivors.
7. HO 215 429 1942. See Colpi [*1991: 271–8*] for full reproduction of this list.
8. The concept of chain migration was defined by the Australian geographers John and Leatrice Macdonald in 1964 as a process whereby families from particular villages or regions move to a new country or to a city, from which they instigate a 'chain migration'

by assisting their relatives to join them. Prospective migrants learn of opportunities, are provided with transportation, and have initial accommodation and employment arranged for them by contacts already established abroad. Before the Second World War, this was the main mechanism by which Italians were able to transfer to Britain.

9. FO 916 2581, folio 548.
10. FO 371 25210.
11. These PoWs were captured in British waters at the declaration of war by Italy in 1940 and are a totally different group from the 150,000 Italian PoWs who were imported to Britain from 1941 after capture in Africa, all of whom were held prisoner in military camps on the British mainland.
12. FO 916 2581, folio 548.

REFERENCES

Cavalli, C., 1973, *Ricordi di un Emigrato*, London: Edizioni, *La Voce Degli Italiani in Gran Bretagna*.

Colpi, T., 1991, *The Italian Factor: The Italian Community in Great Britain*, Edinburgh: Mainstream Publishing.

Colpi, T., 1991, *Italians Forward: A Visual History of the Italian Community in Great Britain*, Edinburgh: Mainstream Publishing.

Di Mambro, A.M., 1989, *Tally's Blood*, play for stage commissioned by the Traverse Theatre, Edinburgh.

Gough, V., 1990, 'Interned Italians and the Sinking of the *Arandora Star*', unpublished M.A. dissertation, Polytechnic of Central London.

Gillman, P. and Gillman, L., 1980, *'Collar the Lot!': How Britain Interned its Wartime Refugees*, London: Quartet Books.

Guida Generale, 1933 and 1939, *Guida Generale degli Italiani in Gran Bretagna*, 3rd ed., London: E. Ercoli & Sons.

Hickey, D. and Smith, G., 1989, *Star of Shame: The Secret Voyage of the* Arandora Star, Dublin: Madison.

Hughes, A.C., 1991, *Lime, Lemon and Sarsaparilla: The Italian Community in South Wales 1881–1945*, Bridgend: Seren Books.

Lafitte, F., 1988, *The Internment of Aliens*, London: Libris (first published Penguin Books 1940).

Lotti, S., 1988, 'Internati e PoW Italiani in Gran Bretagna', *Rivista di Storia Contemporanea*, Vol.17 (No.1), pp.110–17.

Macdonald, J.S. and Macdonald, L.D., 1964, 'Chain Migration, Ethnic Neighbourhood Formation and Social Networks', *Milbank Memorial Fund Quarterly*, Vol.42 (No.1), pp.86–97.

Mack Smith, D., 1959, *Italy: A Modern History*, Ann Arbor, MI: University of Michigan Press.

Maclean, A., 1985, *The Lonely Sea*, London: Fontana Collins.

Rossi, G., 1991, *Memories of 1940: Impressions of Life in an Internment Camp*, Rome: Scoglio di Frisio Foundation.

Sponza, L., 1988, *Italian Immigrants in Nineteenth Century Britain: Realities and Images*, Leicester: Leicester University Press.

Stent, R., 1980, *A Bespattered Page? Internment of His Majesty's Most Loyal Enemy Aliens*, London: Andre Deutsch.

Tolaini, V., 1982, *Voyage of an Alien*, London: published privately.

Valgimigli, A., 1932, *La Colonia Italiana di Manchester 1794–1932*, Firenze: Enrico Ariani.

Zorza, P., 1985, *Arandora Star*, Glasgow: Supplemento a Italiani in Scozia.

Visual Art Behind the Wire

KLAUS E. HINRICHSEN

There was a surprisingly large number of visual artists among the German and Austrian refugees interned in 1940. Apart from those persecuted on 'racial', religious and political grounds, Britain had accepted artists whose work had been branded by the Nazis as 'Degenerate' at the notorious Entartete Kunst Ausstellung of 1937, and who thereby had lost their teaching posts and were forbidden to sell, exhibit, and even work. For artists internment, though irksome, was less onerous than for most other refugees as they could work in artistic freedom. Thus German Art, strangled by cultural barbarians at home, survived in British internment camps.

On 28 August 1940 the *New Statesman and Nation* published a letter from Hutchinson Internment Camp in Douglas, Isle of Man, signed by 16 artists from Germany and Austria. It read, in part, 'Art cannot live behind barbed wire . . . the tensions under which we exist here, the sense of grievous injustice done to us, the restlessness caused by living in close proximity with thousands of other men . . . prevent all work and creativity . . .'. It ends with an appeal to British artists and others 'to help us obtain our liberty again'.

Apart from Ernst Schwitters, the son of Kurt Schwitters, who was a photographer, four of the signatories were sculptors, Ernst M. Blensdorf, Siegfried Charoux, Georg Ehrlich and Paul Hamann; the rest were painters and graphic artists: Hermann Fechenbach, Carl Felkel, Erich Kahn, Fritz Kraemer, Herbert Mankiewicz, Hermann Roessler, Kurt Schwitters, Fred Solomonski, Erich E. Stern, Fred Uhlman and Hellmuth Weissenborn.

One name was missing: Ludwig Meidner, once considered one of the greatest German Expressionist painters. Helped by Augustus John he had only arrived in Britain shortly before the war. In internment he experienced an intensely religious, Jewish Orthodox, phase, and felt safe in this community. Internment also protected him from bombs and financial worries. He did not want to be released and therefore refused to sign the letter. Nor did he join the other artists in their 'artists café' or in their exhibitions.

Hutchinson Camp contained a surprisingly large number of visual artists. Many had previously met at the Free German League of Culture (Freier Deutscher Kulturbund) or the AIA (Artists International Association), which had been formed in 1933, or the Artists Refugee Committee which had been set up by Roland Penrose and members of the AIA, with John Heartfield, Theo Balden and other Communist artists to rescue the members of the Oskar Kokoschka Bund who had fled to Czechoslovakia when Hitler came to power. Some of the artists may have teemed up at any of the transit camps, Kempton Park, Lingfield, Ascot, Huyton, or the notorious Warth Mill near Manchester and had stayed together on the boat from Liverpool to the Isle of Man.

Hutchinson Square in Douglas had been opened on 13 July 1940 and soon accommodated 1,400 men, ranging in ages from 16 to over 70 years. It consisted of a terraced lawn surrounded by streets of former boarding houses which had been requisitioned at short notice and enclosed with double rows of barbed wire, patrolled outside by soldiers with fixed bayonettes. Some of the houses served as the Commandatura and offices (Illustration 1).

The first transport arrived at night. A rather smart Regimental Sergeant Major who in civilian life was the head porter of the Dolphin Square Apartment blocks in Chelsea, counted out 30 men and appointed one of them House Captain of one of the 40-odd houses. They were expected to share double beds and to cater for themselves with rations collected from stores. For afficionados of herrings this was the life.

Entering their houses they found the windows painted blue and the bulbs red; some boffin at the War Office had calculated that blue windows and red bulbs would cancel each other out and thus guarantee a fool-proof black-out. Thus, during the day the internees lived in a fish bowl and at night in a brothel. Naturally, the red paint soon got scraped off the bulbs, to the alarm of the air raid wardens and aggravating the misgivings of the local population; one of the Manx newspapers had already greeted the internees with the headline 'The Huns steal our landladies' houses'.

Of course, not all artists ended up at Hutchinson Camp. Walter Nessler stayed at Huyton, from where he joined the Pioneer Corps; at Huyton there were also Hugo (Puck) Dachinger (later Ramsey, IoM), Martin Bloch (later Sefton, IoM), Alfred Lomnitz, (IoM), and Samson Schames. In Onchan also on the Isle of Man were Jack Bilbo, Henrion, Egon Hersch, Klaus Meyer, Hermann Nonnenmacher; elsewhere, or moved around, were Alva, Erich Bischof, Erwin Bossanyi, A. Gumprecht, Kawé, Theodor Kern, Kurt Lade, Reinhold Naegele, Carlo Pietzner, Albert Reuss, De Roessingh, Julius Rosenbaum, Arthur Segal, Erich and Guenter Wagner, Ernst Wolfsfeld and Richard Ziegler. Among those transported overseas to Canada were Theo Balden, René Graetz and Heinz Worner, while Hans Abarbanell, Georg Adams and Hein Heckroth were shipped to Australia on board *The Dunera*.

Only a small proportion of refugee women were interned. The artists Margarete Klopfleisch, Pamina Mahrenholz and Erna Nonnenmacher for a time were in Holloway Prison before being sent to Port St. Mary or Port Erin on the Isle of Man.

This list is by no means complete; John Heartfield, famous for his photomontages, went through three camps before being released on medical grounds. All these artists, apart from Blensdorf and Schwitters who only arrived in Britain from Norway in July 1940, had been investigated by Tribunals and classified 'C' or an occasional 'B' as Victims of Nazi Oppression.

Not all refugees were interned, the whole exercise had been ill-considered and haphazard, and some were quickly released for more essential tasks – Joseph Otto Flatter to draw anti-fascist posters and leaflets for the Department of Psychological Warfare and Henrion to work on exhibition design for the Ministry of Information. Richard Ziegler's sketches of dictators and their henchmen were published under the pseudonym Robert Ziller with the title 'We made History' and sold in large numbers.

A somewhat obsessive statistician calculated in the *Onchan Pioneer* that in this camp of 1,500 men there were 57 per cent professional people, including 8.6 per cent writers, journalists and artists.

The blue-painted windows of the Hutchinson Square houses provided an unexpected artists' material. By removing the paint with a simple knife or scraper or razor blade Hellmuth Weissenborn, formerly professor of graphic design at the Academy at Leipzig, scraped mythological scenes, the goddess Artemis, centaurs, a unicorn, a dolphin and rider and some arabesques into all the windows of his house. As he also acted as cook he decorated the kitchen window with a mouth-watering still-life of assorted comestibles. Ernst M. Blensdorf, a sculptor who had taught at the Staatliche Kunstschule at Wuppertal engraved into his windows slightly erotic nubile nymphs splashing water over a youth. In other houses one could see parts of the Sistine frescoes, a wishful dream of whisky bottle, lobster and cigars, or Adam and Eve being offered an apple with the price tag 1½d – a reference to the alleged overcharging by the canteen. Houses became known rather by their illustrations than by their numbers. Alas, of all these amusing enterprises nothing has survived but a photograph of Mr Neunzer (also known as Blick), a lion tamer and animal trapper for zoos – who caught mice with a lassoo in the camp, pipe-smoking in front of the window into which he had scraped a large number of exotic animals regardless of their comparative sizes (Illustration 2).

In the early stages of internment artists carried only their sketchbooks and some pens and pencils. Blensdorf and Schwitters arrived shaping branches into a female figure or an abstract object. The sketchbooks of

Walter Nessler and Klaus Meyer have preserved the minutiae of camp life, the improvized latrines, the tents of Prees Heath, and even the unfortunate man who hanged himself there. Artists' requisites were re-invented: oil paint from crushed minerals and dyes extracted from food rations mixed with the olive oil from sardine tins, paint brushes from Samson Schames' strong and wiry beard while in Huyton Dachinger and Nessler collected gelatine from boiled-out bones and mixed it with flour and leaves to size newspapers, and pronounced *The Times* to be the best paper in every respect on which to draw with burnt twigs as charcoal substitutes. By now some of this newsprint has resurfaced and gives the images an additional pattern and depth of background (Illustration 3). And Jack Bilbo's powerful purple is Onchan beetroot juice.

Some ceiling squares of a composite material had been left by builders in Hutchinson camp and on these Kurt Schwitters painted his academic portraits and landscapes; he also dismantled tea-chests for their plywood panels. Lavatory paper, distinctly marked as War Office Property and of poor quality became elevated to a sort of illuminated scroll. H.G. Gussefeld, a businessman with no artistic training, turned tent pegs from Prees Heath into letter-openers in animal shapes, the crocodile being the most suitable. And to general bewilderment Schwitters also picked discarded cigarette boxes, stamps, sweet wrapping papers and throw-away detritus from the streets. For him these were the first tangible examples of British civilization as since his arrival from Norway he had been sluiced from prison in Edinburgh to various camps until he was finally deposited at Hutchinson, and were to become the ingredients of his collages.

When the Hutchinson Commander, Captain O.H. Daniel, discovered that the pianist Maryan Rawicz was one of his charges he asked him to give a gala performance to which all the officers on the island would be invited. At that time Rawicz and Landauer were a famous Viennese piano duo, often heard on the radio and in music halls. Rawicz went from house to house to find a suitable piano among the dozen or so instruments in the camp. One succumbed completely under the impact of his powerful hands, and was quickly cannibalized: the mahogany panels were given to the sculptors, the wires to the Technical School for illicit electric heaters; the castors to needy furniture, and the ivories to the lion tamer who turned them into dentures for fellow internees. For the concert a grand piano had to be hired.

Fortunately, the landladies of these boarding houses had been fond of linoleum in their corridors and kitchens and this became source material for many linocuts. Again it was Hellmuth Weissenborn who manufactured enduring printing ink by mixing crushed graphite from lead pencils with margarine. He also discovered a laundry mangle in the utility room of his house, and the great number of prints produced in Hutchinson Camp have probably gone through this mangle (Illustration 4).

In the absence of canvas or paper the artists in Onchan used the reverse side of wallpaper, and having stripped one room completely, formed a human chain along the walls with each artist drawing a portrait of his neighbour on the bare wall, thus creating a continuous frieze like some Renaissance procession. At Hutchinson the stage designer Erich E. Stern, known as Este, who had worked for Max Reinhard und Charell and was to design for the film *The Red Shoes*, turned the walls of his room into frescoes of Revue scenes and can-can dancers. One Sunday Schwitters surreptitiously decorated the whole staircase of the office building with Miro-like designs, a deed not appreciated by people who like their art to be representational. Of all these emphemera nothing has survived.

Soon art materials began arriving from the AIA and other organizations and, helped by the camp authorities, also from suppliers on the island. In Hutchinson Captain (later Major) O.H. Daniel gave the artists what they desired most: studio space above the Commandatura and in huts between the wire stockades; elsewhere Sir Timothy Eden, elder brother of Anthony, supported particularly Hugo Dachinger, but also other artists; Schwitters, whose studio caught fire, eventually was even allowed to paint in a flower garden outside the camp without any guards.

An important factor for the cultural life in the camps was the arrival of duplicators such as Roneo or Gestettner which enabled the production of camp papers. Complete sets of the *Onchan Pioneer* and Hutchinson's *The Camp* are kept at the Imperial War Museum in London. Others were *The Central Promenade Paper*, the *Mooragh Times*, the *Sefton Record*, while the women produced the *Rushen Outlook* and, allegedly, *The Awful Times*. Camp Hay in Australia had *Camp News*, *Lagerspiegel* and *Boomerang*; papers produced in Canada were probably wallcharts. Generally the papers were typed on stencils and rolled off the duplicators. Some contained roughly scratched in illustrations. The *Onchan Pioneer* was the most informative and printed political commentaries and was illustrated by drawings from *Nonnenmacher*, *Henrion* and *Klaus Meyer* and others. *The Camp* at Hutchinson had a much better layout but less information and was almost entirely written in English and copiously illustrated. Erich Kahn, used to engraving in wood and metal, experimented with the duplicator wax stencils and by using rasps, roulettes and household utensils, developed a technique which makes the prints look like lithographs or etchings. His illuminated initials to various articles enliven the pages as well as the catalogue of the Art Exhibition and other publicity material. He taught his newly acquired technique to the other artists, but although Fred Uhlman, Paul Hamann, Blensdorf and Carlo Pietzner and in a couple of powerful portraits also Schwitters achieved successful work, nobody matched Kahn's technical skill, and no other camp paper discovered the stencil's potential.

For artists life in internment, especially after having been granted studio space, was less onerous than for former lawyers, civil servants, businessmen, clerical or even manual workers. Artists could follow their vocation, albeit in far from ideal circumstances – but then, life in Britain under bombing was far from ideal as well! They enjoyed free board and lodging, had no financial worries, no family obligations and even a chance to show and possibly to sell their work. Hardly any of them had previously found a gallery in Britain to exhibit.

In many camps they lived among brother-artists in congenial company of intellectuals and practitioners in other fields of Art. But they also mixed with people of very different backgrounds both in their own and other houses. Where else could they encounter within half a square mile Yiddish-speaking Chassidim, Spanish Civil War veterans, Prussian ex-ministers, a Protestant pastor of the 'Bekennende Kirche' the

Resistance Church, a Nobel Prize-winner and, indeed, a condom sales-
man by the name of Liebe (Love)? But this understanding worked both
ways: for many of the hard-working men an artist was a bohemian lay-
about, a scrounger fooling the public; now they proved to be good
members of their houses, reasonable and responsible and even clever
with their hands, and not at all elitist or condescending. Paul Hamann
won gratitude and praise for his housekeeping, Weissenborn proved an
ingenious cook, and Schwitters a gardener.

The Artists' Café has been vividly described by Fred Uhlman and
fictionalized in the Roman à clef 'Die Welt in der Nusschale' (The World
in a Nutshell) by Richard Friedenthal. This basement laundry room under
the direction of a famous Austrian pastry cook was indeed the setting for
displays of extrovert artistic temperaments, not least Schwitters
declaiming his Dadaist Ursonata (Sound Sonata) consisting of single
letters or meaningless words. The Scherzo Lanke Trrgl, Lanke Trrgl, Pi,
Pi, Pi, Pi, Lanke Trrgl Ooka, Ooka, Zueka, Zueka . . . became a
greeting whenever Old Hutchinsonians meet.

It was in the Café that the letter to the *New Statesman & Nation* had
been drafted. Apart from visual artists, architects, musicians, writers,
actors, an art dealer and I, then a young art historian, were welcome.

It was also the forum for a diversity of ideas and problems which at the
same time were discussed in all other camps: if the Nazis were to invade
via Ireland the inmates of the Isle of Man camps would be trapped.
Thanks to the bureaucratic accuracy of the camp authorities lists were up-
to-date; any Gestapo officer carrying the notorious 'Black Book' of
named anti-Nazis would have no trouble in picking them up here, and the
others would not be faring better. Even if the camp gates would open
there was no escape from the Isle of Man, and much thought was given to
the least painful method of suicide.

Again like everywhere else in the camps, the main topic was the
prospect of release. A White Paper had been published after a public and
parliamentary outcry against the internment of known opponents of the
Nazi regime, itemizing 20 (later amended to 24) categories under which
internees could apply for release. It was shamelessly opportunist and
utilitarian and the applicant's usefulness to the war effort seemed to
supersede the question of loyalty, which apparently was no longer
doubted. Artists fell under category 20 – not exactly a high priority! They
had to be 'eminent' artists and needed testimonials from the Royal
Academy or similar bodies. British artists were generous in their support,
and so was the Czech painter Oskar Kokoschka. For the younger artists,
though, this criterium of eminence was impossible to meet. If they were
Jewish, or branded as 'degenerate' or known left-wingers they had no

chance of exhibiting in their homelands or being mentioned in art journals. Erich Kahn was supported in the camp by all the artists who wrote in December 1940 from Hutchinson Camp to the Artists Refugee Committee in London:

> We hear that Erich Kahn was already proposed for release by you to the Royal Academy, but contrary to ourselves did not get an official confirmation to the effect that his case has been taken up by the Academy . . . Works exhibited by him in the camp were of outstanding quality and showed an impressive artistic talent.

Kahn was eventually released. A much younger artist, Peter Fleischmann (later Midgley) was not so lucky: his file got lost and as there was no record of his ever having been interned there was no machinery for his release.

Releases were as haphazard as had been the arrests, but they were naturally the main topic of conversation although both this word and the word *Weihnachten* (Christmas) were frowned upon in the Café. What the artists did not share with other internees was their concern with the role of an artist in wartime. Enemy aliens could not become official War Artists or even help with camouflage. Was it morally defensible to continue painting flowers and still-lifes or model the human body in wood or clay? Were they not under an obligation to use their talents in the service of Propaganda? Paint Hitler as Devil Incarnate and Churchill as Avenging Angel? Or to demonstrate the evils of fascism in caricatures? Or should one leave this to the acknowledged masters of the genre, John Heartfield with his photomontages or Richard Ziegler, under the name Robert Ziller with his hard-hitting portraits of the Nazi leaders?

Many artists tried their hand at political art, but in retrospect it seems that one needs special skills which cannot be acquired. And how to react to the depressing facts of internment and life in camps? The cartoonist Mierecki, who signed his work Dol, compared it ironically with a Grand Hotel with uniformed head porter, a table bulging with luxury food and wine, room service and a cabaret of scantily dressed chambermaids, while Weissenborn designed a menu card worthy of the best hotels anywhere.

Some of the artists were Jews, others were not. The painter Fred Solomonski who later became a cantor in Cuba, claimed to be able instinctively to recognize any work by a Jewish artist. This gift, apparently, was denied all other artists let alone the art historians and the general public. The Nazis had funded multi-discipline research projects to determine who and what was a Jew and had failed. The recent exhibition in the Barbican Gallery in London (1991) *Chagall to Kitaj: Jewish Experience in 19th Century Art* seems only to confirm the futility of Solomonski's claim.[1] Solomonski's stencil engraving of God awakening Elijah is one of the very few religious subjects from any camp. The shared experience of all the artists was the loss of homeland and the internment in their country of refuge, and it was irrelevant whether people were Aryans, Jews, half, quarter or one-eighth Jews – such differentiations could only serve to perpetuate the lunatic Nazi race theories.

Fundamental differences of outlook, however, existed between the majority of mostly non-political artists and a small but vociferous group of Communists.

Most refugees felt betrayed and disowned by the nations where they were born and had grown up. The trauma and the sense of loss were too deep to be forgotten. They consciously transferred their allegiance to the nation that had given them refuge and had already begun to sink their roots into the life of their adopted country. Internment was a disappointment but perhaps understandable during the critical stage of the war. The outcry in Press and Parliament against their arrests and for their release proved to them that they had made new friends and were accepted as allies in a common cause. Their despair at not being allowed to help was the root of much depression and the impetus even for older men to enlist in the Pioneer Corps. The desire to assimilate led to *The Camp* in Hutchinson being written almost entirely in English. Yet, the question remained whether one should also abjure one's cultural heritage.

For the Communists, many of whom had already fled from Germany to Prague in 1933, such questions did not arise. They considered themselves temporary exiles from their homeland, ready to return as soon as the Nazi regime had collapsed. They refused to be immigrants or prospective citizen of another country. Up to the time of Hitler's attack on Russia the war had been a contest between capitalist imperialist forces and of no concern to them. Russia's entry into the war would speed up the destruction of the fascist system and the establishment of a Communist state to which they would return and be hailed as guardians of German or Austrian Art and culture when it had been under attack. It was the avowed aim of the Free German League of Culture to keep German culture and language alive. Post-war publications in the DDR accredit a quite unrealistic influence to this organization and also to the Communist artists in the internment camps. Max Zimmering in the *Aufbau* (DDR) of 1948 claims in *Kunst Hinter Pfaehlen* (Art behind the posts) that 'their shared love for German language and culture characterized all artistic products in the camps'. It did not. As it turned out the Communists who returned soon after the war to Eastern Germany were to be bitterly disappointed; after a short honeymoon they were shunned and denounced as tainted by Western formalism. Their work was considered incompatible with the stern Soviet canon of heroic Realism, their murals in public places were overpainted and their teaching assignments terminated. For Theo Balden, Ernst Bischof, Heinz Worner, Margarete Klopfleisch and especially René Graetz and to a lesser degree even John Heartfield their Nazi experience tragically repeated itself. Those artists who stayed were slowly absorbed into British life, some as successful artists and many as influential teachers, foremost Midgley and Weissenborn at Ravensbourne College of Art and Blensdorf in Somerset. It takes a long time for artists to succeed in Britain.

Art exhibitions were the visible proof of what could be done with a limited range of materials and under unpropitious conditions. In Onchan the driving force was Jack Bilbo, a colourful character who had been interned quite early as the author of *Carrying the gun for Al Capone* and *Chicago Shanghai* while in fact he had never been there, let alone met the gangster. He founded the *Popular University* and organized various exhibitions. As a painter he was self-taught and 'his work is full of wild energy and makes few concessions to the viewer'.[2] In fact his stunning colours hide weaknesses in design and are influenced by the German Expressionists while the implied social criticism reminds of Otto Dix and George Gross. In Onchan he deliberately included amateurs in the exhibitions and constantly encouraged youngsters to try their hand. The *Onchan Pioneer* chastises some artists '. . . impressions were perceptible of traditions and concessions, of striving for inartistic objectivity, portrait similarity and propagandistic purposes' and exhorts them 'to sacrifice everything to the purely artistic purpose to form a judgment as to the function of the thing beheld on their minds' journey and to get rid of their vanities, their spiritual inertia and even of their wish for praise'. A tall order indeed! On his release Jack Bilbo was awarded a testimonial scroll from the many internal organizations he had been involved with, reading

> Our dear friend Jack Bilbo has shown to 1500 internees on their way from London via Kempton Park and Bury to Onchan on the Isle of Man how one man with courage and initiative can help his fellowmen. By founding the Popular University and organizing a great many performances as well as exhibitions he enabled us, at a time of great mental strain, to carry our fate in a dignified way and to make internment even a human inspiration to everyone of us.

Small exhibitions were staged at Prees Heath and Huyton with charcoal drawings on primed newspapers by Dachinger: Nessler and Martin Bloch, Dachinger, the inventor of Lettraset, also designed posters for – among others – a performance by the famous ballet company Kurt Jooss who had been stationed at Dartington School before internment. At Peel Kawé, Borchard and E. Fox collaborated. Exhibitions also took place in Canada and Australia.

The best documented event was the second Art Exhibition at Hutchinson Camp in November 1940. The Commander had put an empty building at the disposal of the 'Camp University' – his grandiloquent name for the Cultural Department – and the large first floor became the venue of the exhibition. The opening had all the trappings of a professional art gallery, with Private View invitations, a catalogue and speeches by the Campfather and the Commander, concluded with a performance of chamber music.

Artists always complain about their exhibits being badly hung and their entries unjustly curtailed. During the night before the opening the sculptor Ernst M. Blensdorf, a man of huge hands and tremendous strength, single-handedly carried a large plaster figure of a highly pregnant woman up the stairs and left her standing in the middle of the floor where she endangered the structure of the building. The campfather's address to the Commander is reproduced in *The Camp* on 24 November 1940:

> The artist, more than anybody else, suffers under the stress and strain of adverse circumstances. He might have stupendous and even divine inspirations but he wants an atmosphere of kindness and friendliness around him to materialize that mysterious transmutation: from thought and imagination into a work of Art
>
> . . .

and after protesting loyalty to and love for Britain the speech ends 'by expressing my hope that this will be a very successful exhibition, but our last in internment'.

Thereafter the Commander spoke a few friendly words and with a glass of sherry in his hand, opened the Exhibition. The artists were introduced to him, and it fell to me to give him and his staff a guided tour. At that time, and for a long time after the war, British taste was conditioned by French art, encouraged by educators like Roger Fry. German and to lesser degree Austrian movements like the Bruecke or the Blaue Reiter and Egon Schiele seemed crude and brutal, the colours shrieking and bordering on hysteria, the mood nihilistic and the subject matter often revolting.

The Hutchinson Exhibition represented a range of recent styles, most of them suppressed in Germany, and was difficult to appreciate for a British officer. Yet, whatever he may have felt privately, as guest of honour he looked and listened. The huge pregnant woman worried him as a subject, but he greatly admired Paul Hamann's 'Nude Lady Golfer' statue, and praised Schwitters' large oil portraits and Fritz Kraemers' old-masterly silverpoint drawings which were beautifully mounted and even framed. Somewhat simplified one could describe these as in the Holbein tradition while Georg Ehrlich's sculptures of young Ephebes had a long classical ancestry and the Baroque was represented by Siegfried Charoux whose cellist stands outside the Festival Hall in London. Solomonski, and Schwitters in his landscapes, were late Impressionists, Fred Uhlman and Carlo Pietzner Surrealists and Symbolists, Kahn and Blensdorf undoubted Expressionists as was Martin Bloch in Sefton Camp. Weissenborn and Dachinger might well be described as Romantic Realists, and Fechenbach represented Neue Sachlichkeit (New Objectivity). All were mainstream German art, even Schwitters' abstract collages but for the fact that the Head of State of Germany – labouring under the delusion of being the greatest artist of his nation, who had sacrificed himself for Politics – had imposed his philistine and petit-bourgeois neo-classical codex on the art establishment. The artists themselves accepted their colleagues' mode of expression with reservations only about the quality of the work. And in this respect some were more tolerant than others.

The exception was Kurt Schwitters' Dadaism. In the early 1920s he had been famous/notorious for his Merz collages and large abstracts which had developed into Surrealism. At the Degenerate Art Exhibition in Munich 1937 one of his large assemblages had been hung almost upside down under the heading Total Verrueckt (completely crazy) and Hitler was photographed in front of it, smirking inanely. But the year 1940 was either too late or too early for this kind of work inside an Internment Camp to be appreciated. Exile and War, it was argued, were too serious matters for such frivolous, non-representational, formalistic games as gluing together bits of rubbish found in the streets. Ernst Blensdorf, the sculptor who had fled with him from Norway, summed up this feeling in a letter written after his release to the still interned Schwitters: 'I really cannot understand why you are still there unless Dada itself is being considered dangerous . . . I am sad for you to have produced such stupid stuff.' Furious, Schwitters insisted 'Dada is purely artistic, abstract and non-political. It is as much an aspect of Expressionism as is Blensdorf's work.' Knowing that he would be misunderstood and ridiculed he only exhibited portraits and landscapes and reserved his collages and developing abstract expressionism for the few visitors to his attic studio. I must have been one of only half a dozen people to have seen and smelled the quivering, mouldy heaps of porridge, the left-overs from breakfast in 40 houses which he had collected in buckets. He had festooned this mess with stones, shells, matchboxes, postage stamps and objects trouvées, and foul-smelling liquids kept dripping on the beds of the room below. It was the world's first and possibly only Dadaist porridge sculpture.

For the ordinary internee Schwitters was an enigma. On the one hand he was considered a crank, an eccentric who would not wear socks, could not sleep in, but only underneath, a bed and not before having barked like an angry dog out of his window – thereby releasing a life-long suppressed urge in an Austrian banker on the opposite street of the Square to bark likewise to the dismay of the Military who did not allow animals in the Camp. His recitals in the large hall included poems for stammerers, allowing additional scanning for difficult consonants, poems and grotesque stories as he had performed them decades earlier in Germany and Holland in Merz cabarets.

On the other hand, his portraits could be deemed a worthy addition to anybody's ancestor gallery and would be unexceptional in the Summer Exhibitions of the Royal Academy. He had a long academic training and a businesslike approach: he painted well-known camp personalities on spec to attract commissions. His charges were fixed: £5 half figure with hands, £4 ditto without hands, £3 head and shoulders only. This mercenary approach was not shared by the other artists, but enabled him – having arrived penniless – to live in comparative luxury with wine and cigars and to have his threadbare wardrobe replaced by a tailor in the camp.

His letters to his wife and mother who had remained in Hanover allow a moving insight into the mental state of the 54-year-old man who had been forgotten as an artist by this time but was to become, posthumously (he died 1948 in the Lake District in Cumbria) one of the most admired and influential artists for a whole generation of young British and American painters who saw him as the father of Abstract Expressionism and even Pop Art. On Christmas Eve 1940 he wrote 'Christmas in prison is an ordeal. I went to our Church in the Camp unable to believe any longer in a loving mankind. This cruel war robs me of all my beliefs . . . The old carols were sung, but I could only cry . . .'[3]

At the Art Exhibition Schwitters' portrait of Rudolf Olden took pride of place as a memorial to the great democratic publicist and Secretary of the German PEN Club in Exile who had been drowned together with British evacuee children en route to the USA on the *City of Benares*, torpedoed by a German submarine. On the lawn of Hutchinson Square before a vast audience he used to put political events into a philosophical framework, and Schwitters had caught the sweeping gesture of the arm and the far-away look of the speaker. Like so many other academics he had been invited to an American university as soon as his internment became known.

The Exhibition ranged from accomplished oil paintings, sculptures and graphic work to untutored but moving 'sketches from the German Anti-Nazi fight and the Spanish fight for Liberty' (Exhibition Catalogue) to Punch and Judy puppets, chess sets, stage prospects, boxes, tent pegs turned into figurative letter openers. Bruno Ahrends, a town planner from Berlin, showed plans for a re-designed Douglas, erasing all existing buildings and replacing them with high-rise hotels and 20-storey Apartment blocks. The accompanying text extolled the virtues of green spaces and tower-block amenities. In retrospect Douglas was lucky that he was not at liberty!

As varied as the styles of the artists was the subject matter. Without doubt the largest body of work in all camps was topographical, views of the inside and the surrounding landscape, especially the glorious view over the red-tiled roofs of Douglas to the little Fortress of Refuge, the harbour, and the blue Irish Sea beyond. Then followed portraits and self-portraits, then scenes chronicling events in the Camp. There were many still-lifes and, notwithstanding the absence of models, enchanting and often quite erotic studies of the female nude. Caricatures, Christmas cards, logos, arts and crafts; a few mythological and allegorical works, and interesting examples of Symbolism and Surrealism. One could discover French, Italian and Spanish influences, but with the possible exception of Blake, Fueseli and late Turner these artists felt no affinity with British art of the Camden Town or Euston School groups or even the Vorticists, let alone Ben Nicolson or Henry Moore who was hated by both Georg Ehrlich and Paul Hamann.

It is impossible to list all the interned artists and describe their work created in the camps; most of it is dispersed or lost. Quite unexpectedly, however, a large collection of Hutchinson work has emerged in recent years. After I had given a talk on BBC Radio 3 about being interned with Kurt Schwitters I received a letter from a landscape architect in Scotland telling me that he was the son of the Camp Commander Major O.H. Daniel and that his late father had left him a leather-bound album with weird and wonderful paintings, drawings and linocuts. These had been given to his father with personal dedications by every one of the Hutchinson artists in recognition of the help they had received from him. Surprisingly, Schwitters' contribution was one of his earliest abstract-oval-shaped oils. Peter Daniel also found in his loft several rolls of photographic negatives taken in November 1940 inside the camp, on his

father's instruction, but apparently never printed. Among the subjects
Weissenborn, Hamann and Blensdorf at work in their studios, and several
views of the Art Exhibition. He also owned a hand-coloured copy of the
Almanac for 1941, a raffia-bound effort by the writers and artists still
interned in December 1940. This was a unique find, which was recently
exhibited at the Hatton Gallery of the University of Newcastle in connection with the showing of a TV film made by Bewick Films in Newcastle, a
documentary entitled *His Majesty's Most Loyal Enemy Aliens*.

Are there any works of art which could only have been created in
internment? Primarily, of course, the barbed wire as an integral part of
the landscape. Most artists learnt to ignore it, to look through it, but it
entered the soul of Hermann Fechenbach, and dominates all his linocuts.
For him internment means a prison cell with a straw palliasse as bed and

surrounded by twisted rolls of wire (Illustration 5). Even a sunrise over
the island is fragmented by it and the released internee is watched glumly
and enviously through strands of barbed wire. Fechenbach, a First World
War invalid, who had been in a German concentration camp, emigrated
to Palestine and hence to Britain in search of freedom. At Warth Mill he
had staged a hunger strike and been taken to prison.

Hellmuth Weissenborn's window engravings were made possible by
some crazy bureaucrat's idea of a perfect blackout, neutralizing red bulbs
by blue painted windows. Nowhere but in an internment camp could
Hugo Dachinger have caught the resignation of a young refugee selected
to be shipped overseas watching his luggage being weighed before
embarkation, perhaps on the ill-fated *Arandora Star*. Nor could Walter
Nessler anywhere else have sketched the man who hanged himself.

Fred Uhlman whose first child was born while he was interned invented
an iconographic symbol for Hope, a small child following a balloon from
darkness into light, and the mysterious, 'Madonna of the Barbed Wire'.
His dark, depression-born drawing of a dead man sitting upright in a
rowing boat while in the stormy, moonlit sea a corpse floats past, could
hardly have been conceived in freedom (Illustration 6). These drawings
are now in the Imperial War Museum in London.

Only in internment could Martin Bloch produce the surrealist 'Miracle in Internment' where he and his three friends discover that the herring on the dining table has turned into a mermaid. Solitary and misanthropic Erich Kahn, oppressed by the milling crowds, sublimated this experience into a stencil print of a man with a lamp searching for a human being among the grotesque multitude, among them the artist himself and a large fish skeleton. He inscribed the work 'Aesop' (Illustration 7). Haunted by nightmares he drew and painted visions of burning cities and fugitives, running and crouching in despair, thereby lifting the specific experience of emigration and persecution into an indictment of man's inhumanity.

Ernst Blensdorf, quite apart from the fact that he might not have been able to carve into the sidepanel of a decrepit piano anywhere else, asserted his belief in survival and regeneration by the sculptures of his heavily pregnant women, and the joy of life in his exuberant and provocative dancing girls. But he also drew a stencil print of an emaciated mother whose frightened child seems to witness an air raid (Illustration 8). And finally Peter Fleischmann, a young orphan from Berlin who had only just before the war arrived in a children's transport. But for internment where he enjoyed the guidance of all the artists, his nascent talent would have wilted and he could not have developed into the painter, muralist, engraver and teacher at Ravensbourne College of Art, Peter Midgley.

Art is a solitary occupation, communing with oneself, and in their letter to the *New Statesman and Nation* the signatories specifically

referred to 'the restlessness caused by living in close proximity with
thousands of other men which prevents all work and creativity'. But their
output, both in quantity and quality, contradicts their thesis. The artists
coped and found it an enriching experience as recorded in their work.
Banned from their homelands they had been interned in Britain, but here
their artistic impulses and convictions had not been censored or curtailed.
In 1940 German and Austrian art, strangled on the Continent, survived
and developed in British internment camps.

NOTES

1. Monica Bohm-Duchen, 'The Stranger within the Gates', *Third Text*, No.15 (Summer 1991), Special Issue on 'Art and Immigration'.
2. Jane England, Exhibition Catalogue, London, 1991.
3. Kurt Schwitters, *Wir spielen, bis uns der Tod abholt. Briefe aus fuenf Jahrzehnten*, edited by Ernst Nuendel, Ullstein, Berlin, 1974.

ILLUSTRATIONS

1. Paul Henning: View of Hutchinson Square Internment Camp, Douglas, Isle of Man, Linocut, 1940. Private collection.
2. Exotic animals scratched into blue-painted windows by the animal trapper Neunzer, aka Blick, Hutchinson Camp, 1940. Photograph in the possession of Peter Daniel.
3. Walter Nessler: Stoves in Huyton Camp. Multimedia on prepared newspaper, 1940. Artist's collection.
4. Hellmuth Weissenborn: Still life with kitchen utensils in Douglas. 1940 Linocut. Private collection.
5. Hermann Fechenbach: Internee. 1940 Linocut. Private collection.
6. Fred Uhlman: Ship of the Dead. 1940 Pencil drawing. Imperial War Museum.
7. Erich Kahn: Aesop. 1940 Stencil print. Private collection.
8. Ernst M. Blensdorf: Mother and children. 1940 Woodcut. Private collection.

LITERATURE

This essay is based on personal recollections, conversations, reference books, catalogues and recorded memoirs by former Internees.

History of Internment: François Lafitte; *The Internment of Aliens*, with a new introduction, London: Libris, 1988.
Peter and Leni Gillman, *Collar the Lot!* London, 1980.
Connery Chappel, *Island of Barbed Wire*, London, 1984.

The large literary output from Internment Camps is summarized by Michael Seyfert, *Im Niemandsland-Deutsche Exilliteratur in britischer Internierung*, Berlin: Das Arsenal, 1984.

The Oral History Department of the Imperial War Museum, London, contains a number of recorded interviews, many transcribed, with former Internees under the heading *Britain and the Refugee Crisis 1933–1947*

Compared to the research into Camp literature relatively little has been published about the visual arts in the camps, and then mainly in the FDKB (Freier Deutscher Kulturbund) and DDR papers. More information is to be found in Exhibition Catalogues:

1978 London Artists from Germany, German Embassy, London.

1986 Kunst im Exil in Grossbritannien 1933–1945, Neue Gesellschaft für Bildende Kunst Berlin, Froelich & Kaufman, Berlin 1986. The catalogue lists extensive biographical details and relevant literature.

1986 Art in Exile in Great Britain 1933–45, Camden Arts Centre, London. This is the above Exhibition with several additional names and biographies.

John Denham Gallery, London NW6, has mounted exhibitions of work by Nessler, Dachinger, Hersch, Lomnitz, Kahn and others. English & Co, London have shown Bilbo; the Juedische Museum in Frankfurt, Samson Schames 1991; Museum of Modern Art, New

York and The Tate Gallery, London, Kurt Schwitters; and in Taunton and other places in Somerset the work of Ernst Blensdorf is displayed.

The Manx Museum and National Trust, Douglas, Isle of Man has a permanent section of Memorabilia from internment in two world wars.

The Hatton Gallery of the University of Newcastle in 1991 mounted an Exhibition of work from Internment Camps in conjunction with the TV Film *His Majesty's Most Loyal Enemy Aliens* by Bewick Films, Newcastle.

K.E. Hinrichsen talked about *Interned with Kurt Schwitters* on BBC Radio 3 and contributed an extended version to *Kurt Schwitters Almanach*, No.8, Postskriptum Verlag, Hannover, 1989, '19 Hutchinson Square'.

Conclusion and Epilogue

TONY KUSHNER and DAVID CESARANI

'I don't, to be honest, regard it as a terrible hardship if
you think of the sort of hardships which we subjected
say the IRA in 1939 to when we hanged them or the
French taking the Spanish republican army in 1940 and
interning that and handing it over to the Germans or
the Americans taking the whole of the Japanese
population of California in 1941 and interning that
often with ridiculously hard circumstances and quite
wrong and we're not doing of that kind.'
(Professor Norman Stone on the actions taken against
Iraqis and others in Britain during the Gulf War, 1991).[1]

It is very easy to minimize the significance of alien internment in
twentieth century Britain by use of international comparisons. Compared
to the genocidal campaigns against the Armenians, Jews and Gypsies, the
various internment episodes appear trivial. But there is little to be gained
from comparing like with unlike. The events referred to by Norman Stone
differ so much in context from those in Britain that scant light is shed on
either the British or foreign examples by drawing up league tables of
decency towards 'alien' groups during times of conflict. The merciful
absence of genocide from British soil in the twentieth century should not
be used as an excuse to neglect the study of other, less or non-murderous
forms of racial and ethnic intolerance. Ultimately the significance of alien
internment in the modern British experience has to be found within its
own national context.[2]

The most important aspect of the wartime internments has been the
impact on the groups most directly affected. If it is easy to dismiss the
British cases by using international models, there has also been a
tendency to overplay the episodes through sensationalism, muckraking
and exaggeration. Nevertheless, a close examination of specific examples
concerning the Germans in the First World War and the Italians in the
Second by Panayi and Colpi respectively reveals that the impact of the
intolerant impulses within British society should not be minimized or
casually disregarded. Panayi states bluntly that 'The First World War
destroyed the German communities which had thrived throughout
Britain during the Victorian and Edwardian periods'. Colpi adds that 'To

say that the effect of the Second World War on the Italians in Britain was devastating would not be an overstatement.'[3] So these were neither trivial nor temporary problems; the British state and British society at times of crisis proved itself capable of destroying minority communities by a process of deportation, confiscation of property and removal of individual freedom. In both cases, well-established and seemingly well-integrated communities were ruined. German and Italian groups would be re-formed in Britain after both 1918 and 1945, but pre-war structures, dynamics and identities would never be recovered. As Lidia Capaldi in Edinburgh recalls, even within the Italian community 'there was always a stigma about . . . the old Italians' after 1945.[4]

The case of the internment of refugees from Nazism, the most heavily researched and documented, presents a more complicated pattern than the two examples to which reference has been made. For a small but significant number, imprisonment in Britain or deportation to the colonies proved to be the final mental/physical hardship and resulted in death, sometimes self-inflicted. For the vast majority of refugees, however, as Kochan and Hinrichsen suggest, internment was a difficult experience through which, thanks to their ingenuity and talent, most passed without major traumas. New skills were learnt, some often of great use in future careers (Hinrichsen in his specific case study of the refugee artists actually suggests that 'The artists coped and found it an enriching experience as recorded in their work') but this should not disguise the slur on loyalty that internment and deportation imposed. The marginal status of the refugees, now 'enemy aliens', was highlighted by the episode and it would be a long time (and for some it would never come) before they felt 'at home' in British society. In terms then of the immigrant and minority experience in Britain, the impact of alien internment was of major importance.[5]

In his account *The English: Are They Human?*, published in 1931, the Dutch historian G.J. Renier commented on the place of the foreigner in England:

> The English are owners of their speech, and the man from another country cannot rob them of their right to call him an 'alien'. But when he comes to feel the value of words in the language of his country of adoption, he writhes under the lash of the heinous word, although he is unable to explain the nature of the injury to those English who are so peculiarly unconcerned about the strange and complex beauty of the marvellous language it is their good fortune

to wield. He must consent to be called an 'alien' – *alienus*, an outsider, one who is different – instead of a 'foreigner' – one who comes from outside the country, a word which kindly ignores those notions of difference, of being other than English, which to the English means less-than-English, an inferior. 'Alien' dwells on quality, 'foreigner' only on locality.[6]

Eight years later, Alfred Perlès, an exile from Nazi Germany now in a refugee camp in Sandwich, Kent, commented:

> I do not like that word, *alien*; the word has a derogatory, almost cruel ring. I should have much preferred being called a stranger. But stranger was, perhaps, too vague a term; anybody from Yorkshire, or Dorset, would be a stranger in Kent, without being an alien. Why, then, couldn't we just be foreigners? It would have sounded less humiliating than alien.[7]

The very concept of 'alien' in British society involved at best a patronizing, at worst, a hostile attitude. Moreover, as Cesarani suggests, there was a great deal of continuity in the development of anti-alienism from the late nineteenth century onwards which drew with it earlier notions of 'the alien' as a dangerous, seditious, criminal or diseased presence. The outsider or even pariah status of alien was easily transformed into the still more marginal and despised 'enemy alien' in both World Wars. So it is with good reason that Raphael Samuel has suggested that 'Anti-alien sentiment, though only surfacing occasionally in organised political form, might nevertheless appear . . . a systematic feature of [British] national life'.[8]

The continuity of concept and language found a bureaucratic counterpart, especially in the Home and War Offices. The administrative framework of the First World War, itself drawing on earlier blueprints, provided the model used to intern the enemy aliens in Britain during the Second. Yet as Kushner and Burletson illustrate, internment in the Second World War was carried out under what Colin Holmes has described as the 'myth of fairness'.[9] Prejudice could operate against alien Jews, or as Sponza shows, against the Italians, under the guise of decency and liberalism. The mass internments of both World Wars provoked little or no self-criticism concerning the treatment of marginal groups in periods of conflict at the time or subsequently.

Furthermore, of equal or greater significance, the role of secret, uncontrolled and unaccountable government in the internment process was never seriously questioned. In contrast, greater emphasis on ethnic pluralism in post-war USA society and culture has allowed a much more mature reflection on past instances of state and popular racial intolerance. The American Civil Liberties Union has called the internment of some 120,000 Japanese Americans (including 77,000 citizens of the United States) 'the greatest deprivation of civil rights by a government in [the USA] since slavery'. In October 1989 the House of Representatives fulfilled a pledge made a year earlier to give compensation of $20,000 to each of the 62,000 Japanese American survivors of the wartime internment. The total amount pledged was a massive $500 million per annum to reach a final total of $1,250 million in compensation.[10]

In view of the contrasting treatment of this episode in the official and public memory of the United States, it is hardly surprising that it was only the United Kingdom that repeated the errors of the earlier internments in the Gulf War at the start of 1991. Indeed the United Kingdom was the sole Western country in the anti-Iraqi alliance to take action against 'enemy' aliens in the conflict (although the definition of such aliens was to be wide-ranging and often bizarre).[11]

The continuity of anti-alienism is easy to chart. Nevertheless changes of emphasis and intensity have also occurred. Given what occurred during the Gulf War in 1991, it is ironic that Britain avoided taking any action against Egyptian citizens in Britain during the Suez crisis of 1956 (despite the Egyptians expelling up to 13,000 British subjects) because as Commander Noble said to his fellow MPs 'the House and the country would not wish to meet barbarism with barbarism'. Therefore 'No restriction [was] imposed . . . nor [were] any deportation orders . . . issued against them'. It is true that anti-alienism was not absent. One MP, Captain Kerby, demanded to know with regard to Egyptian educationalists (who had visited Scotland as guests of the British Council), whether 'these aliens took advantage of . . . free [dental] treatment'.

Yet a number of factors contributed to restraining the expression and influence of such sentiment in the Suez crisis. First was the desire to create a moral distance between the policies of the Egyptian dictatorship and liberal Britain. Second was the numerical and absolute insignificance of Egyptians in Britain (Captain Kerby was surely disappointed to find out that the British taxpayer had had to shoulder the burden of financing four temporary and one permanent dental fillings for Egyptian aliens). Finally the mid-1950s were years of government non-interference, at least on a public level, in issues of race and immigration.

Immigration control, especially against those of colour, was seriously considered by the Conservative cabinet in the mid-1950s but it was rejected on pragmatic grounds. Immigrants were still valued for their labour (taking jobs that the indiginous population would not consider), and intervention in immigration control was potentially dangerous as it could be seen as racist both by more liberal sections of British society and, more importantly, the New Commonwealth. Nevertheless there was no desire from government to ease the integration of immigrants into British society or to take measures which would have countered prejudice and discrimination. This was in marked contrast to the situation 35 years later by which time the British state had taken draconian measures to stop the influx of coloured immigration. In turn such changes reflected the contraction of British society since the 1960s and the growing importance of an exclusive English national identity which found one obvious outlet in the expression and practise of racism.[12]

The detention and expulsion of Iraqis and others during the Gulf War, like those of enemy aliens in the two World Wars, would have tremendous comic potential had it not been for the traumatic impact on the groups concerned. Indeed the tragedy of this episode was emphasized by the repetition, if on a smaller scale, of all the features and mistakes of the earlier internments. The detentions laid bare the marginality of non-citizens resident in the United Kingdom and the power as well as the prejudice of the security services. Mistakes were made – often as fundamental as detaining the wrong people – reflecting the inaccuracy, bias and redundancy of information on the basis of which bodies such as MI5 continue to operate. The episode showed the potential dangers facing democratic government if, as is now proposed, MI5 is given even greater powers in British society, although the new statutory basis on which they will operate is surely to be welcomed. The detentions and other measures taken against 176 Iraqis and other Arabs (including seven Palestinians) also revealed the potential for abuse of British immigration control procedures. More generally the sorry affair highlighted the dangers inherent in a country without a charter of individual rights, including the right to a fair trial or even *habeus corpus*.[13]

As in the First and the Second World War, the heaviest blow fell on those who were 'detained' pending deportation (the Home Secretary in 1991 objected to the term 'internment') or expelled. Although only 176 were involved directly, many more were affected through changes in immigration procedures. An even greater number were afflicted with anxiety that the apparently arbitrary measures would extend to equally innocent victims.

Indirectly therefore many different Arab groups resident in Britain were made deeply insecure by the British government's measures. But the impact of the intolerance exhibited by both British state and public was even more widespread. Racial violence increased and, although it

was particularly aimed at Muslim groups, other Asians and even Afro-
Caribbeans came under attack. Britain's vulnerable coloured minorities
were under siege for the brief months of the conflict. The Gulf War thus
gave an outlet to the power of intolerance and showed once again the
narrowing and exclusivity of English national identity in recent decades.
Like the previous internments, the government measures in 1991
represented a climax of earlier hostilities and prejudices; they were not,
therefore, one-off panic measures in specific and self-contained moments
of military crisis.[14]

The origins of this volume were in a conference held in 1990 to mark the
fiftieth anniversary of mass alien internment in the Second World War.
Those involved little suspected that less than a year later Britain would
again indulge in a haphazard round up of 'suspect' aliens guided by little
more than prejudice and suspect information. The otherwise
overwhelming lack of interest in this anniversary was, however, an
indication that the lessons of earlier conflicts had yet to be learnt.

> If you've got a war on and you've got the possibilities of a terrorist
> offensive in your own country [in fact no evidence of this was ever
> provided against any of the detainees held in prison] . . . then civil
> liberties would have to be suspended for the duration . . . you have
> to do this in a war if you want to survive.

These comments from the influential Professor of Modern History at
Oxford University, Norman Stone, *after* the Arab detentions had been
carried out, would suggest that alien internment in Britain may recur in
future conflicts. In 1991 a vocal and significant body of public opinion was
marshalled to contest the measures taken against the detainees. As in
1940, this lobby had some success in reversing government policies.
There is still a long way to go, however, before state and society recognize
the human misery, the abuse of power against innocents, the sheer waste
of resources and, finally, the threat to democratic and accountable
government that represents the true nature of alien internment in
twentieth century Britain.[15]

NOTES

1. In 'The Heart of the Matter', BBC 1, 17 March 1991.
2. For international comparisons, see Panikos Panayi (ed.), *National and Racial Minorities in Total War* (forthcoming, 1993).
3. Panikos Panayi, *The Enemy in Our Midst: Germans in Britain during the First World War* (Oxford, 1991), p.283; Colpi, contribution to this volume p.168.

 4. Capaldi in Tim Edensor and Mij Kelly (eds.), *Moving Worlds: Personal Recollections of Twenty-One Immigrants to Edinburgh* (Edinburgh, 1989), p.196.
 5. Hinrichsen, contribution to this volume, p.207.
 6. G.J. Renier, *The English: Are They Human?* (London, 1931), p.21.
 7. Alfred Perles, *Alien Corn* (London, 1944), p.12.
 8. Raphael Samuel, 'History's Battle for a New Past', *The Guardian*, 21 Jan. 1989.
 9. Colin Holmes, 'The Myth of Fairness', *History Today*, Vol.35 (Oct. 1985), pp.41–5.
10. Roger Daniels, *The Decision to Relocate Japanese Americans* (Philadelphia, 1975); Thomas James, *Exile Within: The Schooling of Japanese Americans 1942–1945* (Cambridge, MA, 1987) and comments of M.Weiner in *Immigrants and Minorities*, Vol.10 (Nov. 1991), pp.103–4. For the later compensation of the relocated Japanese Americans see *Keesing's Record of World Events*, Vol.35 (Nov. 1989), p.37081 and Vol.36 (April 1990), p.37408. On the recognition of American diversity see John Bodnar, *Remaking America: Public Memory, Commemoration, & Patriotism in the Twentieth Century* (Princeton, NJ, 1992).
11. See *The Independent*, 9 March 1991, 'A Clumsy Abuse of Power'.
12. Commander Noble in *Hansard* (HC) Vol.561, cols.30–1, 26 Nov. 1956; Captain Kerby, *Hansard* (HC), Vol.558, col.110 (Written Answers), 29 Oct. 1956. There were 2,019 Egyptian born aliens resident in England and Wales according to the *Census 1951: England and Wales: General Report* (London, 1958), p.110. See Peter Lewis, *The 50s* (London, 1978), Ch.7; Russell Braddon, *Suez: Splitting of a Nation* (London, 1973); Vernon Bogdanor and Robert Skidelsky (eds.), *The Age of Affluence 1951–1964* (London, 1970) and Keith Kyle, *Suez* (London, 1991) for the impact of the Suez crisis on British society, culture and politics; Paul Rich, *Race and Empire in British Politics* (Cambridge, 1986), chapter 8 who argues for state neglect in the 1950s and Bob Carter, Clive Harris and Shirley Joshi, 'The 1951–55 Conservative Government and the Racialization of Black Immigration', *Immigrants and Minorities*, Vol.6 (Nov. 1987), pp.335–47 for an opposing view of the role of the state.
13. For the mistakes made by the security forces see *Observer*, 27 Jan. 1991 and 'Under Suspicion', Channel 4, 18 March 1991. On the abuses of individual rights see the Open Letter of the National Council for Civil Liberties to the Home Secretary published in the national press, March 1991 and the comments of Hugo Young, 'Liberty lost in the fog of war', *The Guardian*, 7 Feb. 1991.
14. For the impact on the Iraqi community ('Fear of internment is haunting Iraqis living in Britain') see Geraldine Bedell, 'The plight of the "enemy within"', *The Independent on Sunday*, 13 Jan. 1991; for the changes in immigration control procedures see *Observer*, 3 March 1991 and *The Guardian*, 19 Jan. 1991; for the impact on Muslims in Britain see the articles by Vivek Chaudhary and Dave Hill in *The Guardian*, 2, 3 May 1991; for the increase in racial violence see *Observer*, 27 Jan. 1991 and *Race and Immigration*, No.243 (March 1991), pp.1–3; Paul Gilroy, *There Ain't No Black in the Union Jack: The cultural politics of race and nation* (London, 1987) for the closing in of British society.
15. Stone quoted on 'The Heart of the Matter', BBC 1, 17 March 1991; for the campaign against the measures see the profile of Jane Coker, solicitor for the most famous Gulf War detainee, Abbas Cheblak, in *The Guardian*, 7 Feb. 1991 and 'Under Suspicion', Channel 4, 18 March 1991. See also the editorial comments in *Observer*, 3 Feb. 1991 and *The Independent*, 9 March 1991.

Appendix

INTERNMENT TESTIMONIES

PAUL COHEN-PORTHEIM

Paul Cohen-Portheim was an Austrian artist and writer who had spent summers in England for many years. He was interned in May 1915 and remained so throughout the war in a variety of places: Stratford, East London, Knockaloe in the Isle of Man and Wakefield before being deported to Holland in February 1918. The following extract is from the camp Cohen-Portheim spent the most time in, Wakefield (the 'gentleman's camp'), and is taken from his *Time Stood Still: My Internment in England 1914–1918* (London, 1931) and is reproduced by kind permission of Duckworth Publishers. After the First World War Cohen-Portheim became a prominent travel writer in Britain and Europe. He died tragically young in 1932. See the appreciation by Raymond Mortimer in Paul Cohen-Portheim's *The Spirit of London* (London, 1950, third edition), pp.v–vi and the obituary in *The Times*, 8 Oct. 1932.

TK

Barbed Wire Air

The process of adaptation to new and difficult surroundings had taken up the first weeks in Knockaloe, the repetition of that process in Wakefield took me many months. Possibly one had already lost some of one's elasticity, but in my case this new adaptation was in itself more difficult because I was entirely out of sympathy with my new surroundings. Knockaloe in its early days, which were the days I knew there, was restless, seething, and anarchical; it was very rough but it was also very alive and stimulating; it was dymanic. Wakefield had settled into a routine long before I knew it and that routine continued in endless monotony for ever after; it was static. Wakefield in fact was dead. Dostoïevski in his marvellous memories of his life as a prisoner in Siberia calls the prison 'a house of the dead', and no better term could be found for Wakefield. That book describes its atmosphere most admirably, and even most of the characters depicted are images of Wakefield prisoners; like causes led to like results.

Wakefield was an extremely orderly place, as orderly, monotonous and drab as a lower middle-class suburb, but it was a suburb without a city, and its inhabitants suburbanites out of work. Everything was organized, everything ordered. The huts had captains, the captains a chief-captain, and he an adjutant with so little sense of humour that he actually signed himself Adjutant L. and wished to be addressed by his ridiculous title. There were committees for everything, and nearly everyone was a member of one or the other or had some sort of post in the PO or the kitchen department or God knows what, and they all took themselves and their activities most seriously. Nearly all took part or desired to take part in the government and administration of this place where there was nothing to govern, as the real governing powers were outside the camp, and there was little enough to administer. It was and became ever more an administration which served no purpose except that of giving its participants a feeling of their own importance, it was full of corruption and protectionism. If anyone benefited by it, it was the real administration of the camp, the British military in command. Whenever in later life people asked one what the existence had been like their first question was invariably: 'Were you treated well?' It would have been difficult to make them understand that the treatment by the military authorities (which their question referred to) was really a very minor matter once the fact of imprisonment had been accepted. There was so very little of it. Soldiers kept guard to prevent prisoners escaping, officers counted their heads twice daily, anonymous authorities issued orders which were mostly restrictive and irritating, and that was all. During my stay in Wakefield there were three or four different commandants, but I cannot say that I noticed any difference whatsoever in the treatment of the prisoners. Very likely things were different in other camps or in other countries; I don't wish to make any general statement, and I believe that all general statements about no matter what aspect of the war are nonsensical. I am prepared to say what British treatment of prisoners of war or of interned civilians was – fair, correct, brutal, inhuman, indifferent – I can only speak of my own experience and that was that the treatment of prisoners was standardized and carried out according to War or Home Office rules and regulations. Either these left no room for personal initiative or else no advantage was taken of existing possibilities, but certainly there was no personal contact between prisoners and gaolers and therefore no like or dislike. The prisoners, of course, professed hatred of their oppressors, but it was really half-hearted and none too sincere, just part of that prescribed hatred of the enemy which had become universal. A prisoners' camp is in many ways similar to a school, and schoolboys do not hate the legislators of compulsory education, but their masters or fellows, and what they suffer most from are not the restrictions of their state but the treatment meted out to them by the other boys. When I look back on the years spent in camp, from 1915 to 1918, I cannot recall a single instance of cruelty or of kindness to me from officers or soldiers. Many of the orders enforced were, I consider, cruel, and many more were quite absurd, but that was the fault of the system, not of the men who might as well have been machines set going. The system was cruel as must be all systems which do not aim at justice; it did not treat or profess to treat people according to their deserts, it was guided by entirely different considerations. The Germans in England, the foreigners of enemy nations in all countries, must not be allowed to join the belligerent forces of their countries of origin and they must not be allowed to endanger the safety of the countries they happened to have been in when war broke out. They were therefore rounded up and locked away in camps because that was the easiest way of dealing with the problem. As a sop to certain qualms of conscience (for thousands of these prisoners had friends who knew them as harmless or likeable people) each government gave out that they were only following the enemies' example. That sufficed as an explanation of anything during the war, and that fact I consider the worst aspect of war mentality. That two wrongs *do* make a right became the accepted moral teaching of all nations, and reprisals a term which excused any crime. And if it happened that one party had no knowledge of what the other really had done, it acted on rumours. In no previous European war had enemy civilians been interned; in 1914 every country interned them and every country gave out that the measure adopted was one of reprisal for similar treatment of their own subjects. The way prisoners were treated varied on that same principle of reprisals. When prisoners at Wakefield complained to the neutral representative who sometimes visited the camp of insufficient nourishment they were told that the 'number of calories' had been reduced to correspond to that given to British prisoners in Germany, and the British there were no doubt told the same tale. If a French city was bombarded by German aeroplanes and women and children killed, then the French bombarded a German city (or more if possible), killing German women and children, and everyone (not quite everyone, to be just) applauded them. No considerations of humanity need deter the governments or fighting forces of the nations from any measure whatsoever, and they did not; but it was always better to convince one's own people that the enemies had been the first to employ any particularly nauseous weapon and that your side was merely taking reprisals. During the war no one could ascertain the truth of such a statement and after the war no one would care.

That, in short, was the origin and the reason of the cruelty of the system of treatment; its absurdity was due to the red tape and utter lack of comprehension inherent in all administrative measures and intensified by the war spirit prevalent. In this, however, the system of treatment of prisoners did not vary in principle from the system of treatment of the nation's own subjects. The first were bundled into camps, the latter into the armies; both to be ruled by systems and regulations, both to be treated as numbers, both to suffer from reprisals for deeds and actions on which they had not been consulted. And as the war progressed, restrictions and coercion gradually enslaved all the civilian population as well, until all the world seemed to lie under the shadow of the words *Es ist verboten*, once supposed to be the true and exclusive expression of Prussianism.

That, then, was the law under which one lived, unchangeable for the time being as a law of nature, and therefore accepted after a short resistance as something inevitable. That law had its executants, and they again were accepted as inevitable. I maintain that after a time they ceased to trouble the prisoners (until some new change for the worse occurred) and that they really gave very little thought to them. Unconsciously they classed them with other necessary evils: cold, disease, death, bereavement, which one deplores but takes for granted. They represented the peculiar form in which war affected prisoners, and war itself was a fact, a sort of unending earthquake from which there was no escape.

This long digression is intended to clear up a misconception of the essential character of life in internment camps shared by everyone I have ever met who had had no personal experience of it. They believe that the interned had 'a good time' (comparatively) when they were 'treated well' and 'a bad time' when they were 'treated badly'. But if bad treatment might have aggravated and good treatment eased the prisoner's lot, neither one nor the other could change its essentials or even modify them to any considerable extent. The evil was inherent in the system and in the way that system affected and changed the prisoners. When people asked me whether I had been badly treated I truthfully said 'No', but when they continued and said: 'Then you didn't have too bad a time' – which seemed the only logical conclusion – the answer should have been 'I had an awful time', or perhaps, in my own case, 'I had what you would consider an awful time.' But that would have led to lengthy explanations and one was as disinclined to talk much of one's experiences as were the soldiers back from the front. Things are different now, twelve years have passed, and one has gained sufficient distance for dispassionate judgment. That, I think, explains the great number of war books written lately and the great success of many of them: the writers feel that they can now write the truth (as it appears to them, for there is no absolute truth and no general truth in such matters) and the public is eager to learn the truth, having realized that what they were told about the war while it was in progress or shortly after it was over bore but a faint resemblance to any sort of truth.

The whole problem of prisoners of war and their treatment was a secondary consideration in all countries while all energies were directed towards winning the war, and the fate and treatment of interned civilians again was but a small and none too important part of that problem, yet a good deal of space was given to it in the papers and in parliamentary discussions. There were two main sides to it; the British public wished to know how their men were being treated in enemy countries, to be reassured about their fate, and to urge the Government to do all in its power to improve their lot. That was the one side; the other was the question of how enemy prisoners were being treated in Britain, and that could not be separated from the first. I do not know how near the truth were the statements about conditions and treatment of British prisoners abroad, but I do know that the picture of conditions and treatment of prisoners in British internment camps given to the public was extremely fanciful. That whole question had become part of the vast system of propaganda attributed, rightly or wrongly, to Lord Northcliffe. The main idea never varied: British prisoners abroad were being treated abominably, German prisoners in England were being treated with foolish generosity. The latter was, to be just, frequently denied in parliament by members of the Government, but this made no difference whatsoever to the continuation of the press campaign against that supposed scandal. There were very few days when the more sensational papers (we got all the English papers, but no foreign ones) did not contain a paragraph under the (invariable) heading: 'Our pampered Huns' and the statements they contained were not mere travesties of truth but simply fantasies. I have read descriptions of dinners (including full menu) which never took place, of prisoners disporting themselves on a golf-course which never existed, of strange happenings between prisoners and women friends who visited them, when in reality officers and soldiers on guard were present on all such occasions, and there were countless other inventions which I have forgotten. Wakefield was their favourite aim of attack, being a 'privileged' camp, together with Donnington Hall which was an officers' camp. There is no need to speak of the impression these accounts made on the minds of the prisoners, but the impression produced on the British public was, of course, such as was desired: they were perhaps mildly angry with the Government, but at the same time not displeased with such a show of characteristically British magnanimity, and any possible sympathy they might have felt with the prisoners was killed outright. How far that propaganda impressed the neutrals, which was always one of its main aims, I do not know, but my own opinion is that at least the European neutral powers ceased to be impressed by any propaganda of either side after a very few months and got bored with the absolutely contradictory statements screamed at them day after day. But as far as the British public went that question was settled. One must remember what a small minority reads the better-class papers which did not join in that particular chorus and how vast a majority the others. The millions knew the truth as they thought: German prisoners in England, interned civilians in particular, were not only treated well, but with quixotic generosity, whereas the treatment of British prisoners in Germany was cruel and barbarous. And all the time the real truth which was never told them was that the treatment in both countries was as nearly identical as circumstances allowed, that both sides were continually receiving reports about the camps from neutral observers and hastened to adjust the conditions they controlled to those reported from the other side. Exceptions to this rule there may have been, there were probably remote camps seldom or possibly never visited by neutrals, and – as we had cause to know – these neutral inspections remained very much on the surface, but such details cannot change the dominating facts. What happened to the prisoners on one side happened to those on the other, and their lot was subject to a system of mutual reprisals from which the authorities dreamt as little of abstaining as – to choose a well-know example – the flying forces refrained from 'punitive expeditions'. But the British public read with horror and loathing that 'the Germans have bombarded the unfortified town of ----' and later with satisfaction 'we have bombarded places of strategical importance behind the enemies lines'; while the German public was given the same news in the inversed terms. Thus, as Georg Brandes had foreseen from the very beginning, Truth was murdered by war and thus every day that hatred was fanned anew without which the war could not have continued.

WERNER MAYER

Werner Mayer was born in 1921 in the German town of Landau, a town with a sizable and long-established Jewish community. After the *Kristallnacht* pogrom of November 1938 he was sent with his father to Dachau concentration camp. After his release he left alone for England on a temporary visa, settling in Manchester where he had distant relatives. His parents and other relatives died in the Holocaust. After the war Werner Mayer became a school-teacher and eventually Deputy Headmaster of King David Jewish High School in Manchester. In his retirement he has played a leading role in the Manchester Jewish Museum.

Further details of his early life can be found in his autobiography, 'To Tell The Story: Recollections of My Youth in Germany 1921–1939' (1990), available from the Manchester Jewish Museum, 190 Cheetham Hill Road, Manchester M8 8LW. His experiences as a refugee in Britain are related in the *Manchester Jewish Telegraph*, 27 Feb., 10 April 1987 and 2 Sept., 4 Nov. 1988.

TK

His Majesty's Loyal Enemy Alien

As the summer months of 1939 passed, the clouds of war were gathering ominously. Yet, the British world was blissfully ignoring the signs. I remember going to the city centre one afternoon and seeing the newsvendors' placards announce 'England in grave danger'. I quickly snatched a copy. Had the inevitable happened? Had Hitler driven the world to the ultimate catastrophe? No such thing. Breathe again, this is more serious, a difficult patch for the English cricket team in the test match.

Driven by curiosity I had once made a pilgrimage to the sanctuary of cricket, the Old Trafford ground, equipped with a sublime ignorance of the rules of the game. Only the English could invent a game which spread over five days! If I was in search of excitement, I had come to the wrong place. A blazing hot sun had lulled the handful of portly spectators in the front row into apparent somnolence. Thirteen men were on the pitch, and one of them at regular intervals pitched a ball at the one with the bat, who would promptly play it into the ground, and that seemed to be the sum total. Once in a while the dinosaurs in front bestirred themselves into wakefulness, gave a polite handclap, calling 'Well played, sir' before resuming their stupor. There was obviously still a lot to learn about the natives.

As the corn was ripening in the fields, the God of War sharpened his scythe for the harvest of men. In late August a pact between Russia and Germany marked the last step towards the war. The government had already issued us with identity cards, and encouraged us to acquaint ourselves with the newly-distributed gas masks, just in case – and, just in case, children were evacuated from the cities, allegedly as a rehearsal.

On the morning of Friday, 1 September, the news broke. Hitler's armies had invaded Poland. And yet, for two frustrating days, Britain and France hesitated. It was on the Sunday morning that we gathered round the wireless set at 11.15, to hear the crackling voice of Neville Chamberlain telling us that Peace in our days had given way to total war.

We refugees had ambivalent feelings. We rejoiced that at long last the free world had squared up to Hitler, yet, would they achieve victory before untold suffering was inflicted on our dear ones? The separation from them was now complete, and we were kept from one another by battlefields.

It had never occurred to us that we had now technically become enemy aliens. Though we had every reason for praying for the Nazis' defeat, the law said that, since we had German passports, we were enemy aliens, however friendly our disposition.

Within hours of the declaration of war all 'enemy aliens' were summoned to the Town Hall, to register, and to be informed that we were now subject to restrictions, which excluded us from a 25-mile-wide strip near the coast, generally controlled our movement without a permit, and forbade us to use bicycles. We felt a bit humiliated, but if it would help to bring victory nearer, so be it.

Now came the turn of the stateless ones. Authority decided to clear up vaguenesses and to allocate such persons arbitrarily to a proper nationality. Some hilarious decisions were made: there was Heinz, who had applied for a Polish passport way back in Vienna, and had received a flat refusal. By accident his stateless passport had the letter of refusal tucked into its pages. The officer studied the document and, proud of his knowledge of the German language, decoded the words 'Polinisches Konsulat, Wien'. Without further ado Harry became Polish, hence a 'friendly alien'. Similarly Bernhardt's passport gave his birth-place as Libshku, and misinterpreting the information, the officer granted him Polish nationality. Libshku, be it said, is Polish for the town of Leipzig.

Tribunals were now set up in order to establish our bona fides as refugees. Discrepancies appeared. There were three categories. Some authorities assumed that all refugees were Category A hostile enemy alien. Others operated on the principle that doubt existed, and therefore tended to award Category B status. I was given the privilege of becoming a Category C Alien, which officially certified me as a friendly enemy alien! Yes, there was still a lot to be learned about the British!

Somehow the war failed to live up to expectations. Once the rape of Poland had been achieved, there was no sign of the expected lightning warfare, the 'Blitzkrieg' we had been led to expect. Indeed, initially as a bit of sarcasm British slang adapted the word Blitz to signify aerial bombardment of towns, and later we were to hear of cities having been blitzed. Our own Air Force was reported to be dropping leaflets over Germany, and a comedian on the wireless told of an airman being reprimanded for forgetting to cut the strings of the packages: he might have killed someone!

The reality arrived that April morning when we heard that German troops had overrun Denmark and were attacking Norway. Once again the French and British appeared paralysed, and within a short period the British Expeditionary Force had given up the unequal struggle.

10 May 1940 saw the unbelievable: German troops invading Holland and Belgium, and thus entering France through the back door, making nonsense of the 'impregnable' Maginot Line. The German High Command had repeated on an extended scale the strategy which in 1914 had brought its armed forces within artillery range of Paris. And the Allies had not grasped the basic lesson! This time the plan succeeded totally: within a matter of weeks the French Republic lay at the feet of the conqueror, and the British army was fleeing in disarray. Two small pinpricks of light shone through the gloom: the British had lived up to their reputation of 'muddling through', snatching their defeated soldiers from the enemy's reach, and in the hour of national danger had called on Winston Churchill to assume the leadership of the government.

We were sublimely unaware of the danger which was building up against us. Reports began to circulate that Holland had fallen largely through the activities of traitors, as had Norway through a man whose name was to become synonymous with betrayal, Vidkun Quisling. DORA turned out not to be a girl's name but the acronym of Defence of the Realm Acts, paragraph 18b of which provided for internment of individuals who were potentially enemies of the state.

The safety afforded by my previous classification of 'friendly' was inadequate, and one morning detectives arrived at our home to take me into custody, along with thousands of other refugees.

It is difficult to describe my feelings at the time. Certainly humiliation was uppermost. To suspect us, whose only hope was for the defeat of Hitler, of lack of loyalty! To have to face for the second time in my young life the view of barbed wire from behind! But then, there was a war to be won, and if our incarceration in a bizarre way would contribute to the downfall of Hitler, it had to be accepted.

It was a confused nineteen-year-old who in June 1940 arrived in His Majesty's Internment Camp in nearby Bury, a former cotton factory called Warth Mill.

Internment

Warth Mill was above all a place of squalor. The former cotton mill had been hastily prepared to receive hundreds of internees (civilian). We were introduced to the comfort(?) of palliasses scattered on the floor. Toilet and personal hygiene facilities were totally inadequate, and relations between us and our guards were that bit tense. The latter regarded us with a certain amount of suspicion – after all, were we not 'Jerries'? – and throughout the time I spent behind British barbed wire I felt a certain hiatus between the soldiers and us. In their view we were 'toffee nosed', with some justification. The camps contained eminent scientists, famous musicians, and men of many vocations, and we in no way resembled the preconceived image of the 'native'.

By and large we accepted the inevitable, still resentful at the humiliation, worried about the dear ones we left behind, and frightened out of all proportion.

Some genius at the Home Office had ruled that we were to be deprived of all news. Not only were newspapers banned, and radio sets prohibited, but when internees were occasionally transferred from one camp to another, motor-cycle patrols went ahead to remove any posters or placards referring to the raging battle. Of course, predictably, rumours began to circulate. The Germans had landed in Britain; the British government was suing for peace, and one of the conquerors demands was the handing over of internment camps to the Germans. I do not know how true it was, but stories of suicides began to go round.

Whatever the shortcomings of the arrangements, there was no doubt in our minds about the difference between British and German barbed wire. Having experienced both, I realized that British incompetence and chaos were preferable to German cruelty and barbarity.

There were also comical aspects, and I was to experience those particularly at the next camp, Prees Heath in Shropshire. We were housed in bell tents, and the place resembled a holiday camp in the beautiful summer days of 1940.

Our relationship with the guards was more relaxed. Rumour had it that two internees due to be transferred to Huyton Camp near Liverpool were sent off without guards, because of manpower problems, on their sincere undertaking that they would report at the other camp upon arrival. The incredible happened: they went missing. The powers-that-be delayed making a hue-and-cry, and their hesitation was rewarded when one of the missing internees turned up at Huyton. Where had he been? Well, having been interned for some months, Liverpool's temptation had induced him to linger a bit – where was his mate? He still had some money left, but he would be along in due course, and so he was.

Making the best of the situation, we began to organize our camp life. There was much talent available, and soon the 'Heath University' flourished, under whose aegis seminars on an astonishing variety of subjects were addressed by eminent speakers who had once been the pride of German and Austrian universities.

More dramatic was the arrival of workmen, who set about erecting arc-lights around the perimeter. Our representative was told by the Commanding Officer that the Home Office had decreed that under international law Britain was obliged to inform 'our' government of our whereabouts, and to mark the camps by night, 'to prevent the enemy bombing his own nationals'. We were not amused. Prees was on the main flightpath to Merseyside, and we saw little benefit in indirectly helping the Luftwaffe to find its targets, and we explained that we were by no means convinced that the Germans would experience anything but delight in sending us a few stray bombs. However, as the CO said, orders are orders; on the other hand he also gratuitously informed us of the date and time of the proposed illuminations. It took little enough time for us to rectify the situation with a few well-aimed stones, and the safety of darkness returned.

The morrow saw an Order of the Day from the CO talking about wilful destruction of His Majesty's property. As a punishment the whole camp was to be deprived of telephone and telegraph facilities for two weeks. Since we had never enjoyed such privileges in the first place, justice was seen to be done by all!

In due course the camp was depleted as the internees were being transferred to other camps. I was fortunate not to be placed on an overseas transport: we had all heard of *The Arandora Star*, packed with internees bound for Australian camps, which had fallen victim to German torpedoes with large loss of life. My destination turned out to be the Isle of Man. I was put into one of the large hotels in Douglas which, in better times, had been the holiday venue for visitors from the mainland. Camps were scattered across the island, and Port Erin and Port St Mary were the receiving centres for internees civilian and female.

Conditions in Douglas were much more civilized than in my previous camps, but I had little time to draw comparisons. Within little time I was informed that my American visa was now available, which meant another transfer, this time to Lingfield racecourse in Surrey, where we were actually accommodated below the stands, and there can be few who can vie with me for having had literally a grand-stand view of the Battle of Britain.

My visit to the consulate, then in Epsom, was a brief formality, and I returned to camp with my official permit to take up residence in the United States.

The official mind works in its wondrous ways. I was now released from internment, but my Aliens Registration Book was endorsed with the remark 'may reside in the United Kingdom', provided that he emigrates at the first available opportunity.

So I made my way back to Manchester, pondering on the logic, if any, of the situation. My internment had been ordered on the remote suspicion of my being an enemy of the realm. My key to freedom had been the American visa. Since, predictably, there was not the slightest chance of my having any 'available opportunity' of abiding with the provisions of my release, I was left to ponder by what magic the visa had changed me into a more trustworthy 'enemy alien'. But my freedom proved the point!

RANDO BERTOIA

Rando Bertoia was born in Montereale, Pordenone province in northern Italy, in 1920. Both he and his father before him in 1914, came to Scotland under the patronage of the well-known Toffolo family to work in the *terrazzo* industry. Today, Rando, a survivor of *The Arandora Star*, is 72 and still works in his clock and watch repair business in the city of Glasgow. His personal account of his internment and views on this, as recounted to Dr Terri Colpi in an interview in June 1990, just before the 'Internment Remembered' Conference, are transcribed below.

When Germany brutally and savagely attacked Poland on 1 September 1939 and in doing so sparked off the Second World War, Italy remained neutral for the time being at any rate, but it was on the cards that she would fling her lot in with her newly acquired unprincipled partner. It was a period in which I, and probably most of my compatriots in Britain, lived in a state of apprehension and anxiety awaiting that fateful day to arrive. What will become of us? was the question which was ever present and uppermost in our thoughts as we carried on with our daily tasks praying and hoping that somehow sanity and common sense would prevail. Alas this was not to be. The temptation of military glories on the cheap over-rode all sentiments of sanity and commonsense and Italy deliberately declared war on fallen France and on a Britain which seemed on the verge of collapsing. The day I so much feared and dreaded had finally arrived and I accepted and resigned myself to what I had sadly visualized to expect. I became, overnight and through no fault of my own, an enemy of the people who yesterday were my friends. The 10th of June 1940 is a day I will always remember. Being Italian, residing in this country for many years, I was in consequence interned as soon as Italy declared war on Britain on 10 June 1940.

I, along with my father, was awakened at 6 am next morning by two policemen who took us to the local police station where me met other Italians many of whom we knew. I was 20 then. We remained in the cells there for about eight hours and then we were transferred to the military barracks in Glasgow where we spent the night. The next day we were transported, by train and by bus, to our first internment camp which was at Milton Bridge near Edinburgh.

In this camp I remained until the 24th June when along with some of my fellow internees, chosen at random it seemed, I was tranferred to Bury in Lancashire where we joined a few hundred other Italian internees from England. There was also a cousin of mine from Newcastle. We were very friendly and it was nice to meet one of the family, a nice boy. On the 30th June a few hundred of us, again it seemed chosen at random, were taken away from Bury and transported to Liverpool where we embarked on the ill-fated *Arandora Star*, a pre-war luxury liner converted to comply with wartime requirements. This liner which was bound for Canada carried on board Italian, German and Austrian internees for internment there. It will always remain a mystery to me how I was picked for *The Arandora Star*. We were just picked at random. Some were very old men and they were taken away. They should have been left to go to the Isle of Man. My father was left. But other old men came with me. At that time Britain was in turmoil, a panic and all the rest of it. So I think they just grabbed some here and some there. Probably they took the names if people were *fascisti*. But they were just picked at random, I wasn't in the *fascisti* or anything. I was nothing. I wasn't registered anywhere and I hadn't joined anything. As a matter of fact some of the real *fascisti* remained out. The nation was in panic awaiting day by day for an invasion so they just picked on anybody that they could think of.

We thought we were going to the Isle of Man. Of course when I saw the big ship I gathered I wasn't going to the Isle of Man, not with a big ship like that, a 15,000 tonner. But we had no idea.

Just over a day's sailing from Liverpool on the early morning of the 2nd July *The Arandora Star* was torpedoed by a German U-Boat and sank within 40 minutes taking with her hundreds of internees and many British soldiers who were on board to guard us.

I was one of the lucky ones – I can't even swim – who, with the help of some of my friends, was able to scramble into a life-boat without even getting my feet wet. I can't believe, even today, how lucky I was when I think about it because they were here and there in the water, all over the place. When the boat was lowered it was heavily overloaded but, as the sea was reasonably calm, the risk of overturning or sinking was not very serious. Around us we could see debris of the disaster and a number of life-boats and rafts floating about. I was very seasick and I remember bobbing up and down but I was lying on the floor of the life-boat. As we floated aimlessly on this great expanse of ocean and sky, I became aware of a strange and uncanny silence surrounding us; only the gentle lapping of the waves against the boat could be heard now and then to break this silence. For hours we drifted in this manner anxiously hoping that some help was on its way.

As time dragged a thought entered by mind – what was the purpose of all this suffering and misery? This thought gnawed at me continually and after much pondering the only answer I could come up with was that I was an innocent victim, as were millions of others like me, of a great human tragedy deliberately created and skilfully engineered by wicked people who cared nothing what happened to their own people and far less for humanity, as long as they furthered their own personal ill-conceived ambitions of military glory and military conquests. It's all as simple as that, that's how I look at it. I was just a victim so I wasn't thinking very good things about my leader in Italy. Unfortunately for the little people, in order to attain or achieve such grandiose ambitions, nations have to resort to war and when a nation embarks on war it follows that many of its people are bound to get hurt; a fact that I, unlike many of my countrymen, accepted and resigned myself to. It was part and parcel of the harsh realities of war.

My thoughts were suddenly interrupted at about midday by the drone of an aeroplane at a distance and within minutes, to our great relief, an enemy [British] plane came into view; a most welcome enemy plane – it was a Sunderland flying boat. It flew around overhead for sometime dropping foodstuffs and other essentials and then made its way back to its base. Our hopes now rose in the knowledge that we had been located and our plight discovered; rescue should not be far away now. And right enough, in the late afternoon, a vessel appeared on the horizon and seemed to be heading towards us. As it got nearer we recognized it as a Canadian destroyer and were so happy to see it! Hanging from its sides were rope ladders and as it came alongside our lifeboat we, with the help of the destroyer's crew, scrambled on to these ladders and tumbled into the safety of the vessel.

The destroyer continued searching around the disaster area for some time picking up survivors from rafts and pieces of debris and then after making sure there was no more sign of life headed for the mainland. Those who were already dead were simply left behind to a watery grave even when we had hung onto them for hours because we knew them.

At about 6.30 next morning, 3rd July, we landed at Greenock in Scotland. It was a lovely morning and as the pitiful gathering of dejected humanity made its way along the quayside someone in charge ordered us to stop and line up. This person, with a handful of papers in his hand, presumably a list of all the people who were on the *Arandora Star*, began to call out names. Sometimes the word – *'presente'* – greeted his call and sometimes his call was greeted by heartbreaking silence. When my cousin's name came along there was no answer. I think I broke down then. There were about 200 of us survivors anyway.

We remained at Greenock for the night and next day, 4th July, we left for Birkenhead, Arrowe Park and then after a day or two we were taken to Liverpool where we remained until the 10th. On this day we embarked on the motor ship *Dunera* which, unknown to us, was bound for Australia. When it sailed away I was trying to be fly and work out the direction we were taking. Seeing the sun above and so on. But we didn't know where we were going. There were Germans on there too, I could hear German voices and I could make out 'Africa, Africa'. They were sailors, you see, and they could figure out where we were headed. And, right enough, we landed at Freetown in Sierra Leone, where they picked up supplies and things. From there we went to another place, Takoradi, on the Gold Coast, and from there we landed in Capetown. There, I could just see the lights of Capetown, that's all. From Capetown we crossed over to Perth in Australia. And from Perth to Melbourne. After a voyage lasting 55 days in lamentable conditions, we finally arrived at Melbourne, on the 3rd September. And for four long years from one internment camp after another, Australia was to become my new home.

Once arrived in Australia, internment was to me and to probably many of my fellow internees, more or less a kind of a holiday and I was reasonably happy. I found myself thousands of miles away from the war and the hardships we had suffered seemed now behind us and I considered myself lucky to be alive. For many, time must have dragged on boringly, but I made the best of the time I had on my hands by attending drawing classes, playing chess, studying Italian, woodworking, metal working and scribbling down my private thoughts for a future day.

The Aussies turned out to be, once they got to know us, quite a friendly lot and were not very strict towards us. Life was bearable, food was adequate and we had our happy moments. We organized our own entertainments in the form of concerts and plays. Football matches were played between us and the German internees who were permitted to enter our compound from theirs which was adjacent to ours. Bowls and tennis tournaments were held which eased the monotony of the day. Some Italians were 100 per cent anti-British, so they deserved to be interned. Even today. I had to keep quiet; some of them were very hot-headed. The ones from Scotland, I found them to be less interested, but some of the ones from London were real *fascisti*. They kept us on our toes, but most of us were not that way minded: we were just Italians.

In July 1943 *Il Duce* fell from grace and was deposed. Some weeks later on 3 October Italy switched sides and went over to the Allies. Our status then changed from being enemy aliens to become, overnight, friendly aliens. In keeping with this new label we were offered our release from the internment camp and the opportunity of working in the Australian bush cutting down trees. I volunteered, as many of my mates did, and worked in the bush for about a year. Then I found employment in my old trade as a terrazzo worker in Melbourne. A man from my area of Italy gave me a job. Terrazzo and mosaic workers were all from my region of Italy: Friuli. I had a girlfriend in Melbourne who worked in an ice-cream shop. She was born in Australia but she was from my part of Italy.

The opportunity, which I took, to return to Britain was offered to me when I was informed that the liner *Mauretania* was about to sail for Britain in August 1946. I boarded this liner at Sydney and I am happy to say that my return journey home was quite different from the terrible conditions on *The Dunera*. The *Mauretania* docked at Liverpool on the first week of September and a day later I was back in Glasgow. My colourful and unasked-for adventures had come to an end.

My father, Ermenegildo Bertoia, was away for about nine months to internment on the Isle of Man. When he came back he started work and was able to go back to what he was doing before; terrazzo was a semi-essential sort of job. My brother was born here but he was too young at the time of war to be interned, so he stayed at home.

The treatment I received during my internment was, on the whole, to my way of thinking at any rate, not unreasonable for a nation dazed and bewildered by the magnitude of the disastrous events which overtook her and plunged her into a state of disorder and confusion. France, in six momentous weeks had unexpectedly fallen and the victorious German Armies seemed poised and ready to invade Britain from across the English Channel. The invasion of unprepared Britain seemed imminent, day by day and hour by hour. It was in this abnormal atmosphere of panic and invasion-scare that many hasty decisions and judgements were rightly or wrongly made regarding refugees, prisoners of war and us Italians. Some of these decisions turned out to be not to Britain's credit. In particular, regarding the refugees who had fled from the Nazi tyranny and found asylum here and were now thrown into concentration camps and treated as would-be enemies. To them it must have seemed like jumping out of the frying pan into the fire. But this is quite understandable at the time as it would probably have been very easy for a spy to pose as a refugee and filter his way into Britain. There was, however, no evidence of this ever having happened but Britain could not afford to take the risk and consequently all refugees were rounded up.

Britain's image as being a champion of freedom was severely damaged by these mishandlings, as was the rounding-up, in a higgeldy-piggledy manner, of the Italians and deporting many of them overseas. It was not quite in keeping with Britain's image of fair play. There were, though, many people in very high places in this country who were seriously concerned and continually protested at this treatment of the prisoners. In doing so they went some way to restoring Britain's fair play way of life. The efforts of these people were not in vain as the situation of the internees and prisoners gradually eased and sometime later many of them were released. Major Layton was very fair in the tribunals he conducted with us in Australia.

While the terrible experience of *The Arandora Star* will remain in my memory for ever, the harrowing journey to Australia on *The Dunera* will be the period of my internment I will never forget. But my nature is such that I came to terms, without much difficulty, with the conditions presented and imposed upon me and I therefore endured the hardships as best as I could. After all, it was war and my country chose deliberately to go to war against this country when Britain seemed to be on the verge of collapsing after the unexpected fall of France.

In the sordid surroundings on *The Dunera*, being a thinker and noting that my fellow internees continued to vent their wrath on the British for their sufferings, my private thoughts and sentiments descended instead elsewhere – on the two sinister individuals [Hitler and Mussolini] who by their crafty machinations, deliberately created, engineered and set in motion the catastrophe which befell humanity. They were the ones who were entirely responsible for our sufferings and for the sufferings of millions of other innocent people.

The guilty two, one more guilty than the other, who menaced and threatened the peoples of Europe with war if their demands were not met, were determined to lead their nations to war in order to satisfy their yearning for grandiose ambitions of military glories and conquests.

Tragic historic events must, or should, be kept alive otherwise they will be disappearing in the distance and Mankind will not learn from them; understanding the past will or should enable us to prevent a similar repetition of folly in the future.

Rando Bertoia kept, on a scrap of lavatory paper, a blow by blow account of the main events of his internment. He still has this today, 50 years on, and it is reproduced, in enlarged form – the original writing is minute – below.

Tues. June 11	Arrested at 4·30 am. and taken to Strathbungo Police Station. Left in the evening for Maryhill Barracks.
Wed. June 12	Left Maryhill Barracks for Milton Bridge Midlothian.
Mon. June 24	Left Milton Bridge for Bury. Arrived at Bury at 6 pm. Cousin Luigi here.
Sun. June 30	Left Bury for Liverpool where we embark on the Arandora Star.
Tues. July 2	Arandora Star torpedoed by a U-boat at 6 am. Picked up by a destroyer at 3 pm.
Wed. July 3	Arrived at Greenock at about 8 am.
Thur. July 4	Left Greenock for Arrowe Park Birkenhead.
Sat. July 6	Left Arrowe Park for Mason St. Barracks Liverpool.
Wed. July 10	Left Mason Street Barracks and embark on motor ship Dunera.
Wed. July 24	Arrived at Freetown Sierra Leone Africa. Left again in the evening for Takoradi.
Sat. July 27	Arrived at Takoradi West Africa.
Mon. July 29	Left Takoradi at 7 am for Cape Town.
Thur. Aug. 8	Arrived at Cape Town at 9 am.
Friday. Aug 9	Left Cape Town for Fremantle Australia. at 8 pm.
Tues. Aug 27	Arrived at Fremantle.
Wed. Aug. 28.	Left Fremantle for Melbourne.
Tues. Sept. 3	Arrived at Melbourne after 55 days on Dunera. Taken to №2 Internment Camp Tatura.
Friday. May 16, 1941	Transfered to №4 Internment Camp.

ANNA SPIRO

Anna Spiro was born in Augsburg, a city with an ancient Jewish community numbering about 1,200 in the years after World War One. She grew up and was educated there until 1936, when she left Germany and came to England on a student visa. In 1938 she married Ludwig Spiro whom she had met in Augsburg. Both Anna and Ludwig were interned on the Isle of Man. Ludwig quickly rose to a leading position in the camp administration making good use of his managerial training. The first of their two children was born in 1942. Ludwig worked in an engineering company and Anna as a homemaker. Both are intensely involved with the community of former refugees. The details of Anna's experiences are contained in *Years to Remember* (published privately, 1988), a copy of which is deposited at the Wiener Library where she works as a volunteer.

DC

For us the first months of the war seemed unreal. There were none of the expected air raids, very few shortages and life for a time had settled to a routine which differed little from peacetime except that more and more people had either to leave for the forces or change over to war work.

All this changed completely when the Germans, after the occupation of Denmark and Norway, attacked Holland and Belgium and fought their way across into France. The Blitzkrieg had started with German parachutists causing major disturbances all over those countries making defence difficult. The British press at the time blamed much of the military disaster on the activities of fifth columnists operating in the invaded territories who, according to the press, had sabotaged the efforts of the defending armies.

We know today that the activities of the 'fifth columnists' have been greatly exaggerated. However, in May 1940 it led to a strong campaign in the British press demanding the immediate internment of all aliens. Newspaper headings such as 'Intern the Lot' became the order of the day. The fact that people in our position were much more opposed to Hitler and the German armies counted for little and was very often not understood even by some of the more intelligent people.

Against this background the Government decided to take action and decreed the internment of all male aliens who had been classed 'B'. On the evening of 5 May the police knocked at our door and collected Ludwig. Two days later the internment of all women who had been categorized 'B' was decreed and so they came to collect me. This left my parents-in-law for a few days on their own in our house as, due to their advanced age, theirs was a lower internment priority.

I was taken to Wembley Police Station where many women had already been assembled. We were taken by coach to Fulham Hospital Prison where we spent the night not knowing what would happen to us. Things were pretty chaotic. There were women with small children and with young babies who had just come out of hospital and were far from well. I met another 'fifth columnist' Hilde Jacobi who winced with toothache and whom I could help as I had a few aspros in my handbag. There were few facilities, just a few bunks, and most of us had to sleep on the floor. Next morning all of us were again put on to coaches, by now we were a few hundred, and taken to Euston Station where a train was waiting for us. Once we were inside the doors were locked and we departed. After some hours the train stopped and we realized that we had reached Liverpool. Now we were ordered to disembark and, after repeated counting and checking, we were marched through the streets of Liverpool to the docks to board a boat.

On our march we were spat at by people who managed to line the roads in considerable numbers and who obviously had been told that we were enemy aliens under police guard. Some of the bystanders vented their feelings by shouting 'Bloody Germans' and the like. Gradually our procession reached the harbour where there was a ferry boat which we boarded and which was soon filled, and by the time of departure there was standing room only. We soon realized that we were being taken to the Isle of Man. Three hours later we landed at Douglas where, after a great deal of repeated counting, we were put on board a railway train; the doors were locked and we travelled to our destination Port Erin.

This little town, normally a holiday resort, was to be our 'home' for many months to come. We were distributed amongst boarding houses and hotels, all of which had been virtually emptied as far as normal residents, staff and equipment were concerned. The whole place seemed like a ghost town which we now began to fill very rapidly. Throughout most furniture, bed linen and carpeting had been removed. The rooms were filled as we came along, and three of us were allocated a room with one large and one narrow bed; I shared the double bed with another woman.

The running of the hotel, where we were now sixty women, was our responsibility. All services were severely restricted; hot water was available once a week when we could have a bath and wash our smalls. The floors had to be scrubbed every day according to a duty rota which prescribed all our domestic duties. Our hotel was called 'Towers'. The food was reasonable under the circumstances and apart from breakfast, lunch and dinner even included an obligatory nightcap consisting of cocoa which we suspected contained a fair amount of bromide. There was curfew from eight in the evening to eight in the morning, and twice a day we had to line up for roll call.

The whole operation had stunned most of us. Here we were a great deal more anti-German and anti-Nazi than many of our guards and administrators. We had to leave our homes and in many cases members of our families who normally depended on our care and attention. We, the victims of the Nazis, were suddenly lumped together with non-Jewish German and Austrian girls, not only in the same hotel but often they shared the same room with us. They were looking forward to a German invasion and seemed certain that the boats which were passing on the horizon were part of a German invasion fleet. It took some time until we managed to sort ourselves out and avoid much of the friction which had made the first days so very difficult.

Things were not helped by the fact that the Home Office had selected Dame Cruickshank for the position of camp commander of Port Erin, by now a camp which housed some 5,000 women of whom the vast majority were Nazi victims. She had been in charge of one of Britain's largest women prisons, and it was not particularly pleasant to meet her walking with a horse whip through Port Erin. If she saw any internee who did anything which disturbed her, such as walking in the road and not on the pavement, she would use her whip to redirect the villain.

A few days after my arrival, when I was in the street, I suddenly met my mother-in-law who was looking for me. She had been billeted in a small hotel where she met Mrs Rachwalsky and her daughter-in-law Carla whom she knew from Berlin and with whom we became very good friends. Carla had with her her daughter Alice who was then four years old.

Most of us realized how important it was to be occupied and to keep ourselves busy. We therefore did a great deal to organize talks on subjects of general interest, language courses and the like. All that seemed fine and made life tolerable, especially as the weather during those summer months was very pleasant. However things were very different in the evenings when there was plenty of time to think and to consider our position. Here we were a sitting target if ever the Germans were to come. What had happened to our husbands? Who was going to pay the rent for our house? The place was full of rumours, after all none of us had seen a newspaper or had been allowed to listen to the radio. All this created an atmosphere which was far from agreeable and gave us much to worry about.

At last after some five weeks we were allowed to receive newspapers. Now we realized the seriousness of the country's position and it felt even worse that there seemed nothing for us to do in order to help. From now on we were allowed to write and to receive three letters a month. At last came the first letter from Ludwig from which I learnt that he was alright and that he got to the Onchan camp, one of the three male camps on the Isle of Man. I knew now where he was and that his father, who was almost 70 and who was suffering from angina pectoris, had also been interned and was in another camp on the island and that Ludwig was hopeful of getting him shortly transferred to his Onchan camp.

After some months the authorities gave serious consideration to the transfer of male internees on a voluntary basis to Australia. The men requested to meet with their wives to discuss this important move. A two hour meeting in Port Erin was organized for husbands and wives. The scheme was subsequently dropped but at least we had seen each other for some two hours. Later during the autumn and winter months we had once a month a meeting with our husbands in a large hall in Douglas. Whilst this was not a very private occasion, at least we could look at each other and assure oneself that one's husband was alright. Ludwig's friend Peter Katzenstein even brought a rug to these meetings in case some of the ladies would find the unheated hall too cold.

There seemed little doubt that the men coped better with their fate than most of us. Ludwig had many interesting people amongst the two thousand in his camp. There were well known scientists, people who had the Nobel Prize, musicians of international repute and the like which helped to support a great deal of learning and a good class of entertainment.

Ludwig had been elected Camp Suvervisor and was thus in charge of the camp administration and responsible for the relationship with the outside world. This was a very demanding appointment which absorbed him greatly. He was in daily contact with Sir Timothy Eden, his Camp Commander, the brother of Anthony Eden, and various members of Parliament who visited the camp and whom he could influence to further the release of people who were able to make contributions to the war effort. He was particularly impressed by Eleanore Rathbone who took so great an interest in the internees at a time when Parliament was largely absorbed by the war's most serious phase.

Things were very different in the womens' camp; here were constant rumours suggesting that our husbands would be sent to camps in Canada or Australia, and from one of Ludwig's letters I gathered that he thought that this was a distinct possibility on which he expected an early decision. He had therefore written to Margot Rosenberg asking her to send him a case with some of his clothing. We learnt later that Margot, upon receipt of this request, proceeded to 31 Valley Drive and selected some of Ludwig's clothing for sending to him. Now she needed a suitable case, and in the knowledge that all the family's numerous luggage was in the loft, she found a ladder and climbed into the roof space where, after a little while, she discovered a suitable empty case. As she wanted to descend, the ladder slipped and she was marooned in the loft. There was nothing she could do when suddenly she heard the front door opening and

Tatjiana Riester entering the house. She had a key of the house and, having heard of the possibility that internees were to be sent overseas, had decided that some clothing should be sent to me.

With Tatjiana's help the ladder was repositioned and Margot climbed down and the case was packed and despatched! When it arrived, together with lots of similar consignments, at Onchan Camp everything had to be opened in the presence of one of His Majesty's Officers and a representative of the internees. At that time Ludwig was still in charge of the camp's post office. He attended the opening and was rather embarrassed to find that the contents of his case was covered with a Union Jack. The officer lifted the flag shaped like a set of underwear with detachable legs which I had made for Ludwig's birthday at the time of the coronation in 1937. Lt. Shaw took it all in the right spirit. When a few weeks later Ludwig was elected Camp supervisor, members of his house had got hold of the 'flag' and hung it fixed on a broomstick out of his window, visible to the whole camp and the guards on the other side of the barbed wire.

Suddenly the overseas transports materialized and many men from the various camps were sent to Canada and Australia. These transports have since been fully described in the post-war literature, and represent a most unfortunate chapter of the British war history. Refugees, who had fled from Nazi persecution and who had thought that they had found shelter in Britain, were herded on to ships ill-equipped for the transport of humans, locked by the hundreds into the holds of the boats and treated much worse than prisoners of war. One of these ships *The Arandora Star*, which was to take hundreds of internees to Australia, was torpedoed and sunk with the loss of much life. Ludwig was very fortunate that he was heavily engaged in the administration of his camp which saved him from being selected for any one of the overseas transports.

All this happened at a time when the war passed through one of the most critical phases and one could understand that our fate and our problems were of little importance under the then prevailing conditions. It was therefore even more remarkable that Members of Parliament, and of all parties, made time available to raise the internment of refugees in the House. These debates soon led to the release of the most elderly and sick, and were followed by various measures which, admittedly very slowly, led to the reconsideration of our position on a very individual basis.

Thus my father-in-law was released at the end of July, having been interned for just over two months. He returned to our house, and having never in his life done any domestic chores, did not find living on his own unduly easy. However, the neighbours rallied to his help. They cooked an extra portion when they made lunch and handed it across the garden fence. In the process my father-in-law lost a great deal of weight which had not been achieved in earlier years and which much improved his well-being.

He was on his own for just over six weeks which was the time when there were many heavy air raids on London. He had made himself, with the help of a large bookcase and some corrugated iron, a makeshift shelter in one of the downstairs living rooms. Lying on a mattress he managed to creep into this shelter during day raids and sleep there at night.

My mother-in-law's release from the Isle of Man, which had been granted together with that of her husband so that she could look after him, took another six weeks until her discharge papers came through. Ludwig's employers, C.P. Jackson, had early on applied to the Home Office for his release as they needed him for war work. These applications were considered on their merits, and all internees had to be cleared by a fresh tribunal. Ludwig and I had a very friendly hearing by a committee which sat in Douglas presided over by a judge who readily re-classified us as 'friendly aliens'. Thereafter it still took four weeks until the papers for Ludwig's release came through. Three weeks later my release followed; I was to leave the camp at 6 a.m. on 10 February 1941 to catch the 7 a.m. boat from Douglas for Liverpool. When I got to the boat we were advised that due to the severity of the storm the sailing was cancelled and I had to return to my 'hotel' for another day. Next morning the elements had calmed down and we sailed on time towards the mainland without any further delay.

I must admit that it took me a very long time to get over the experience if being interned with some 5,000 women under conditions which, for most of us, despite the country's emergency, were very difficult to accept. The departure from the Isle of Man was a marvellous moment which I will never forget. I had looked out over the sea for very many months and now this had passed and I felt that never again did I wish to stay at the seaside nor did I wish again to see so many women around me.

ABBAS SHIBLAK

Abbas Shiblak is a Palestinian writer and senior researcher at the Arab League in London. He was born in Palestine in 1944 and has lived in Britain since 1975. In 1987 he was given indefinite leave to remain in the UK and at the time of the Gulf War his application to become a naturalized British citizen was under consideration. On 17 January 1991 he was detained in Pentonville prison pending a deportation order. Abbas Shiblak was released on 6 February 1991 after a sustained campaign by individuals and organizations.

The legal details of the case are reported by Duncan Campbell in *The Guardian*,

24 January 1991 and by Shiranika Herbert in *The Guardian*, 7 February 1991. For details of the release campaign and the role of Abbas Shiblak's friend, Simon Louvish, see *Jewish Chronicle*, 22 February 1992 and more generally, 'Under Suspicion', Channel 4, 18 March 1992. The following account first appeared in *Index on Censorship*, Vol.20 (April/May 1991). A briefer version appeared in *The Guardian*, 11 February 1991.

TK

Out of Pentonville

Thursday, 17 January. It was the second day of the Gulf War. My Adult Education class on sailing finished at 9.30 that evening. It took me less than 15 minutes to drive to my house in Kilburn. My wife Farehan was standing in the entrance, shaken and in tears. 'Four security men came and asked about you. They're carrying an order to detain and deport you. They said they will be back at 10.'

I tried to hold myself together and to calm Farehan down. 'It's probably a mistake', I said. 'No, no,' she said, 'they showed me the order.'

I tried to think what to do. 'We'll have to call someone, a lawyer, someone from the office.' There was not much time. A knock soon came at the door and Farehan let the four men in. I was in my study on the first floor making telephone calls. I asked the men to come to the lounge upstairs. My two children were sleeping on the ground floor.

The four men showed me the order. I noticed there were mistakes in the spelling of my name and of the street in which I live. The men did not search the house or ask me any questions. They had no answers to my questions either. We are simply carrying out Home Office orders, they said. They were polite and gave me a few minutes to finish the phone calls and pack a few clothes and some books.

I have never experienced prison life before. But from that moment I became a number. They took me first to Willesden police station. I spent the most terrifying night of my life in a detention cell not half a mile from my home. The conditions were quite appalling.

Next day they took me to Pentonville prison. There I met the other detainees. The majority were Iraqis, mostly postgraduate students, many in the final stages of their studies. I had never met any of them before. I made my views on the war and my opposition to Saddam Hussein clear to them from the first day. I was apprehensive at first, but later I discovered that I had gained their trust. They began to talk to me more openly about their predicament and their own views. Many were either of a religious persuasion opposed to Saddam or non-activist Ba'athists, who had to be members of the Ba'ath Party in order to have any chance for further education. They were mainly worried about their families. With almost no contact, no source of income, many with poor English, their wives and children outside were in serious trouble.

On the second day I met a Palestinian, Mahmoud Ayyad, who had worked as a public relations officer in a Gulf state embassy for many years. The only contact I had with him was in the mid-70s when I was still a student. He offered me a driving job with the health section of the Embassy during one summer holiday. He is a completely apolitical person whose main interest is to lead his own life. Ayyad couldn't believe what had happened to him. He remained very pessimistic right up to his release, keeping his hopes well hidden. When he put on his shorts, as we were allowed to play volley ball one day, he appeared to me like a character from *Dad's Army*. 'What kind of sleeper are you? You never wake up!' I used to joke with him.

The second Palestinian I met was Ali al-Saleh, whose English friends called him 'Nemo' (after his family name al-Nīmr). When I first came to London in 1975, Ali was the leader of the Palestinian Student Union in Britain. After this period Ali abandoned politics and for the past 12 years he has lived in Bedford, got married and raised a family, pursuing a career first in journalism, then in management. Ali is a highly sociable person, with a beautiful voice. When we were in neighbouring cells, he used to ask me if I minded if he sang. He seemed tuned to very sad songs.

I had never met the third Palestinian detainee, 'Mr B', before. He seemed to be an innocent, lonely person with a quiet voice, who had committed only one unforgiveable sin, that of being born the nephew of a man who is hated and feared throughout the world.

The one thing we all had in common was our background as refugees. To have a home, a family and a job in a peaceful environment, free from fear, was an achievement Palestinians, in particular, value highly. The idea that we would do anything to endanger this was completely foreign to us. The experience we were living through made us feel even more keenly our unique vulnerability and the need to preserve this refuge.

For the first two days we had not even an inkling of what lay behind our detention apart from the vague grounds of 'national security'. But on the third day we read a leak to the newspapers that the security services had broken a cell of seven Palestinian terrorists who were planning bomb attacks in Europe and the USA. I realized suddenly that these seven were in fact ourselves: Me, Ayyad, Nemo and his wife, Mr B and his wife, and a businessman of Palestinian origin who was released early on. A very gloomy picture started to emerge before my eyes. They were trying to stamp us as terrorists! But this was very strange, as the authorities never interrogated us, they never searched any of our homes, and no one was ever asked about his links to any of the others. We found ourselves in a nightmare situation in which all the legal channels were closed. Our lawyers were trying desperately to bring our case to a court, to require the charges and evidence to be produced, but all these challenges failed. We appeared to have no legal rights whatsoever.

Our only hope seemed to lie with the British and other friends who visited us in Pentonville, the fellow writers and journalists who started to write about my case and the other detainees. This initiated a wide debate on the rights of people in Britain, and on civil rights in time of war. They began to highlight the issue that the only way people caught in our predicament could be properly treated would be to have the right legal procedure, in which we would have an opportunity to make our voice heard beyond the walls of Pentonville prison. We felt we were in a dark tunnel from which there was no way out. It was under these circumstances that my case came before the advisory panel of the Three Wise Men. I had a very short time to state my case before them, and was lucky to have articulate friends who could support my statements. But other detainees may well not have such advocacy, or know any UK citizens well enough, or even have a proper command of English.

I was relieved that the Home Secretary decided to revoke his order of deportation and to release me and a few others, including Ayyad, Nemo and Mr B. But sad to have discovered the other face of a system I had always assumed was just and fair. This was a terrifying experience for my family and myself. After losing two countries, Palestine and Lebanon, Britain has been our home for the last 17 years. It is a country which gave me an education, shelter, and a sense of freedom.

Out of this episode, two facts emerged for me, which I will not find easy to forget for many years. The first is this: here we are in a democratic and free society, yet suddenly I found myself completely helpless and defenceless, held in prison and threatened with the destruction of my future without any reason being given, without any legal defence. It is a terror I do not wish on anyone. Political deportation seems to me like cot death syndrome – it strikes suddenly, without warning, and is completely devastating. The second fact is a brighter one: unlike a third world dictatorship, there are democratic institutions, a long-standing tradition of free speech, a free press, civil liberty groups and many individuals who are ready to stand up and speak out for these rights. The support I received from neighbours, colleagues, fellow writers, academics, journalists, MPs and civil liberty activists – PEN, Liberty and Amnesty International – was overwhelming, and gives me hope and faith for the future.

Notes on Contributors

Louise Burletson is a History graduate of the University of Southampton where she won the dissertation prize for her work on alien internment. She is now studying Management Studies at Oxford University.

David Cesarani is Director of the Institute of Contemporary History and Wiener Library. His publications include *Justice Delayed: How Britain Became a Refuge for Nazi War Criminals* (1992).

Terri Colpi (D.Phil, Oxford) is a specialist writer and commentator on the Italian Community resident in Great Britain and Research Fellow at King's College, University of London. Recent publications include *The Italian Factor: The Italian Community in Great Britain* and *Italians Forward: A Visual History of the Italian Community* (1991).

Klaus E. Hinrichsen was born in Luebeck, Germany. After obtaining his doctorate in History of Art he worked as a researcher for Art Encyclopaedias in Germany. He arrived in England shortly before the Second World War. Apart from lecturing he has been involved with exhibitions and radio and television documentaries both in Britain and Germany.

Miriam Kochan is an independent researcher and translator based in Oxfordshire whose publications include *Prisoners of England* (1980) and *Britain's Internees in the Second World War* (1983).

Tony Kushner is Parkes Lecturer at the University of Southampton. Recent publications include (ed.), *The Jewish Heritage in British History: Englishness and Jewishness* (1992).

Panikos Panayi is lecturer in history at De Montfort University. He was temporary lecturer in history at the University of Keele in 1989–90 and Alexander von Humboldt Research Fellow at the Institut für Migrationsforschung und Interkulturelle Studien at the University of Osnabrück in Germany during the 1991–92 academic year. He is author of *The Enemy in Our Midst: Germans in Britain during the First World War* (Berg, Oxford, 1991). He is also editor of *Minorities in Wartime: National and Racial Groupings in Europe, North America* *and Australia during the Two World Wars* (Berg), and *Racial Violence in Britain, 1840–1950* (Leicester University Press), both of which will be published in early 1993.

Lucio Sponza is Lecturer in the School of Languages, University of Westminster. He is the author of *Italian Immigrants in Nineteenth Century Britain: Realities and Images* (1988).

Index